MAJOR CONCEPTS IN SPANISH FEMINIST THEORY

SUNY series in Latin American and Iberian Thought and Culture
———————
Jorge J. E. Gracia and Rosemary G. Feal, editors

MAJOR CONCEPTS IN SPANISH FEMINIST THEORY

ROBERTA JOHNSON

Published by State University of New York Press, Albany

© 2019 State University of New York

All rights reserved

No part of this book may be used or reproduced in any manner whatsoever without written permission. No part of this book may be stored in a retrieval system or transmitted in any form or by any means including electronic, electrostatic, magnetic tape, mechanical, photocopying, recording, or otherwise without the prior permission in writing of the publisher.

For information, contact State University of New York Press, Albany, NY
www.sunypress.edu

Library of Congress Cataloging-in-Publication Data

Names: Johnson, Roberta, 1942– author.
Title: Major concepts in Spanish feminist theory / Roberta Johnson.
Description: New York : State University of New York Press, [2019] | Series: SUNY series in Latin American and Iberian thought and culture | Includes bibliographical references and index.
Identifiers: LCCN 2018021841 | ISBN 9781438473697 (hardcover) | ISBN 9781438473703 (perf.)| ISBN 9781438473710 (ebook)
Subjects: LCSH: Feminism—Spain. | Women's rights—Spain. | Women—Employment—Spain. | Sex role—Spain.
Classification: LCC HQ1692 .J64 2019 | DDC 305.420946—dc23
LC record available at https://lccn.loc.gov/2018021841

10 9 8 7 6 5 4 3 2 1

I dedicate this book to my husband, Ricardo Quinones, who showed great forbearance during the many years it took to write it, and to Ben Quinones, Laurel, Sarah, and Cecilia, who never tired of asking me how the work was coming along.

Contents

Introduction		1
Chapter 1.	Solitude	25
Chapter 2.	Personality	59
Chapter 3.	Social Class	89
Chapter 4.	Work	117
Chapter 5.	Difference	149
Chapter 6.	Equality	177
Epilogue		205
Notes		209
Works Cited		225
Index		235

Introduction

The Concepts and the Women Who Formulated Them

Is Spain different? Many have argued that Spain's geographical position between Europe and Africa and its 800-year-domination by Arabs (711–1492) have molded the country in distinctive ways. Its literature and philosophy seldom appear in major surveys and anthologies of Western cultural production. Such is the case with Spanish feminist theory. Mary Nash points out, for example, that "el feminismo igualitario, basado en el principio de la igualdad entre hombres y mujeres y el ejercicio de derechos individuales, no representa la fundamentación teórica exclusiva del feminismo español sino que coexiste con un fuerte arraigo de un feminismo que se legitimiza a partir del presupuesto de la diferencia de género y del reconocimiento de roles sociales distintos de hombres y mujeres" ("Experiencia y aprendizaje" 158) [egalitarian feminism, based on the principle of equality between men and women and the exercise of individual rights, does not represent the exclusive foundation of Spanish feminism but coexists with a strong basis of a feminism that is legitimized on the presupposition of sexual difference and the recognition of different social roles for men and women]. And Maria Aurèlia Capmany notes that Spanish feminists, unlike their Anglo-American sisters, did not form an ideological front. Campany points out that each region in Spain had different social, economic, and political circumstances that demanded different solutions (see *De profesión mujer* 23–24). (*A New History of Iberian Feminisms* takes this situation into account.) In Spain, late eighteenth- and early nineteenth-century liberalism (especially the notion of representative government) of other Western countries such as France and England was weak. The ancien régime was prolonged in a medieval landholding system, in the top-down socioeconomic and political hierarchy, and in the relatively small and slow-growing bourgeoisie. Only a few wealthy men had the right to vote. The general lack of confidence in electoral democracy did not inspire women to place the vote at the center of their agenda for change. Rather, education became the motivating force, education that would provide women the means to work and gain economic independence from men. Mary Nash also points to another factor in Spanish society that steered early Spanish feminism in directions other than suffrage—"el claro predominio del discurso de la domesticidad" (160) [the clear preponderance of a discourse of domesticity], which forms the basis of Spanish feminism and shapes its course. Understanding this fundamental difference between Spanish feminism and that of other Western countries is important to contemporary debates between "difference" feminists and "equality" feminists that have characterized recent Spanish feminist theory.

A number of studies exist on French, American, English, and Italian feminist thought, but there is only one monograph on Spanish feminist disc ourse—Estrella Cibreira's *Palabra de mujer: Hacia la reinvindicación y contextualización del discurso feminista español* [Women's word: Towards the vindication and contextualization of Spanish feminist discourse]. Cibreira's is a valuable initiation into the topic, but it is written in Spanish and includes commentary on both essays and fictional works. The many histories of women and histories of feminism in Spain are likewise written in Spanish and have not been translated. Catherine Davies's "Feminist Writers in Spain Since 1900: From Political Strategy to Personal Inquiry," a useful survey that treats Carmen de Burgos, Margarita Nelken, Clara Campoamor, Federica Montseny, Carmen Laforet, Carmen Martín Gaite, Lidia Falcón, Monsterrat Roig, Esther Tusquets, and Rosa Montero, includes both essayists and novelists. *Spanish Women Writers and the Essay: Gender, Politics, and the Self*, edited by Kathleen M. Glenn and Mercedes Mazquiarán de Rodríguez, contains in-depth considerations of specific women writers who wrote essays, although not all of them on feminist topics. The volume includes Emilia Pardo Bazán, Carmen de Burgos, María Martínez Sierra, Margarita Nelken, Rosa Chacel, María Zambrano, Carmen Martín Gaite, Lidia Falcón, Montserrat Roig, Soledad Puértolas, and Rosa Montero. *Constructing Spanish Womanhood: Female Identity in Modern Spain*, edited by Victoria Lorée Enders and Pamela Beth Radcliff, contains a number of useful essays on significant topics related to Spanish feminism from the early nineteenth to the mid-twentieth century—motherhood, Catholicism, work, and politics; I reference the articles on women's work in chapter 4. Most recently, *Recovering the Spanish Feminist Tradition*, edited by Lisa Vollendorf for the Modern Language Association of America, marks another milestone, as it contains important analyses of specific authors of all literary genres from the Renaissance forward. Lastly, I mention two volumes I have coedited and that I hope the present volume complements—*Antología del pensamiento feminista español 1700–2012* (with Maite Zubiaurre) [Anthology of Spanish feminist thought 1700–2012] and *A New History of Iberian Feminisms* (with Silvia Bermúdez). The first supplies a sampling of texts of Spanish feminism across three centuries, and the second chronicles the history of Spanish and Portuguese feminist thinking with special emphasis on the particularities of feminist thought in the key Spanish territories—the Basque Country, Castile, Catalonia, and Galicia.

While these studies move chronologically from author to author, *Major Concepts in Spanish Feminist Theory* is organized around six central concepts that mark the focus of its chapters: (1) solitude, (2) personality, (3) work, (4) social class, (5) equality, and (6) difference.[1]

The six concepts are intertwined, but pairs of concepts—solitude and personality, work and social class, and equality and difference—bear particular affinities, in part because they share the same historical time frame. Work and social class were important topics of Spanish feminist thinking in the 1920s and 1930s, when leftist political parties were gaining ground in Spain leading up to the Second Republic and during the Republic's brief rule. Equality and difference feminism, while they have precedents in earlier Spanish feminist thinking, are especially linked to the democratic era. These two concepts, in fact, became identified with particular Spanish feminist schools of thought that engaged in open and sometimes hostile public debate, a debate that continues to smolder today (See my article "The Concept of Gender Equality in Constitutional Spain"). The concepts of solitude and personality can be found throughout the modern history of Spanish feminist theory. The importance of these concepts in Spanish feminist theory can be attributed to the fact that Spanish women were not traditionally considered persons in their own right, but rather as appendages of the men in their lives—fathers, brothers, husbands, sons. Given that certain writers focused on one or another concept, they are treated only in the chapters of their particular focus. Such is the case, for example, of Rosa Chacel and Maria Zambrano in the chapters on solitude and personality. In addition, since these writers are more philosophically inclined, their approaches to feminism are less sociological than others treated in later chapters. The book's themes are arranged in a roughly chronological format (1700 to the present). Thus early mid-twentieth-century authors, such as Zambrano and Chacel, are less likely to appear in later chapters, especially the chapters on difference and equality that come to the fore in democratic Spain (1975–present).

Within each chapter I also follow a roughly chronological format to analyze the work of several writers who have treated the chapter's subject. Although *Major Concepts* is not a comparative study, the concept approach allows me to highlight the important contributions of Spanish thinking to Western feminist theory. Questions I address are not necessarily those that shaped the development of feminist theory in other countries. For example, as the chapters on solitude and personality reveal, education and personal development, rather than suffrage, were the galvanizing issues in early Spanish feminist thinking. My format also allows comparison of several authors' views on a particular topic. Geraldine Scanlon's *La polémica feminista en España* also employs a topics format, but Scanlon's is more a factual history of the Spanish feminist movement(s). Nonetheless, Scanlon does discuss a number of theoretical matters that fueled feminist debates between 1868 and 1974.

Although *Major Concepts* is structured thematically, to take into account the importance of history and politics to Spanish feminist thought, I also consider the chronological development of Spanish feminist philosophy. This is a story of revival and recovery, and its perspective must be historical. Each chapter notes the recurrence of certain themes in Spanish feminist thought at different times that register the vicissitudes of Spanish history's somewhat circular path. Thus I trace the modifications each concept has undergone in various periods from the eighteenth century to the present. Despite the existence of significant feminist writings in nineteenth-century Spain, the first Spanish feminist movement flowered during the Second Spanish Republic (1931–1939).[2] This movement, which gained women the vote and social and political equality, was stymied by the Spanish Civil War (1936–1939) and the conservative, repressive dictatorship of Francisco Franco (1939–1975) that followed the war. When the dictator died in 1975 and Spain transitioned to a democratic form of government, the Spanish feminist movement recovered some of the ground women had lost between 1939 and 1978, when under the new constitution women once again gained the vote and equality before the law. Themes such as work, social class, and women's solidarity that had been muted in women's nonfiction writing from 1939 to 1975 reappeared. Even toward the end of the dictatorship, a timid thaw witnessed the emergence of some feminist writing, such as Lidia Falcón's *Mujer y sociedad* (1969), Geraldine Scanlon's landmark book *La polémica feminista en la España contemporánea, 1868–1974* (1975), and other more recent studies such as Pilar Folguera's and Nash's; such writings provide a great deal of the historical background in which I situate the development of the six major concepts I address. Unlike my book, these historical studies do not engage in detailed analyses of specific theoretical topics, and Scanlon's important book ends with the demise of the Franco dictatorship in 1975.

Major Concepts includes prominent Spanish feminist thinkers from the eighteenth century (Father Feijoo, Josefa de Amar), the second half of the nineteenth century (Concepción Arenal and Emilia Pardo Bazán), the early twentieth century (Carmen de Burgos, María Martínez Sierra, Margarita Nelken, Hildegart Rodríguez, and Federica Montseny), those who began writing in the 1930s and continued to write in exile after the Civil War (Rosa Chacel and Maria Zambrano), the Franco era (María Laffitte, Lilí Álvarez, Carmen Laforet, Lidia Falcón, Montserrat Roig), the transition to democracy (Rosa Montero and Carmen Martín Gaite), and democracy (Celia Amorós, Victoria Sendón de León, Alicia Puleo, Carmen Alborch, Milagros Rivera, Marina Subirats, Alicia Miyares, and Lucía Extebarria), among others. Given the ultraconservative, restrictive religious, social, and political milieu in which Spanish feminist thinkers of the nineteenth century until the 1980s lived and worked, their achievements as feminist thinkers are especially remarkable.

Concepción Arenal (1820–1893), whose liberal father was imprisoned and died shortly thereafter, defied her very Catholic mother and dressed as a man to attend university classes on law. Countess Emilia Pardo Bazán (1851–1921), a prolific writer of essays and fiction, founded and wrote her own journal, *Teatro Crítico*, and published a book series intended for women. Joyce Tolliver believes that despite her prolific production in fiction, Pardo Bazán should be considered primarily an essayist, remarking that "she was never timid about expressing her sympathies with the feminist movements that were gaining momentum in Europe and the United States" (14). Pardo Bazán spoke and wrote vehemently in favor of women's education, despite the dominant male culture's ridicule of her. As was the case of María Laffitte (1902–1986) and Lilí Álvarez (1905–1998)—both titled aristocrats and feminists during the reactionary Franco regime—Pardo Bazán's social class was important in making her feminist ideas heard. Carmen de Burgos (1867–1932) broke several social taboos by leaving her husband at the turn of the twentieth century to move to Madrid, where she lived as a single woman journalist and teacher. She wrote numerous popular novelettes on feminist themes, in addition to her feminist essays and speeches. María Martínez Sierra (1874–1974), married to Gregorio Martínez Sierra, a theatrical impresario, penned well-received plays as well as feminist essays and speeches, which Gregorio signed or delivered in public. Margarita Nelken (1894–1968), art critic and single mother, was first a socialist, then a communist political militant; she was one of the first women to be elected to the legislature under the Second Spanish Republic. Federica Montseny's parents Joan Montseny and Soledad Gustavo were important anarchist activists, as was Federica (1905–1994), who lived according to the ideology she preached. Hildegart Rodríguez (1914–1933) was a prodigy conceived by her mother out of wedlock to be schooled in and to propagate her mother's ideas on feminism, sexual liberation, and eugenics. Ironically, her mother shot her when at age eighteen she began to show some independence of spirit. Rosa Chacel (1898–1994), self-taught philosopher, and María Zambrano (1904–1991), with a doctorate in philosophy, published daring feminist essays in a philosophical milieu dominated by misogynist José Ortega y Gasset. Both continued their feminist writing in Latin American exile when the Franco regime made life in Spain impossible for Republican-sympathizing intellectuals. Interestingly, they both moved away from feminist writing after the early 1950s, when it became clear that the Allies were not going to vanquish Franco, and they would not be returning to Spain anytime soon, where they might have had an opportunity to make a feminist impact on their nation. Clearly, both writers were anxious to universalize their philosophical themes and ensure that their work would have wider appeal. As detailed in chapter 2, Zambrano left women's concerns to focus on humanity in general via her notion of "person," especially in *Persona y democracia* (1955, Person and Democracy), and after *Saturnal* (1970) Chacel left essay writing to concentrate on fiction, which she probably perceived as more lucrative in her penurious exiled state.

The relationship of the individual to society is one of the themes that bind together the chapters on the concepts of solitude, personality, social class, work, equality, and difference, as these themes have developed in Spanish feminist thought over the course of nearly three hundred years. Two rival positions emerge—one emphasizes women in their social milieu and the other focuses on women as individuals. In the nineteenth century, Concepción Arenal exemplifies the first position when she defends education for women as a means to better society as a whole, while Emilia Pardo Bazán argues that women should be educated for their own personal improvement and enjoyment. Arenal's argument from the exterior is continued in 1920s and 1930s feminist writing by Carmen de Burgos and Margarita Nelken in favor of legal parity for women. In this period and into the 1940s through the 1970s from their exile in Latin America, Rosa Chacel and María Zambrano looked to women's inner selves as the loci of their strength and place in the world. In the late Franco era and the democratic period, these two positions, with important modifications, can be detected in thinkers such as equality feminist Celia Amorós and difference feminist Milagros Rivera (who often relies on María Zambrano's insights).

"Feminism" and "Theory" in the Spanish Context

I employ the term "feminist" for writing that addresses women's condition to expose or attempt to correct inequities. Lidia Falcón defines feminism within the Spanish context: "[l]a mujer está sometida al hombre desde que nace. Vive las condiciones que le han sido dadas por sus padres, por su ambiente, por su escuela, por la sociedad entera. Salir de ello requiere lucha y sacrificio y preparación que no la tiene" (qtd. in Vollendorf, "Introduction" 4) [women are subjected to men from birth. They live within the conditions they have been given by their parents, by their ambience, by their school, by their whole society. Struggle, sacrifice, and further education are required for women to move beyond this condition].[3] I would add to this definition that feminism and especially feminist thought pertain not only to the struggle, but to the attempt to reveal the conditions that maintain women in a subjugated position. As Najat El Hachmi argues, while feminism is a global phenomenon, it has specific manifestations in different areas of the world: "El feminismo es una lucha global de las mujeres que en cada una de sus realidades socioculturales tienen que encontrar el mecanismo más adecuado para cambiar el machismo particular que les ha tocado" ("La discriminación positiva" 1) [Feminism is a global struggle of women who in each one of their sociocultural realities have to find the most appropriate means to change the particular masculinism that pertains to them]. Sometimes the arguments are ontological; other times they are political, legal, social, or refer to personal practices. María Ángeles Durán reminds us that the dictionary of the Royal Spanish Academy defines *feminism* as "una doctrina, un sistema elaborado de pensamiento. . . . probablemente en el uso actual dominan las connotaciones relativas al estilo de conducta, a prácticas sociales" ("Introducción," *Mujeres y hombres* 12) [a doctrine, an elaborated system of thought. . . . probably in today's usage the connotations relative to a style of conduct, to social practices]. As I do here, Durán recognizes that the term *feminism* changes with the time and place in which it is used.

While in the Anglo-American world, few who write about or work for the improvement of women's situation would contest the label "feminist," such has not been the case in Spain. "Feminist" has been a troubled category, even for the women such as Federica Montseny, Rosa Chacel, María Zambrano, and Soledad Puértolas, who fit most definitions of feminism but who were or are reluctant to be called feminist. For example, Kathleen Glenn reports that "Soledad Puértolas rejected the idea that as a female author she should shed light on the world of women" ("Voice" 374). At the same time, Mercedes Mazquiarán de Rodríguez finds feminist statements in Puértolas's *La vida oculta*: "Puértolas's self-acknowledged inability to respond quickly and cogently in front of an audience is the result of social conditioning, and her own annoyance regarding the fact is an indication of her awareness of the limitations patriarchal societies have imposed on women. Uneasiness when facing the public eye has traditionally been a woman's reaction in male-dominated cultures" (237).[4] Mazquiarán de Rodríguez also cites Puértolas on women's writing: "Why should it be acceptable, she wonders, for male writers to write about anything they desire without anyone questioning the reasons for their choices, while all women are expected to write about the same things. Once again she poses a rhetorical question laden with irony: 'Is it that women perhaps and within that category, women writers, are condemned to be exactly the same?'" (238). In Spain, women such as Emilia Pardo Bazán, many of whose writings could be identified as feminist, run the risk of being considered masculine. According to Geraldine Scanlon, Pardo Bazán's *Nuevo Teatro Crítico*, the journal she wrote and published entirely on her own, "demonstrates, wrote a contemporary biographer, the capabilities of her 'varonil espíritu' [manly spriritl] (Anon.); Gómez de Baquero affirms that few contemporary male writers would be equal to the task she has undertaken, and Mariano de Cavia refers to her as 'La Madre Feijóo [Mother Feijóo], calling her an 'autor' or author rather than authoress because 'es mucho hombre esta mujer' [that woman is some man]" ("Gender and Journalism" 244–45).

It is not entirely clear why the label "feminist" should have such negative connotations in Spain. Often those who resist the feminist label pit feminism against what they consider more universal human concerns. Some writers and activists, such as Federica Montseny, were "double militants" who did not believe that matters relating specifically to women should take precedence over what they considered larger issues, such as class oppression. Lidia Falcón countered that argument by declaring women to be a social class. Central to some Spanish feminist thought is that the sexes are absolutely equal in abjection of all sorts, including what they consider bourgeois marriage. Spanish feminists, whose society has traditionally and institutionally maintained highly differentiated sexual roles, have often had to find ways of mediating between feminist ideals in other countries and ones that can be accepted in Spain. As Mary Lee Bretz points out, one of María Martínez Sierra's contributions to Spanish feminist theory is her wedding of the notions feminine and feminist. Martínez Sierra argues that no woman should reject the label "feminist," because being feminist does not subtract from a woman's femininity (that is, her domesticity, maternity, and care-giving):

> Toda actividad generosa que le haga traspasar por un momento los lindes encantados de su propio hogar, acercarse a la vida, ponerse en situación de comprenderla, de darse cuenta de que hay un más allá, o un más abajo, hecho de injusticias tremendas y de dolores insospechados, lejos de hacer perder femininidad a su espíritu, la aumentará, ensanchándole el corazón a medida que acrezca el conocimiento. Por saber más no es una mujer menos mujer . . . no puede dar de sí más que un perfeccionamiento de sus facultades naturales, nunca un cambio de su naturaleza. (*Feminismo* 13)

> [All generous activity that makes her leave the enchanted borders of her own home for a moment, approach life, place herself in a situation to understand it, to realize that there is something beyond, or below, full of tremendous injustices and unsuspected pain, far from causing a loss of femininity in her

spirit, will increase it, enlarging her heart as her knowledge grows. Just because a woman is more learned, does not mean she is less of a woman. . . . she can only perfect her natural faculties; she cannot change her nature.]

Maryellen Bieder notes that early in her career, Carmen de Burgos was a master of holding feminist positions and carrying out feminist activities, while strategically rejecting the label "feminist": "As she frequently does in her public statements, she takes both sides of the issue, opposing feminism but recognizing its fundamental role in enacting social change" ("Carmen de Burgos" 250–51). By the 1920s, however, Burgos unequivocally declared herself a feminist (Bieder, "Carmen" 251).

In many cases one suspects that in rejecting the feminist label, Spanish women writers wish to avoid the kinds of ridicule leveled at feminists, who were caricatured from the earliest years of the twentieth century onward in the popular press and in novels such as Pío Baroja's *Paradox, rey* [Paradox, king] and *El mundo es ansí* [That's the way the world is]. In these novels the feminist characters are foreign (English or Russian), and thus a latent nationalism may be operating in Baroja's and other male writers' depictions of feminism as a foreign movement that could invade Spanish soil where traditional womanhood formed part of the nation's identity. These caricatures persisted in the scorn heaped on Carmen de Burgos, whose pseudonym Colombine [Buttercup] was transformed into Colombone [oversized buttercup; Burgos was a large woman], and in the ostracizing of highly militant late-Franco-era feminists such as Lidia Falcón. Some women writers learned to shun any association that would similarly attempt to marginalize them, although others, including Carmen de Burgos, María Martínez Sierra, Margarita Nelken, Montserrat Roig, Rosa Montero, and Lucía Etxebarria, openly called or call themselves feminists. However, some male public figures, such as dictator General Miguel Primo de Rivera and novelist Felipe Trigo, who readily adopted the feminist label, may be suspect.[5]

Double militancy, that is, militancy for a political ideology as well as for feminist causes, is another aspect of Spanish feminism that complicates women's identification with the feminist label. Mireia Bofill highlights the importance in Spain of the intertwining of political ideology and feminist thinking, contrasting the Spanish situation to that in the United States:

Claro, en América, hay antologías de textos u otros de redacción, pero, vamos, no los hay desde nuestro punto de vista que a lo mejor es más politico. A nivel de divulgación general, seguramente es más politico y entonces hay que ver la relación de la lucha política con la situación de la mujer, si una está subordinada a la otra, si son dos luchas independientes, si las mujeres deben luchar sólo por las mujeres y prescindir de la lucha política, o luchar sólo políticamente y dejar lo de las mujeres o intentar coordinar las dos cosas. (Levine and Waldman 49)

[Of course, in America, there are anthologies of texts or others of essays, but, for us they don't exist; our viewpoint is more political. At the level of popular dissemination, surely it is more political, and then we have to consider women's situation in its relation to the general political struggle—if women should fight only for women and not engage in the political struggle, or enter only into the political fray and leave behind women's issues or try to combine the two things.]

In the pre–Civil War era, many Spanish feminists were identified with one or another of the leftist parties or ideologies and militated to varying degrees within them—Margarita Nelken, first with the Socialist Party and later with the Communist Party; María Martínez Sierra with the Socialist Party (at least in the 1920s and 1930s); Federica Montseny with anarchism. Thus Spanish feminist theorists often feel the need to prioritize their several interests. In Monstseny's case, for example, what she considered to be universal human concerns took precedence over issues she deemed more narrowly pertaining to women. María Martínez Sierra, while not directly addressing the division between more universal political militancy and feminist militancy, devoted most of her essays to feminist matters.

Double militancy was a divisive issue in the 1970s after the long oppression of both women and leftist political parties allied with the working class. In an attempt to overcome the theoretical dichotomy between gender and class, Lidia Falcón argued that women are a separate social class: "[n]osotros consideramos que la mujer es una clase oprimida, por lo tanto, entra dentro de la problemática de la lucha de clases evidentemente y hasta que la problemática ésta no se haya resuelto, tampoco se resolverá la de la mujer. Para mí, no tiene importancia una cosa que otra, tiene la misma. La lucha debe llevarse al mismo nivel y además no es imposible" (Levine and Waldman 71) [we believe that women are an oppressed class, and therefore they clearly enter into the problematics of the class struggle, and until it has been resolved, women's situation will not be resolved. As far as I am concerned neither is more important than the other; they carry the same weight. It is not impossible to take the struggles to the same level]. Carmen Alcalde saw women's struggle as the overriding one, and like Falcón, she viewed women as a social class whose interests should take precedence over all others: "para mí es más importante la lucha de la mujer. Para mí, es la primera lucha de clases que existe. . . . es más importante, la lucha de sexos, la lucha sexista. Mientras esto no se solucione la mujer seguirá colaborando con los partidos, con sus presidentes y directivas" (33) [for me the women's cause is the most important. For me, it was the first class struggle to ever exist. . . . the battle of the sexes, the sexist battle is more important. As long as that issue remains unsolved, women will continue to collaborate with the political parties, with their precedents and directives].

The term "theory" presents another set of problems for the Spanish case. Scholars have not been accustomed to considering Spanish thought when theorizing about feminist issues in Spanish writing, partly because that writing often does not resemble theory as we understand it—namely, engaging in pure abstraction. Many Spanish feminist writings, such as Carmen de Burgos's book on divorce in Spain (1904) and her *La mujer moderna y sus derechos* (1927), Margarita Nelken's *La condición social de la mujer en España* (1919), and Lidia Falcón's *Mujer y sociedad* (1969) are more historical, sociological, or political in nature. Of course, there is theory behind historical, political, or sociological essays, but sometimes it is submerged and latent. One must tease it out and foreground it. Spanish feminist thinkers often distinguish between theory and practice, with some tendency to favor the latter. Lidia Falcón mentions a woman acquaintance who became disillusioned with attending feminist meetings in the early 1970s, because those present devoted the time to "una comparación de teorías feministas" (Levine and Waldman 75) [a comparison of feminist theories]. Eva Forest points to the need to base theory on experience:

> Nosotras no queremos partir de textos; más bien los problemas que surgen en cada sesión

nos llevan a los textos. Por ejemplo nos preguntamos después de una discusión: ¿cómo respondieron las mujeres de cierta clase social a estos problemas? Entonces cada una se encarga y hace un poco un resumen de lo que se ha dicho sobre ese problema. Eso nos obliga a estudiar mucho y ver el problema como vinculado con todos los demás problemas. (Levine and Waldman 104)

[We do not want to begin with texts; instead the problems that come up in each session take us to the texts. For example, we ask ourselves after a discussion: how did women of a certain social class respond to these problems? Then each one of us takes responsibility and summarizes a little of what has been said about this problem. This obliges us to study a great deal and to see the problem in relation to all the other problems.]

Feminist theorists from France and the United States, such as Luce Irigaray, Julia Kristeva, Hélène Cixous, Nancy Chodorow, Carol Gilligan, and Judith Butler, take a mostly ahistorical "universalistic" or abstract philosophical or psychoanalytical approach to the study of matters relating to women and gender. By contrast, Spanish feminist theory is more directly tied to specifically Spanish situations, and Spanish feminist writers for the most part begin their analyses and arguments with a historical review as background to understanding a current situation. The emphasis on history may be attributed to the fact that since modern feminism began to emerge in the late nineteenth century, Spanish political history has varied more than that of France, England, or the United States.

This situation does not mean that Spanish feminist theory is not philosophically informed. Most Spanish feminist thinkers reveal the influence of one or more (usually male) thinkers, whose ideas they have employed or modified for their own purposes. Krausism—a Spanish neo-Kantianism—and John Stuart Mill's liberalism are evident in Concepción Arenal and Emilia Pardo Bazán's feminist writing. In fact, Krausism is perhaps a singularly important source of difference between Spanish feminism and other European and American feminisms. Krausism is an odd blend of God-centered German rationalism and ethical social reformism that sought to reconcile the several strands of modern thought that had been seeping through the cracks of the Spanish Catholic hegemony since the late eighteenth century. Concepción Arenal, born in 1820, was a contemporary of Julián Sanz del Río (born in 1814). Sanz del Río popularized Karl Christian Friedrich Krause's ideas in Spain with his courses at the University of Madrid from 1854 to 1867 and with the publication of his *Lecciones para el sistema de filosofía analítica de K.Ch. F. Krause* in 1850 [Lessons for a system of analytical philosophy of K. Ch. F. Krause] and *Ideal de la humanidad para la vida* [Ideal of humanity for life] in 1860.

Arenal's intellectual formation took place in an atmosphere and historical circumstances similar to those of Julián Sanz del Río (except for Sanz del Río's sojourn in Belgium and Germany). And while Sanz del Río garnered a well-recognized following of distinguished thinkers, among them Francisco Giner de los Ríos, Gumersindo de Azcárate, Nicolás Salmerón, and Pedro Dorado, it has long been forgotten that Arenal was also an inspiration to the younger Krausists. She was a close friend of Francisco Giner de los Ríos, with whom she carried on an extensive correspondence.[6] Pedro Dorado wrote a book on her, and Gumersindo de Azcárate, who wrote essays on Arenal,[7] professed a "verdadero culto . . . hacia la excepcional y admirable personalidad de doña Concepción Arenal" [a real cult . . . for the exceptional and admirable personality of Concepción Arenal], this according to Pedro de Azcárate.[8] I consider the coincidences between Arenal's thought and that of the Krausists as parallel developments, especially in the 1860s, when according to Juan López Morillas, "Sanz del Río's influence was extraordinary" (8).[9] By the 1880s, however, when the heyday of Krausism was over and parodies of it began to appear (for example, Galdós's *La familia de León Roch* [1879; Leon Roch's family] and *El amigo manso* [1882; The docile friend]), Arenal adopted a more specifically Krausist vocabulary to her feminist purpose. Her first feminist book, *La mujer del porvenir*, employs Krausist-sounding concepts, such as *perfección humana* [human perfection] and *armonía universal* [universal harmony], in a fairly general way to argue for women's education, while in the later work, *La mujer de su casa* [The stay-at-home woman], she moves to a more philosophically intricate argument for women's involvement in the public sphere, which she regards as essential to the health of the nation. Her use of Krausist concepts and vocabulary is more technical and precise in *La mujer de su casa*, although I speculate that her recourse to Krausist concepts in 1883 is perhaps ironic and not a little subversive. As we will see in some of the pages that follow, Arenal may have adopted the "equal but different" stance with regard to the genders that is at the heart of Krausist thinking on the matter (see Labanyi, *Gender and Modernization* 83).

Krausism likewise melds what might seem to be conflicting impulses in its rationalistic theism. It is possible that Arenal's early contact with Enlightenment and Romantic thinking in the libraries of her father and his family began to be colored with Krausist tinges as early as the 1840s, when several of Arenal's biographers have determined that she was dressing in men's clothing in order to sit in on law classes at the University of Madrid and attend intellectual café *tertulias*. 1841 saw publication of the Spanish version of *Cours de Droit naturel* by German jurist Heinrich Ahrens, who, according to Juan López-Morillas "taught, from his chair at the University of Brussels, a system of philosophy of law directly inspired by Krause's doctrines" (5). If, as López Morillas states, Sanz del Río's "first contact with Krausism [via the translation of Ahren's book] . . . seems to have aroused in Sanz del Río an interest bordering on obsession" (5), what attracted Sanz del Río to Krausism, and what Arenal must have found equally appealing, was its "progressivist and humanitarian ethics" (5). Its "harmonic rationalism" allowed for the wedding of traditional Spanish spiritual values and modern secular science and reason. Such an accommodation particularly suited Arenal, whose family background was a microcosm of Spain in the early nineteenth century. Her father was a liberal supporter of the Constitution of Cádiz, and he died after a debilitating term in prison for conspiratorial activities when Fernando VII's reign breached its promise to maintain the tenets of constitutional monarchy and reverted to absolutism and repression in 1823. Arenal's mother was more conservative and traditional; her views were at odds with those of her daughter, whose avid reading in secular literature and attendance at the University of Madrid she strongly opposed.

Mill's concept of the servitude of women looms large in the work of Carmen de Burgos, María Martínez Sierra, and Margarita Nelken, although each adds significant dimensions to Mill's ideas that fit the Spanish context. José Ortega y Gasset's ratio-vitalism and Max Scheler's notion of "person" are central to Rosa Chacel's and María Zambrano's formulation of (female) personhood. Marxism, socialism, and anarchism inform Margarita Nelken's and Federica Montseny's writings of the 1920s and 1930s and Lidia Falcón's conception of women as a social class in the late 1960s and 1970s. In the late Franco and democratic eras, existentialism, Enlightenment rationalism, and French, American, and Italian feminist theory are important philosophical sources and methods.

Betty Friedan's notion of the feminine mystique had a major impact on Lidia Falcón's writing in the late 1960s, and Carmen Martín Gaite discovered US feminist ideas about women's writing, especially those of Sandra Gilbert and Susan Gubar, Judith Fetterly, and Adrienne Rich, which inspired her to theorize about Spanish women's literature in new ways (see especially her *Desde la ventana*). Spanish equality feminism from the 1980s to the present rejects the premises of poststructuralism in favor of the critical reason of Enlightenment thinker François Poulain de la Barre. Poststructuralism, however, can be indirectly related to Spanish difference feminism of the same period via the traces it bears of French and Italian feminist theory. Although my study is not comparative, I do note wherever possible influences of foreign feminist theorists on Spanish thinkers (for example, Simone de Beauvoir, Betty Friedan, Luce Irigaray, and Luisa Muraro have had significant impact on Spanish feminist thought since 1960).

A Circular History and Arguments from History

As I have noted, unlike the more linear trajectory of feminist thought in other countries, Spanish feminist thinking has traversed a circular path that follows the vicissitudes of twentieth-century Spanish history. Catherine Davies divides her study of twentieth-century Spanish feminist writing into four parts that follow the swings in Spanish political life in the last century. The first section from 1900 to 1930 covers the last years of the Restoration (1875–1931) and the Primo Rivera dictatorship (1923–1930), especially the crucial post–World War I era in which Spanish women entered the workplace in larger numbers and thus gained greater consciousness of their inferior social and legal status. The second part focuses on the Second Republic (1931–1939), when women achieved the vote and equality before the law and entered political life as *diputadas* [congresswomen] and government officials. The third period encompasses the dictatorship of Francisco Franco (1939–1975), when all the gains made under the Republic were rescinded and earlier legal codes reinstated. Even worse, some aspects of women's roles that were formerly a matter of social convention (e.g., domesticity) became institutionalized through the Sección Femenina de Falange that required women to attend courses in cooking, housekeeping, and child-rearing. Finally, during the period of transition and democracy (1975–1990), women once again gained the right to divorce, to limited abortion, and to equality before the law. My chronology begins with Benito Jerónimo Feijoo's *Defensa de la mujer* (1729) and Concepción Arenal's *La mujer del porvenir* (1869) and thus adds a period (1729–1900) to Davies's periodization. All six of the concepts I analyze here have their beginnings in the pioneering work of Father Feijoo, Josefa Amar y Borbón, Inés de Joya, Concepción Arenal, and Emilia Pardo Bazán in the eighteenth and nineteenth centuries.[10] Arenal's and Pardo Bazán's thought draws on Feijoo's; they both wrote essays on Feijoo's thought, although not necessarily on his feminism. Curiously, however, Spanish equality feminists of the democratic era have passed over their own Enlightenment countrymen and women to find inspiration in the French Enlightenment. Following the chronological scheme allows me to perceive the gaps and repetitions in the development of Spanish feminist theory.

In the 1970s Spanish feminists had to "reinvent the wheel" after the forty-year hiatus in legal and social progress for women during the Franco era. Many feminist issues of the pre-Republican and Republican eras (1920s and 1930s) resurfaced in the late 1960s as Francisco Franco approached death. The pre-Republican years were governed by the Civil Code of 1889, a series of legal statutes that severely restricted women's legal independence. In *La mujer moderna y sus derechos*, Carmen de Burgos is particularly eloquent on the "legal construction" of Spanish womanhood, which she defines as a relegation to the status of "eterna menor" (144) [eternal minor]. Unmarried women could not live alone without parental permission and were legally prohibited from becoming pregnant. If a woman became pregnant out of wedlock, the law forbade paternity investigations. A married woman's husband had to authorize any work or travel she wished to undertake, and the husband controlled the woman's money. The infamous article 438 dictated that the man who killed his adulterous wife was only sentenced to exile; if he beat her there was no punishment. Lidia Falcón's *Mujer y sociedad* (1969) revisits the legal construction of womanhood forty years after Carmen de Burgos's *La mujer moderna y sus derechos* appeared. Both women appeal to nationalist instincts by comparing Spanish legal structures to those in other countries. Burgos emphasizes the gains made by women in England, while Falcón includes a chapter on "Tío Sam" [Uncle Sam], which bears the heavy imprint of Betty Friedan. In *Feminismo*, María

Martínez Sierra also compares Spain and the United States, although in her pre–Betty Friedan world, she views women's situation in the United States in a more positive light.

There were, of course, some feminist threads that were not severed during the Franco years, although, on the whole, Franco-era feminists were only vaguely aware of the work feminists had done in the pre-War period, if at all. When Franco-era feminists cite pre-War feminist thinking, they seldom mention specifics. Carmen Alcalde comments, for example, that

> [n]os quedamos un poco cortas. No supimos ver de verdad todos los valores que hubo en los años veinticinco, treinta y treinta y cinco, y en la Guerra, la gente de un valor extraordinario como Victoria Kent y Margarita Nelken o digamos «La Pasionaria», que ya es mito, y Federica Montseny y una cantidad de gente anónima con unos esfuerzos tan grandes y tan pioneras que verdaderamente no se puede decir que no hubo feminismo, tal como se dijo en este libro [her *El feminismo ibérico* co-authored with María Aurèlia Capmany and published in 1970]. (Levine and Waldman 27–28)

> [we came up a bit short. We really were unable to see all the value of the years 1925, 30, 35, and during the War, people of extraordinary merit such as Victoria Kent and Margarita Nelken or "La Pasionaria," who is now a myth, and Federica Montseny and a large number of anonymous people who made enormous efforts and were so pioneering that truly one cannot say that there wasn't feminism, as was stated in this book.]

When asked if the work of feminists like Margarita Nelken and Victoria Kent in the 1920s and 1930s was known to postwar feminists, Elisa Lamas replies that there was an "ignorancia total" (Levine and Waldman 117), because the younger women were all educated under the Franco regime, which recognized nothing that happened in Spain before July 18, 1936, when army generals, including Franco, revolted against the Republic. She remarks that a few highly educated women were aware of the feminist movement in the prewar period, "pero son una parte pequeñísima de la población" (117) [a very small part of the population].

As Catherine Davies points out, the concern for issues that had occupied feminist writing in the 1920s and 1930s did not completely disappear between 1939 and the late 1960s; they went underground and found publication outlets in the novel: "fiction [from 1940 to the 1970s] provided virtually the only means by which women . . . were able to express their preoccupations, to affirm their identity, to arouse public awareness, and yet avoid . . . arbitrary censorship" (208). Openly feminist discourse disappeared from public view in the early years of the Franco regime, to be replaced by the traditional rhetoric and ideals on women's domesticity, wifehood, and maternity propagated by the Sección Femenina de Falange.[11] Concerns about women's education, work, and class can, however, be found embedded in novels such as *Nada* [Nothing] by Carmen Laforet (1945), in which Andrea, an eighteen-year-old girl, narrates a year she spent in Barcelona attending the university immediately after the Civil War. Andrea fits the "chica rara" [odd girl] type defined by Carmen Martín Gaite in an essay by that title. The odd girl goes against the grain of womanhood promoted by the Franco regime—the traditional wife, mother, and homemaker. She is not looking for a husband, likes to be alone, and is studying for a career. She breaks any number of social taboos. Even though her family is from the upper middle class, Andrea interacts comfortably with her lower middle-class Aunt Gloria, a working woman. It is the women of the household—Aunt Gloria, Aunt Angustias, the maid Antonia—who work steadily and keep the family afloat economically; the men are useless in the working world. Laforet herself lived in Spain under the Franco regime for its entire thirty-six years (twenty-one of those as a married woman); she continued to work, often as an important supporter of the family, when her husband's income did not cover expenses. She diverted her creative writing talents to journalism, which was quicker to produce and brought a more steady income than her preferred fiction writing. However, the income she received from *Nada* and her other novels and stories provided a source of support when she separated from her husband in 1970.

Countess Campo Alange María Laffitte's *La secreta guerra de los sexos* (1948) [The secret war of the sexes] was an important exception to the ban on publishing "subversive" feminist essays in the most restrictive years of the Franco regime (1939–1953). Notably, this work appeared a year before Simone de Beauvoir's *The Second Sex*, which exercised its most important impact on Spanish equality feminism in the 1980s and 1990s. In the cover blurb for *La secreta guerra de los sexos*, Laffitte provocatively challenges the traditional female stereotypes the Franco regime enforced legally through the Sección Femenina courses in domesticity all women were required to complete before they could pursue studies, travel, or work (provided these were approved by her father or husband): "La idea de escribir este libro surgió en mí del choque brusco entre dos mentalidades distintas: aquella que sirvió de fondo a mi niñez dentro de un ambiente provinciano y tradicional y la que se ha producido recientemente en un mundo en plena evolución social. . . . Mi vida apersonal se nutre: en un principio de tradiciones seculares que vienen a morir entre convulsiones al borde mismo de mi plenitude vital" [The idea of writing this book arose from the sharp contrast between different mentalities: that which was the backdrop of my childhood in a rural, traditional environment and that which has come about more recently in a world in full social evolution]. María Laffitte's social position as a titled noblewoman surely helped garner her the government censors' blind eye when they reviewed her feminist manuscript.

In a pale reflection of the emergence of feminist writing and feminism in other Western countries, Spain saw a timid flowering of feminist essays in the 1960s. María Laffitte published *La mujer como mito y como ser humano* [Woman as myth and as a human being] in 1961, and Lidia Falcón's *Los derechos civiles de la mujer* [Women's civil rights] and *Los derechos laborales de la mujer* [Women's labor rights] appeared in 1962 and 1963, respectively. In 1962 María Laffitte and Lilí Álvarez formed a group (Seminario de Estudios Sociológicos sobre la Mujer [SESM]) of aristocratic and upper-middle-class women, including Concepción Borreguero, Elena Catena, Consuelo de la Gándara, María Jiménez Bermejo, Carmen Pérez Seonae, María Salas, and Pura Salas, to conduct feminist research. They met often at María Laffitte's home and produced several books of feminist sociology, which they signed collectively. According to María Salas, their ideology was characterized by "1. Una actitud visceral, vivencial y reflexiva ante la vida, que compromete a toda la persona y se refleja en su comportamiento, 2. Un sistema de ideas que, partiendo de la problemática de la mujer, afecta a todas las dimensiones de la sociedad: educación, familia, trabajo, política, economía, religión, ocio, etc. 3. Una acción movilizadora que lleva en sí el cambio social" ("En memoria de Consuelo de la Gándara," *Consuelo de la Gándara*, 14) [1. A visceral, experience-based, and reflective attitude toward life that involves all persons and is registered in their behavior; 2. A system of ideas that, starting from the problematics of women, affects all aspects of society: education, family, work, politics, economy, religion, leisure, etc. 3. A mobilizing action that carries within it social change].

The feminist publications of the 1960s did not receive much public attention, and most feminist issues only resurfaced as part of the public discourse in 1976 after Franco's death. According to Linda Gould Levine and Gloria Feiman Waldman, in May of that year

> varios grupos feministas organizaron una manifestación 'el Día de la Madre,' para pedir la legalización del aborto, la venta libre y gratuita de anticonceptivos, derechos iguales para hijos legítimos, ilegítimos y naturales y la abolición de la funesta *patria potestad paterna*. Se recogieron firmas para un escritor solicitando del Ministerio de Justicia la abolición de la figura delictiva del adulterio. (17)
>
> [various feminist groups organized a "Mother's Day" demonstration to demand the legalization of abortion, open and free sale of contraceptives, equal rights for illegitimate children and the abolition of the terrible *patria potestad paterna*. They collected signatures for a petition requesting that the Ministry of Justice abolish the law making adultery a crime.]

Some issues, such as contraception and abortion, are new to post-1976 feminist writing, but illegitimate children, adultery, and *patria potestad* all echo questions that had been launched by feminists in the 1920s and 1930s. In the 1970s Carmen Conde even repeated Carmen de Burgos's 1904 survey on divorce.

If historical circumstances inform the legal structures so prominent in Spanish feminist thought, they also strongly influence the style of argumentation we find in both pre-Francoist and post-Francoist feminist thinking. Some of the most frequently mentioned early-twentieth-century feminist essays—Carmen de Burgos's *La mujer moderna y sus derechos* and Margarita Nelken's *La condición social de la mujer*—as well as the more recent (late Franco-era) Lidia Falcón all emphasize the historical situation of Spanish women, especially aspects of Spanish women's condition that derive from Roman patriarchal law, Moorish customs, and Islamic law. All contributed in different ways to the Catholic Church's strong domination in matters relating to women's lives that make argumentation for Spanish theorists more of a minefield than it might have been for feminists in other countries.[12] While both Burgos and Falcón argue from history, Falcón foregrounds the history of women's oppression beginning in the Bible in order to explain women's situation in Franco's Spain.[13] Burgos, incorporates history into the specific chapters of *La mujer moderna* that center on the nature of gender and the rights she believes women should enjoy in the present (1920s). These include education, work, financial independence, divorce, equality in the religious and military realms, suffrage, and freedom of dress. Thus Burgos is more prescriptive, while Falcón more descriptive. Even Rosa Chacel's "Esquema de los problemas prácticos y actuales del amor" [Outline of practical and contemporary love problems] and *Saturnalia*, which are closer to the abstract philosophical style of feminist theorizing we associate with most French and Anglo-American feminist thought, include a historical dimension. Chacel argues from José Ortega y Gasset's notion that one lives enmeshed in one's historical circumstances. Thus, according to Chacel, women have not necessarily suffered injustice in any particular era; their situation is synchronous with the times in which they happen to live. She does find certain thinkers (especially Georg Simmel) to be out of synch with the times (the 1920s and 1930s) in continuing to assert that culture is male.[14]

Post-Franco Spanish feminism is dominated by a debate that is unique to Western second-wave feminism—a sharp divide between difference and equality feminism. If earlier manifestations of Spanish difference feminism are ambiguous and seem to straddle the fence between difference and equality feminism, by the early 1980s as Spain transitioned to democracy in the wake of the long antifeminist Franco regime and under the dual influence of Celia Amorós's Madrid Seminar and several groups in Barcelona under the influence of Italian difference feminism, the divide between the two orientations became more radicalized. The debate between equality and difference feminists has dominated Spanish feminist theoretical writing for much of constitutional Spain's thirty years.[15] Many contemporary feminist thinkers are academic women whose strong philosophical backgrounds inform their arguments about equality, although some have found means of popularizing their views as well.

Chapter 5 centers on the notion of difference in Spanish feminist theory, a concept that, along with the concept of equality, became the center of a heated debate in the 1980s and 1990s. However, the difference/equality split in Spanish feminist theory has historical roots that antedate the recent democratic era by several centuries. As I noted, Mary Nash argues that the history of Spanish feminist thought is best understood within a difference rather than a equality framework, especially given that Spanish feminism did not receive its initial impetus from a desire to achieve the vote. According to Nash, as a whole, early Spanish feminism subscribed to a proto-difference feminist position. She argues that Spanish feminism arose in the nineteenth century from the cult of difference and that the predominance of the discourse of domesticity in the configuration of value and models of feminity in contemporary Spanish society was central to Spanish women's lack of interest in achieving political parity with men (for example, there was no Spanish suffrage movement). Thus early Spanish feminists such as Concepción Arenal and Emilia Pardo Bazán argued for equal education but not for equal political rights.

Chapter 6 chronicles the long history of arguments for women's equality with men, beginning in the eighteenth century and continuing to the present day with the debates between difference and equality (or Enlightenment) feminists. Some early Spanish feminists, including Concepción Arenal and Carmen de Burgos, while ostensibly favoring equality, perhaps to make their arguments more palatable to a skeptical Spanish audience, include difference in their argumentation. The chapter ends with an assessment of the current state of the democratic-era debate over difference and equality. The epilogue summarizes some of the new directions Spanish feminist theory has taken since the turn of the millennium.

CHAPTER 1

Solitude

When we think of the notion of solitude in Spanish letters, usually male writers come to mind—Luis de Góngora, Miguel de Unamuno, Azorín, Pío Baroja, Antonio Machado, Juan Ramón Jiménez, Juan José Millás, among many others.[1] Perhaps unconsciously we consider solitude as masculine existential territory, since women are traditionally situated within their relationships to others, above all to family members. As Alda Blanco puts it, "[a] la mujer se le articuló principalmente como un ser relacional subordinado al hombre—ser hija, esposa, y madre era su cometido—se le adscribió el hogar como espacio propio, el único ámbito para su existencia" ("Teóricas" 446) [women were articulated principally as a relational being subordinated to men—their role was to be daughter, wife, and mother—she was assigned to the home as her own space, the only ambiance for her existence]. Here, following a line of inquiry Linda Chown initiated when she argued for "a revitalized look at culturally influenced concepts such as 'solitude' and 'self' and/or 'identity' [in Spanish women's writings]" ("Self/Identity" 198), I trace the concept of solitude in Spanish feminist thought from the end of the nineteenth century to the present to highlight the importance the notion of solitude for many Spanish women writers.[2] These writers consider solitude a necessary condition for women's forming their own identities and fully realizing themselves as independent individuals—workers, intellectuals, writers, artists, or even companions for men. I begin with nineteenth-century thinkers Concepción Arenal (1820–1893) and Emilia Pardo Bazán (1851–1921), who initiated a dialogue on women in relation to family and society. I then move forward in time to Rosa Chacel (1898–1994), who wrote a ground-breaking article in 1931 in answer to José Ortega y Gasset and other male European thinkers who doubted women's intellectual capacity. María Zambrano (1904–1991), approximately the same age as Chacel and also formed in José Ortega y Gasset's intellectual circle, wrote her key essays involving the concept of solitude during her exile from Spain after the Civil War (1936–1939); thus her theories on the subject are surely colored by her own personal solitude in exile. I continue with Carmen Laforet (1921–2004), Montserrat Roig (1946–1991), and Carmen Martín Gaite (1925–2000), who began their careers during the restrictive Franco regime, and conclude with Rosa Montero (1951–) and Carmen Alborch (1947–), somewhat younger women who began writing in the later years of the dictatorship. They offer a new approach to solitude that reflects women's situation during the transition to democracy and the democratic era.

Solitude has a variety of meanings for the authors mentioned above, but in every case solitude is a positive, affirming state replete with possibilities for human development; it lacks the negative connotations—isolation, alienation, melancholy, and even desperation—that men often associate with the solitary state.[3] As Linda Chown notes, "many Spanish writers consider solitude an unavoidable, inevitable condition of MIND for all people, a condition which, if developed, becomes a place of richness" ("Solitude/Identity" 197). Here Chown does not distinguish between male and female writers, but her quotations are from women such as Carmen Martín Gaite ("[la soledad no es] una condena, sino una gracia" ["Solitude/Identity" 197]) [(solitude is not) a condemnation, but a gift]. In a previous article Chown observes that Martín Gaite wrote repeatedly of interior incarceration and her capacity to escape through imagination. Chown also reminds us that Elena Quiroga (1921–1995) evokes the interior journey behind the mask ("American Critics" 97): "Our vision of liberation for women very often presupposes work, creation, activity, and the right to change. . . . Solitude has been a troublesome issue for American critics, who stress the fact that Spanish fiction reflects a preoccupation with the aloneness of people" (Chown, "American Critics" 98). Chown cites an interview she conducted with Ana María Matute (1925–2014): "It is a reflection of something personal but not exclusively because often I realize that many people are alone, terribly alone. . . . I confess that solitude pleases me" ("American Critics" 99; English translation is Chown's).

The concept of solitude that Spanish writers deploy can be divided into two general categories: (1) a vision that derives from a social or exterior perspective in which the woman searches for her own physical space (in the sense of Virginia Woolf's "a room of one's own"), although Spanish thinkers almost never limit themselves to a place apart where they can read, think, and write; (2) an exploration from an interior perspective in which physical space is linked to consciousness that allows one to develop as a person, to be oneself, and to forge one's own independent personality. Neither of these approaches denies the importance of being related to other people. Frequently, solitude in Spanish feminist thinking is viewed as a state of mind. Even when a Spanish feminist author adopts the Anglo-Saxon individualistic model of the self, as does Emilia Pardo Bazán, it does not take on the same connotations as it does in American and English thought (for example, Elizabeth Cady Stanton's sense of absolute solitude in the company of God, as I discuss below).[4]

Concepción Arenal and Emilia Pardo Bazán, the two great Spanish feminist theorists of the nineteenth century, differ on how a woman should be viewed in her relationship to the rest of the world. Emilia Pardo Bazán articulates this difference in the two women's thought in the speech she gave at the Madrid Congreso Pedagógico of 1892: "Lo que doña Concepción Arenal pide principalmente en interés de la colectividad lo pedimos otros principalmente en interés del individuo . . ." (*La mujer española* 111) [What Concepción Arenal asks principally for the collective good, we ask principally for the individual's benefit]. Concepción Arenal, champion of early Spanish feminist Benito Jerónimo Feijoo and follower of a number of his Enlightenment strategies in her arguments for women's education and role in public life, understands women as well as men in their relationship to the rest of society. Emilia Pardo Bazán, on the other hand, student of Kant and Schelling and above all of John Stuart Mill, focuses more on the woman as an individual.[5] It is revealing that Pardo Bazán was an admirer of Kant, who emphasized individual subjectivity and employed highly abstract arguments. The practical application of a philosophy to concrete social problems, of the kind evident in Francisco Giner de los Ríos's Krausism, surely influenced Arenal's thinking, as I noted in the introduction. Throughout her career as a social theorist, Arenal's underlying philosophical style is rationalist, and has much in common with Benito Jerónimo Feijoo (1676–1764), on whom she wrote an essay in 1876.[6]

Some commentators have called Arenal a romantic thinker (see particularly Juan Antonio Cabezas), but even though her topics—sympathy and social concern for the poor, the incarcerated, and the infirm with an emphasis on emotions such as pity—are certainly consonant with romantic liberalism, she rationalizes the passions. She employs Cartesian reason to analyze the role of the emotions in human life, arguing that the emotions are important for specific reasons, and in so doing attempts to reconcile the overlapping eighteenth-century rationalism and romantic liberalism of her day. She considered Spanish women's situation—the lack of education and vocation—within a network that encompassed a whole series of social problems, including poverty, prostitution, and delinquency. Woman in her social being, "al no tener un oficio, no puede auxiliar a sus padres ancianos; esposa, no puede ayudar al esposo; madre, se ve en el mayor desamparo, si la muerte la deja viuda o la perversidad de su marido la abandona" (*La mujer del porvenir* 85) [when she does not have a profession, cannot help her old parents; as a wife she cannot assist her husband; as a mother she is quite helpless, if death leaves her a widow or her husband, in his perversity abandons her]. For Arenal, it is impossible to understand a woman as an isolated entity[7]: "La mujer sin ocupación ni educación para sus facultades superiores va por el mar de la vida sin timón y sin brújula; el sentimiento que puede salvarla, si no es muy puro, puede extraviarla también, y cuando se estrella hace víctimas, porque no va sola" (*La mujer del porvenir* 104) [The woman without occupation or education for her superior faculties travels through the sea of life without rudder or compass; if the sentiment that can save her is not very pure, it can derail her, and when she crashes, she takes victims with her, because she does not travel alone]. Arenal's social approach to woman's selfhood continues in *La mujer de su casa* (1883), albeit now from the perspective of society as a whole, not just as a member of a family. Arenal argues against women's confinement to the home, because the woman who is limited to the domestic sphere looks at social ills as a mere spectator and thus does not participate in remedying them.

Although when she writes of Spanish women's situation, Arenal's arguments usually tilt toward its social dimension, in some passages she considers women as individuals. For example, she points out the need for women to affirm "su personalidad, independiente de su estado" (*La emancipación* 67), but this affirmation of an independent personality serves social purposes:

Dadme una mujer que tenga estas condiciones, y os daré una buena esposa y una buena madre, que no lo será sin ellas. ¡Cuánta falta le harán, y a sus hijos, si se queda viuda! Y si permanence soltera puede ser muy útil, mucho, a la sociedad, harto necesitada de personas que contribuyan a mejorarla aunque no contribuyan a la conservación de la especie. . . . Nada más propio para dar gravedad al carácter y consistencia a la personalidad que la contemplación compasiva de tantos dolores como entraña esa cuestión de cuestiones que se llama la cuestión social. (*La mujer de su casa* 67–68, 70)

[Give me a woman who has these qualities, and I will give you a good wife and a good mother, who would not be able to fulfill these roles without those qualities. How greatly she needs them, as do her children, if she is left a widow! And if she remains single, she can be very useful to society, which certainly needs people to contribute to its betterment although they do not contribute to the preservation of the species. . . . Nothing is better for lending gravity to the character and constancy to the personality than the compassionate contemplation of the many pains inherent in that question of questions—the social question.]

The short version of *La mujer de su casa* that Concepción Arenal sent to the 1892 Congreso Pedagogica further highlights women's personality formation.

This development in Arenal's thought is noteworthy because the Congreso Pedagógico was the forum in which Emilia Pardo Bazán disagreed with Arenal over whether the purpose of women's education is social or individual. Doña Emilia argues fervently against considering women as relational beings; at the end of her talk, she specifically mentions Arenal: "[e]l error fundamental que vicia el criterio común respecto de la criatura del sexo femenino . . . es el de atribuirle un destino de mera relación; de no considerarla en sí, ni por sí, ni para sí, sino en los otros, por los otros y para los otros. . . . Siempre tropezamos en lo mismo, en el concepto relativo del destino de la mujer" (*La mujer española* 158, 160) [the fundamental error that tarnishes the common view of creatures of the feminine sex . . . is to attribute to her a destiny based on mere relationality; to not consider her in herself, by means of herself, or for herself, but in others, by means of others and for others. . . . We always run into the same thing when it comes to the relational concept of women's destiny]. In defining her philosophical position, Pardo Bazán aligns herself with John Stuart Mill's essay *The Subjugation of Women* and against Jean Jacques Rousseau's concept of the social contract:[8]

¿Y quién es Stuart Mill?

—Un politico. Su opúsculo *De la libertad* es tan excelente, como detestable el *Contrato social* de su Rousseau de Uds.

—Son palabras mayores.

—Pues no exagero. Mill saca triunfante la independencia del individuo, mientras Rousseau implanta el despotismo del Estado. (*La mujer española* 114–115; emphasis in original)

[And who is Stuart Mill?

—A political thinker. His treatise *On Liberty* is as excellent as your Rousseau's *Social Contract* is detestable.

—These are serious words.

—Well, I'm not exaggerating. Mill triumphantly saves the individual's independence, while Rousseau implants the State's despotism.]

Emilia Pardo Bazán was very familiar with Mill's *The Subjugation of Women*, which she had translated into Spanish for publication in her Biblioteca de la Mujer series in 1893. *The Subjugation of Women* ends with a section that emphasizes the individual nature of women and the importance of their happiness as a good in itself: "the most direct benefit of all, the unspeakable gain in private happiness to the liberated half of the species; the difference to them between a life of subjection to the will of others and a life of rational freedom" (211), a point that Pardo Bazán also emphasizes.[9] Doña Emilia takes Mrs. Taylor, who inspired Mill to write his feminist essay, as a female model: "en nombre del individualismo Mill reclama la igualdad de los sexos. . . . la señora Taylor . . . aunque esclava por la ley, como las demás de su sexo tenía alma independiente, digna de la libertad" (*La mujer española* 128) [in the name of individualism, Mill demands equality of the sexes. . . . Mrs. Taylor . . . although a slave in the eyes of the law, like others of her sex has an independent soul, worthy of liberty].

Oddly, for the emphasis that Pardo Bazán places on the individual woman, she structures her essay "La mujer española" (1889, English version; 1890, Spanish version) around Spanish women's social-class groupings. She observes, for example, perhaps alluding to Arenal's "la mujer de su casa," that middle-class women are especially prone to going out shopping, visiting, to the theater, or to church to pass the time. This behavior, according to Doña Emilia, is motivated by women's horror of solitude:

> No puede dudarse que este afán de *callejear* revela ciertas deficiencias en la vida de familia. No es que yo crea, como Luis Vives, que la mujer al salir frecuentemente pone en peligro su honra: solamente digo que la salida, «por huir de la casa», indica falta de intimidad doméstica, y algo como aborrecimiento de la soledad, que es indicio claro de tener la cabeza mal amueblada. De todos modos, con el hermoso cielo y el radiante sol de España, el «echarse a la calle» lo considero pecado venal. ("La mujer española" 127)

> [Doubtless this love of walking on the city streets reveals certain deficiencies in family life. It isn't that I think, as did Luis Vives, that women who go out frequently are in danger of losing their good reputation: I only say that going out 'in order to escape the house' indicates a lack of domestic intimacy and something akin to a loathing of solitude, a clear indication that the head is poorly furnished. In any case, with the beautiful sky and the radiant sun in Spain, I consider 'going out into the street' a minor sin.]

In none of Emilia Pardo Bazán's essays do we find the analysis of women's interiority that Mill advocates. Although María Martínez Sierra (1874–1974) refers to interior states such as happiness (as does Pardo Bazán), in

Spanish feminist theory, a genuine analysis of interior states only emerges with writers associated with phenomenology such as Rosa Chacel and María Zambrano. Of course, Emilia Pardo Bazán's vast fictional output provides plenty of examples of the workings of female subjectivity.[10]

Woman's interiority acquired in solitude is perhaps first expressed in the poetry of the *Románticas* (as Susan Kirkpatrick calls them). In the 1843 edition of her *Poesías*, Carolina Coronado published a hymn, "A la soledad," in which she outlines what would become a constant in Spanish feminist thought even to the present day—solitude not as an anguished state, but as a necessary condition for recovering from the trials of living: "Al fin hallo en tu calma, / Si no el que ya perdí contento mío, / Si no entero del alma / El noble señorío, / Blando reposo a mi penar tardío. / Al fin en tu sosiego, / Amiga soledad, tan suspirado, / El encendido fuego / De un pecho enamorado / Resplandece más dulce y más / templado" (Kirkpatrick 308) [Finally I find in your calmness, / If not my own lost contentment, / If not the noble domain / of the inner reaches of the soul, / Soft repose in my latent pain. / Finally in your peacefulness, / much desired Friend solitude, / The lighted fire / Of a loving breast/glows more sweetly and more/measured].[11] That peace and tranquility are required for a woman writer to express her interior feelings and project a vision of her existential being recurs as a theme in Rosario de Acuña's (1850–1923) writings from the 1880s onward (see especially her "Discurso pronunciado en el acto de la instalación de la logia femenina *Hijas del Progreso*" [1889]) and in more recent Spanish feminist writers such as Carmen Laforet and Carmen Martín Gaite.

Interestingly, Elizabeth Cady Stanton made the same argument more than a hundred years before it appeared in Spanish feminist thought. In 1892, the same year that Concepción Arenal and Emilia Pardo Bazán participated in the Madrid Congreso Pedagógico, Stanton gave a speech before the US Congress called "The Solitude of the Self." The main point of her speech was that each human soul is individual and that each person, man or woman, has the right to individual conscience and judgment: "In discussing the rights of woman, we are to consider, first, what belongs to her as an individual, in a world of her own, the arbiter of her own destiny, an imaginary Robinson Crusoe, with her woman Friday on a solitary island" (372). Stanton relates the isolation of the human soul to the fact that at the moment of death both women and men are alone. Stanton associates this way of understanding the person with Protestantism, thus it is possible that the late entry of the concept of solitude into Spanish feminist thought could be in part attributed to the Catholic view of the soul as mediated by the Church. At the end of Mrs. Stanton's powerful speech before Congress, woman in her individuality remains alone before God. Thanks to the intervention of priests, Catholic women are never alone before God or in the face of death. Although as I noted above, in 1892 Emilia Pardo Bazán defended the importance of women's education, not so much to improve her contributions to the welfare of society as a whole, but for her individual good. She does not elaborate on this individual benefit as does Stanton, who affirms that "viewed as a woman, an equal factor in civilization, her rights and duties are still the same; individual happiness and development" (372). Pardo Bazán could have known Stanton's speech, which was delivered in January of 1892; 10,000 copies were published and widely distributed. Doña Emilia's talk at the Pedagogical Congress was delivered in October of 1892. However, the most likely reason for the coincidence is that both thinkers had a common source in John Stuart Mill.

In her *Nuevas cartas a las mujeres de España*, María Martínez Sierra moves the consideration of women and solitude to the interior realm. In an all-knowing way, Martínez Sierra affirms that even if a woman has a husband, she is alone, a situation she gives a positive cast.[12] According to Martínez Sierra, the soul's only refuge is its solitude: "la única fuerza que realmente capacita al ser humano para seguir siendo «hombre» es la posibilidad de quedarse un instante a solas con su alma" (*Nuevas cartas* 52; here "hombre" is a synonym for "ser humano") [the only force that really enables the human being to continue being "man" is the possibility to remain alone with his/her soul for an instant]. As Carmen Martín Gaite will argue some thirty years later, solitude is the only state that can allow a woman to achieve full personhood. In a rather Cartesian move, Martínez Sierra exhorts women to contemplate themselves in the world, because they are the only ones that exist for themselves. Even though women sacrifice themselves all the time to accommodate the whims of the men in their lives, they are unique and irreducible: "Te prestas, te das, sí ¡mas con qué soberana afirmación de personalidad!" (*Nuevas cartas* 53) [You lend yourself. You give yourself. Yes, moreover with sovereign affirmation of personality]. The sacrifices themselves are an unconscious affirmation of women's existence. She further argues that women do not want men to understand them; they only need the "other" to approve of (or possibly admire) them. Solitude (and incomprehension) is the spirit's salvation, and in another letter she affirms solitude's fortifying qualities: "Nunca es más fuerte el alma que cuando está sola. Y sólo los cobardes forman rebaño" (*Nuevas cartas* 71) [The soul is never stronger than when it is alone. And only cowards join a flock].

In considering women as individuals, Rosa Chacel continues the path marked out by Emilia Pardo Bazán, although she approaches Spanish women's situation from an interior perspective and takes the argument into existential terrain. Chacel reintroduces woman as a relational being, reformulating the configuration as a problem of her relationship to men as lovers.[13] Chacel understood her own life from the standpoint of the radical solitude of her youth as a child prodigy who did not fit into the society of other girls her age and as a sickly child who had to spend long periods alone confined to her house and her bed (See *Desde el amanecer*). In her feminist essay "Esquema de los problemas prácticos y actuales del amor" from 1931, she puts forth a theory of social change that begins in people's interior life. In this assertion, she counters Carl Jung's notion that the political events—wars and revolutions—of the first decades of the twentieth century had caused the changes and tensions between men and women. According to Chacel, first an internal change occurs in human beings and then social change ensues:

> No es que la acomodación a un medio con su gradual proceso de conquista vaya creando un reducto anímico resultante de determinada combinación de sensaciones y resistencias, labor primaria, elemental en lo psíquico, sino al contrario, que el alma saturada de su medio, tranquilamente vencedora de todas las hostilidades naturales, anula en sí toda vida de relación tradicional y se queda frente a frente con su soledad. El conflicto se crea de esta autocontemplación. (157)

> [Accommodation to an environment with its gradual conquering process does not create a spiritual state as a result of a certain combination of sensations and resistances, primary work, basic to psychic conditions, but rather the contrary; the soul saturated by the environment, tranquilly conquering all natural hostilities, annuls in itself all traditional relations and remains face to face with its solitude. The conflict arises from this self-contemplation.]

Chacel's 1931 essay is a direct challenge to the theories of women proposed by eminent men of the era, especially José Ortega y Gasset,

Gregorio Marañón, and Georg Simmel. Ortega insisted on women's intellectual inferiority, and Marañón defended the "equality" of men and women, but in separate spheres—women in their maternity and men in their public role. In the face of these powerful and influential thinkers, Chacel defends women's spiritual and intellectual dimension. To Ortega's statement "el espíritu es siempre solidario de sí mismo; no puede en unos órdenes comportarse de una manera y en otros de otra" (Chacel, "Esquema"140) [the spirit is always in solidarity with itself; it cannot conduct itself one way in some realms and in other ways in another], she responds that "[u]na de las cosas que con mayor evidencia pueden demostarnos la adhesión de la mujer al mundo espiritual, a la cultura, es precisamente su primera manifestación de rebeldía a ella" ("Esquema"140) [one of the things that provides greatest proof that women participate in the spiritual world, in culture, is precisely the first sign of her rebellion against it]. In other words, the rebellious woman distances herself from the culture that surrounds her. Chacel likewise argues vigorously against Simmel, who denies women an individual, spiritual life [by spiritual, she means transcendent, culture-producing]: "Creer que lo esencialmente femenino psíquico no tiene un fundamento inexpugnable como lo fisiológico, es igual que temer la influencia de los cataclismos sociales en los fenómenos cósmicos, es ese complejo de temor y soberbia que hace a la pequeñez humana montar la guardia al tabernáculo de la eternidad por creerlo en el fondo eterna merced a su custodia" (153) [Believing that the essential feminine psyche does not have an immutable foundation as does the physiological aspect is the same as fearing the influence of cataclysmic social events on cosmic phenomena. It is this complex of fear and arrogance that makes human smallness mount guard at the tabernacle of eternity, believing it to be eternal mercy under its custody]. Chacel employs Max Scheler's concept of an "absolute individual" to formulate her own idea of a being's identity (man or woman): "Mediante la posesión y reconocimiento de su yo íntimo, el hombre concibe la identidad y diferencia de otros orbes externos" (163) [By possessing and recognizing his/her inner self, a person conceives the identity and difference of other external orbits].[14]

Chacel also resituates what Ortega, Marañón, and Simmel called the "masculinization" of women's social role (women's leaving the domestic realm to enter the wider world of the workplace and the street). She does so by abandoning the consideration of woman as a social entity, which leads to notions of "woman as related to others" and provides the opportunity for the male philosophers' concern with women's masculinization. Instead, Chacel focuses on women's ontology and individual consciousness:

> [N]o es la galantería como expresión social, no es la idealización más o menos ilusionista de la mujer hecha por nuestros inmediatos antepasados, ni es tampoco la supervaloración dada por los feministas a la importancia social de la mujer lo que ha dificultado sus relaciones con el hombre. No es ni mucho menos la virilización de los valores de nuestra época, en cuanto esta expresión significa cerebralización, tecnicismo ni siquiera practicismo o finalismo. . . . Es, sí, esa virilización en cuanto esto supone de vigorización espiritual, de exigencia, esfuerzo y autenticidad en los contenidos íntimos. ("Esquema" 166)

> [[I]t is not gallantry as a social expression, nor is it the more or less illusionary idealization of women by our immediate ancestors, nor is it the supervalorization feminists give to women's social importance that has made women's relationships with men difficult. Much less is it due to the masculinization of values in our times, inasmuch as this expression means cerebralization, technicism, or even emphasizing practical ends. . . . Rather it is masculinization in its spiritual invigorization, exigency, effort, and authenticity in intimate contents.]

María Zambrano (born in 1904 and thus just six years younger than Chacel) was likewise formed in the misogynistic philosophical milieu dominated by José Ortega y Gasset, who directed her doctoral dissertation on Spinoza at the University of Madrid. As a Republican activist, like Chacel she went into exile in Latin America after the Spanish Civil War. I speculate that Zambrano's philosophical trajectory would have been somewhat different had she remained in Spain instead of embarking on her long peregrinations, which took her from France to Mexico to Cuba and Puerto Rico, and back to France and back to Cuba and Puerto Rico, to Rome, and Switzerland. Going full circle she finally returned to Madrid in 1984. Surely the development of María Zambrano's concept of solitude was bound up with her exile experience and her (not so unhappy) separation from Ortega's Madrid circle.

Solitude is an ancillary concept in Zambrano's philosophy, although it emerges in some of her major writings—*La confesión: Género literario*, *El hombre y lo divino*, and *Persona y democracia*—as an important condition of philosophical thinking and very likely the possibility of philosophizing by a woman in her day and country.

Unlike the other women thinkers I address in this chapter—Concepción Arenal, Emilia Pardo Bazán, Rosa Chacel, Montserrat Roig, and Carmen Martín Gaite—who also consider solitude a necessary precondition to the formation of the self, Zambrano does not gender solitude and self-formation. This coincidence reminds us that María Zambrano's political exile was already preceded by her gender isolation as a lone woman philosopher in an intellectual milieu dominated by strong men such as her teacher José Ortega y Gasset. Although Zambrano does not link solitude per se with female selfhood as do Arenal, Pardo Bazán, Chacel, and Martín Gaite, Zambrano's path to the notion of the person, which includes solitude, can be traced to her overtly feminist writings during her early exile in the 1940s. Zambrano's ontology builds on some of Ortega's fundamental ideas—"yo soy yo y mis circunstancias" [I am myself and my circumstances] and "ensimismamiento" [self-contemplation]—but it gradually evolves into an independent view of the self and the other that lends itself particularly well to her ideas on the female self in such works as "Eloísa o la existencia de una mujer" [Heloise or women's existence] and "Respuesta a *La grandeza y servidumbre de la mujer* de Gustavo Pittaluga" [Reply to Gustavo Pittaluga's The greatness and servitude of women]. As we will see in chapter 6, Zambrano's philosophy, while not always referring specifically to women, has become foundational to difference feminism in Italy and Spain.

Well before she went into exile in 1939, in the essay "Por qué se escribe" [Why one writes] published in *Revista de Occidente* in 1934, Zambrano alludes to the solitary condition as essential to becoming a thinker and a writer. The essay begins with the observation that "[e]scribir es defender la soledad en que se está; es una acción que sólo brota desde un aislamiento efectivo, pero desde un aislamiento comunicable, en que precisamente por la lejanía de toda cosa concreta se hace posible un descubrimiento de relaciones entre ellas" (*Hacia un saber* 31) [to write is to defend the solitude in which one finds oneself; it is an action that only comes from real isolation, but in a communicable isolation, since it is precisely due to the distance from concrete things that one can discover the relations between them].[15] While solitude as a necessary prerequisite to writing echoes Virginia Woolf's feminist essay *A Room of One's Own* published just five years before Zambrano's "Por qué se escribe," the latter's development of the topic reflects Ortega's temporal and spatial proximity. In her distinction between speech and writing, Zambrano notes that speech is governed by immediate circumstances, although in a move that already signals a divergence from the master, she endows speech with the possibility of liberating one from one's circumstances. Speech, however, cannot create one's self: "vencemos por la palabra al momento y luego somos vencidos por él" (31) [we conquer via the word at the moment, and then we are conquered by it]. Written words, on the other hand, emanate from the center of the self "en recogimiento, irán a defendernos ante la totalidad de los momentos, ante la totalidad de las circunstancias, ante la vida 'íntegra'" (32) [in self-communion, they come out to defend us before the totality of all moments, all circumstances, life as a whole]. While the liberation of the spoken word is ephemeral, the liberation writing accords is permanent.

Because writing is conducted in solitude, the writer is able to discover "el secreto" ("the truth," in more common philosophical parlance), albeit only partially and in a progressive unfolding. In the process of writing, the writer emerges from solitude to communicate the secret in an act of faith. These secrets only visit the writer in solitude and isolation, provoking the writer's thirst ["sed"]: "Solitario de sí y de los hombres y también de las cosas, pues sólo en soledad se siente la sed de verdad que colma la vida humana" (37) [Solitary in regard to oneself and to humanity and also in regard to things, since only in solitude does one experience the thirst for truth that is at the core of human life]. Zambrano coins the enormously suggestive term "soledad sedienta" [thirsty solitude] for the writer's state in which hidden truth appears. The description of this state foretells Zambrano's last philosophical stage of the 1970s, which has been described as mystical (see especially Ana Bundgård). The solitude in which ideas and the urge to write come forth seems to parallel mystical quietude before the journey toward union with the divine: "y se le muestra a él, aprovechando su soledad y ansia, su acallamiento de la algarabía de las pasiones" (37) [and reveals itself to Him, taking advantage of its solitude and anxiety, its calming of passion's clamor]. The final purpose of writing likewise hints at a mystical union, since the writer writes to communicate the discovered secret "a quien en verdad se muestra es a esta comunicación, comunidad espiritual del escritor con su público" (38) [to whom in truth one reveals is this communication, the spiritual community of the writer with his/her public].

Zambrano's forced separation from Spain in 1939 deepened her thinking about solitude. In the same year she moved to Mexico (1939), she wrote a short essay, "La soledad enamorada" [Solitude in love], which centers on Nietzsche, portraying the late-nineteenth-century German iconoclast as "[c]ondenado en vida a la soledad más desalojada" (*La confesión* 73) [condemned to a life of the most desolate solitude], a state she doubtless also experienced teaching in Morelia, Mexico, removed both from her native Spain and from the hub of Spanish exile intelligentsia in Mexico City. Her own recent exile and Ortega's historical emphasis weigh heavily on the Nietzsche article's meditation on the individual's relationship to historical circumstances: "El destino de un hombre cae sobre él, pero no nace de él, no depende de él, sino que le sobrevive porque es cosa de la historia" (75) [Man's destiny falls upon him, but it is not born of him, nor does it depend on him; rather it survives him because it is an historical entity]. Echoing Ortega, Zambrano takes issue with individualism's belief that a person can isolate him- or herself from history, that "abstrayéndose de las circunstancias concretas que presiden con la inexorabilidad de los astros, su pobre vida. El creer en suma, que la separación es absoluta. El creer que puede determinarse a sí mismo" (75) [extracting oneself from concrete circumstances that preside with the inexorability of the stars over his/her poor life. In sum, to believe that the separation is absolute. To believe that one can determine oneself]. For Zambrano, Nietzsche's solitude allowed him to overcome traditional social paradigms to envision the new man, the superman. Only by setting himself apart from his contemporary circumstances, which condemned him to live in absolute solitude, did he arrive at his most influential concepts, which aggressively attacked that from which he had separated himself.

In 1941, now established in Cuba and Puerto Rico, Zambrano expanded on her ideas on solitude in her essay *La confesión: Género literario* (published in 1943) [*Confession* 2015]. There she meditates on solitude in connection with the confessional genre as it was developed by St. Augustine and Jean Jacques Rousseau. External circumstances and history are less preponderant here, and her concept of the self becomes more interiorized. Not that Orteguian *circunstancias* disappear (she asserts that confession arises from certain situations (circumstances), but these circumstances cede to a more subjective orientation. She understands the confessional genre as "the language of someone who has not erased his condition as a subject; it is the language of the subject as such" (tr. Valis, *Confession* 22). Confession, however, executes a double movement; it is both a flight from oneself and a search for something to sustain and clarify the self. Confession reveals the fragmentary nature of life; it searches for unity. The flight from the self and the search for unity again suggest the mystic experience, and also the Catholic sense of community that is so different from Protestant isolation before God. Recall North American feminist Elizabeth Cady Stanton's famous speech "The Solitude of the Self," in which she argues for women's equality before the law, because men and women alike stand alone before God at the moment of death.

According to Zambrano, St. Augustine offered himself to the divine gaze "hungering to be seen" (tr. Valis, *Confession* 30), and we hear once again echoes of the "soledad sedienta." In the confessional genre, what is important is not to be seen, but to offer oneself up to be seen "that we feel ourselves beheld, gathered up and united by that gaze" (tr. Valis, *Confession* 32). Being seen helps overcome the nightmare of existence (this observation is prior to Sartre's *Being and Nothingness*), in which we feel isolated without the possibility of communication, as when we cry out in a dream in which we are being pursued and no one can hear us: "While we are feeling alone, we cannot act. All action born of solitariness is anarchic, that is, violent and destructive" (tr. Valis, *Confession* 35). In that sense, Zambrano considers Dostoyevsky's *Crime and Punishment* the true confession of our time (interestingly, Rousseau, Zambrano's other major example of a confessional writer, may have been Dostoyevsky's model for his confessional novels, although Dostoyevsky, unlike Zambrano, found many confessions to be examples of bad faith). In a few pages, she returns to St. Augustine and to a more positive view of the solitary confession writer. She was incapable of accepting the terror implied in true existentialism. St. Augustine discovered reality (which in 1934 she called "el secreto") in solitude "en ensimismamiento" [in self-contemplation]. She echoes Ortega's notion of "ensimismamiento," but adds a Schelerian note by pointing out that neither Augustine nor anyone else can find truth "for himself alone, for when truth is found, it is already shared truth" (tr. Valis, *Confession* 36). Only in discovering oneself can one discover the truth. Although Zambrano does not mention Augustine's intellectual life outside his *Confessions*, we can recall that not only did St. Augustine communicate his illuminations in solitude through his writings, he founded intellectual communities based on the notion of shared solitude.

For Zambrano, the Cartesian "I" prepared the way for Jean Jacques Rousseau's confessions by establishing the "immediacy of awareness: acts of awareness and, in its ultimate center, as the ultimate, inner oneness, the self, the self in solitude" (tr. Valis, *Confession* 44). According to Zambrano, Descartes's solitude is the endpoint, rather than the starting point as it was in Saint Augustine. She affirms that the cogito is "human solitude affirming its own existence" (tr. Valis, *Confession* 44), because it eliminates everything that cannot be subsumed into it. It is a completely existential solitude—bound up with being—that gives rise to creativity. Rousseau's confession was the necessary result of humanity's new condition of radical solitude and the urge to create. Thus, Rousseau offers his soul, and the notion of the heart is born. The heart is the subject of Zambrano's important essay "La metáfora del corazón" [The metaphor of the heart], published in the Cuban journal *Orígenes* in 1944, a year after the book on confession appeared. Here Zambrano moves beyond the mystic quietism of solitude to the next state; the heart now wishes to live only for itself and on its own: "Vida pasiva que se alza en soledad, desprendida de todo objeto, pues a imagen y semejanza del yo, o confundiéndose con él, se ha erigido en principio" (53) [passive life that rises out of solitude, unhooked from all objects, as an image and likeness of the self, or becoming confused with the self, has established itself in principle]. One imagines Zambrano comparing herself in exile in Cuba to Rousseau, who at age forty-four, beleaguered with accusations and persecutions, retired to Madame de Épinay's remodeled cottage outside Paris where, according to Zambrano, "se encuentra a solas consigo mismo y siente, precisamente en la holgada paz de sus días, en la felicidad, la insatisfacción, la presencia de lo que no había podido hallar" (55) [he found himself alone with himself and felt, precisely in the leisurely peace of his days of happiness, the dissatisfaction, the presence of what he had not been able to find], a condition that gives rise to his imagination.

Zambrano continued her journey to the interior self with a substantial section on the subject in her 1955 *El hombre y lo divino*, probably written in Rome. Picking up from where she had left off in 1943 with humanity's radical solitude in the wake of Descartes and Rousseau, she now returns to and more fully develops the notion of community through solitude. She associated this idea with St. Augustine in the book on confession, although she does not explicitly mention him in the 1955 essay. Solitude is an existential state that has nothing to do with external conditions such as isolation, abandonment, or lack of communication. Her example—Miguel de Unamuno's play *El otro*—helps situate her idea. In the depths of his solitude, the protagonist El Otro feels himself to be the shadow of another, "ser a medias [que] tropieza con su mitad, con su alter, siempre en el asecho; obstáculo insuperable de su supremo anhelo: la unicidad" (*El hombre y lo divino* 290) [a half being who stumbles over his other half, with his other, always lying in wait; an insuperable object of supreme desire for unity]. Only when that oneness, unity, or identity is experienced can one achieve love, communion, and community: "Vivir en la identidad es estar a salvo del infierno; del infierno de verse en lo otro, de ver lo otro y de ver lo otro que imita a lo uno" (294) [To live within an identity is to save oneself from Hell; Hell is seeing oneself in another, to see the other and to see the other reflecting oneself]. While Zambrano, like Unamuno, argues for individuality in solitude before the Divine, rather than remaining in the solitary state, Zambrano's solitary individual, unlike Unamuno's, can achieve community. In the essay "Eloisa o la existencia de la mujer" (1946) from ten years earlier, Zambrano singles out Heloise as the first woman to create and maintain a separate identity for herself.

Zambrano's ideas on solitude culminate in *Persona y democracia: La historia sacrificial*, published in 1958. Forged in solitude, the person is more than an individual, "es el individuo dotado de conciencia, que se sabe a sí mismo y que se entiende a sí mismo como valor supremo, como última finalidad terrestre" (103) [it is the individual endowed with consciousness that knows him/herself and understands him/herself as a supreme value, as the most important terrestrial being]. Once again, she returns to the interior realm, where the person is developed from the inside out, "este interior como san Agustín dijera, donde reside la verdad—es soledad" (119) [as Saint Augustine would have said, this interior where truth resides is solitude]. She follows Ortega (and Scheler) in distinguishing humans (persons) from animals by the former's ability to retire from living minute to minute in the world and remove themselves from sociohistorical life, but the historical circumstances of her 1930s essays concerning solitude have vanished. As I noted earlier, Zambrano's apprenticeship in thinking about what constitutes a person began in her feminist essays written in her early exile in Cuba and Puerto Rico.

Since the feminist writings of Republican thinkers such as María Martínez Sierra, Carmen de Burgos (1867–1932), Margarita Nelken (1894–1968), Federica Montseny (1905–1994), Rosa Chacel, and María Zambrano were almost completely unknown in Franco's Spain (Carmen de Burgos's work, for example, was banned under the Franco regime), those women thinkers who remained in Spain had to pick up more or less where Emilia Pardo Bazán had left feminist thinking at the turn of the twentieth century, defending women's right to some education, to her own space, and to her own identity. Under the Franco regime, women were once again conceived as purely relational beings. In addition to women's inferior legal and social status, after 1939, as I noted in the introduction, girls were officially obliged to study the domestic arts in classes offered by the Sección Femenina de Falange, designed to socialize them into the role of housewife and mother that the regime envisioned for them. After the brief parenthesis of the Second Republic (1931–1939), during which Rosa Chacel could imagine a completely autonomous female subjectivity, official institutions once again reduced women to a dependent status. This new incarceration of women within the home and domesticity provoked a renewed desire for solitude on the part of many intellectual and creative women—a solitude that would afford them a space of their own and free them from the chores of caring for a home, a husband, and children. (Virginia Woolf's famous book was beginning to be known in small women's circles in Spain and to be read by important thinker-writers such as Carmen Martín Gaite and possibly Carmen Laforet.)

Martín Gaite's "chica rara" [odd girl] begins to appear in novels by Carmen Laforet and other women writers, as does the image of the island as a refuge for this character who has intellectual or artistic qualities. Andrea of Carmen Laforet's *Nada* (1945) likes to wander the streets of Barcelona alone, an escape from the claustrophobic house where she lives with relatives. Ana María Matute's Matia of *Primera memoria* (1960), exiled from mainland Spain during the Civil War and enclosed in her grandmother's home on the island of Mallorca, finds myriad means to escape her traditionalist grandmother's stern vigilance, thus converting her island prison into a space of freedom. In Carmen Martín Gaite's *El cuarto de atrás* (1978), the protagonist and a friend invent *Bergai*, an imaginary island where they fantasize adventures that take them away from the grim reality of the Civil War and early postwar Spain. Significantly,

Gloria Fuertes (1917–1998) titled her first book of poems *Isla ignorada* (1950) [Unkown island]. According to Sylvia Sherno, "Fuertes declared her identification with that island, 'en el centro de un mar / que no me entiende, / rodeada de nada, / —sola sólo' (OI, 21) [in the center of a sea / that doesn't understand me / surrounded by nothing / —only alone]. These early words prefigure the poet's reiterated theme of solitude and her insistence on self-definition" (312).

Although Carmen Laforet made solitude a central component in all her protagonists' development, she did not theorize about solitude in works she published during her lifetime. However, now, thanks to the Laforet correspondence Israel Rolón-Barada recently compiled in his doctoral dissertation, I have been able to locate statements by Laforet, married with five children during the Franco era, about the importance of solitude to her as a creative writer who struggled to maintain a sense of her own identity. Laforet was married in 1946, a year after her first novel *Nada* appeared, and her five children were born in quick succession. By 1961 she began to feel the strain of a woman with a writer's vocation and significant family responsibilities in the social climate created for women by the traditionalist Franco government. In a letter to Father Arrizabalaga she reveals that at that moment in her life and work "en que después de haber estado de espaldas a las cosas durante muchos años [ahora quiero] hacer uso de esta experiencia en soledad para opinar sobre ellas y ayudar—en lo que pueda hacer—todo lo que [le parece] justo, hermoso e interesante, todo sin limitación ninguna" (Rolón-Barada, "Letter 15," 15 January 1961) [in which after having turned my back on things for many years, I now in solitude want to make use of that experience to form opinions about them and help—as much as I can—all that seems just, beautiful, and interesting, without any limitations whatsoever]. She says that she bases this concept on "el derecho natural" [natural law]. Laforet majored in legal studies at the universities of Barcelona and Madrid, although she never completed a degree. Interestingly, Elizabeth Cady Stanton based her philosophical position on natural law, although she does not name it as such.

If Laforet does not openly recognize her synchrony with the North American feminist world in this letter, in other instances she is conscious of her identification with US customs relating to women. In fact, over the years, Laforet came to appreciate the United States as a paradise where she felt freer than in any other place. She made her first trip to the United States in 1965, invited by the State Department, and in the 1980s she made five separate US visits during which she spoke at a number of universities and colleges.[16] Her struggle to continue writing the novels she had outlined in her head, despite the conflicts created by home, husband, children, and lack of money, occasioned the following comment on Jack and Jackie Kennedy, whom she saw as an ideal couple:

> Jacqueline Kennedy que a mí particularmente me parecía una especie de maniquí a través de las fotos y la propaganda ha resultado a través de esas otras fotos y telefotos sin la más mínima preparación, una mujer de cuerpo entero, llena de valor. Y se comprende perfectamente su papel de trabajadora incansable junto al marido. Y alrededor de ella una serie de mujeres que, al parecer, son clave de lo mejor de la vida americana que gira alrededor de la confianza—y la importancia—de la pareja humana, como tal pareja. (Rolón Barada, "Letter to Father Arrizabalaga," 29 November 1963)

> [Jacqueline Kennedy particularly seemed to me a kind of unstudied mannequin in the photos and propaganda that resulted from these photos and telephotos, a woman made of a whole cloth, full of courage. And one can completely understand her role as an indefatigable worker alongside her husband. And around her a series of women who, apparently, are the key to the best in American life, which centers on the shared confidence—and the importance—of the human couple, as a couple.]

This is the kind of couple (viewed from the exterior) that Rosa Chacel theorized from within, from intersubjective consciousness.

The many other references to solitude found in Laforet's letters focus on the need for a solitary state to undertake creative work, a solitude she refers to in a letter to her friend Emilio Sanz de Soto as "la más salvaje soledad" (Rolón-Barada, "Letter 27," 17 March 1965) [the most savage soltude].[17] When Laforet separated from her husband in 1970, she immediately sought solitude as the essential condition to finding her authentic self, buried under years of marriage to a traditional man and a motherhood conditioned by the social norms imposed by the Franco regime (like Concepción Arenal, Laforet employed the term *personalidad* to render the concept of an authentic self): "En cuatro meses últimos—y sobre todo los casi tres meses de soledad de aquí—han sido de aprendizaje (aún no terminado, la verdad) en la recuperación de la personalidad. Es como si hubiera vivido a otra luz durante 24 años, y con mis círculos mágicos de tiza alrededor . . . Así que estoy aprendiendo" (Rolón Barada, "Letter 69" to Father [now "Bernardo"] Arrizabalaga and his wife Carmen, 1 February 1971) [In the last four months—and above all the nearly three months of solitude here—have been an apprenticeship (in truth, not yet over) in the recuperation of my personality. It is as though I had lived in another light and with magic chalk circles around me for 24 years. . . . So, I am learning]. Following a line of thought we find in other Spanish feminist thinkers, Laforet connects the solitary state with that of being accompanied: "Al principio me hizo mucha falta este silencio absoluto, este aislamiento. Ahora ya creo que es contraproducente" (Rolón Barada, "Letter 69") [At first I really needed the absolute silence, the isolation. Now I think it is beginning to be counterproductive]. In a letter to her friend Emilio Sanz de Soto, also written shortly after her separation from her husband, Laforet expresses in another way how difficult it is to find a balance between being oneself and being for others (here Sartrean or even Beauvoirian existentialism may have influenced Laforet's thinking on the self, as it possibly did María Zambrano's and certainly does Carmen Martín Gaite's and that of equality feminists in the 1980s and 1990s): "Ya sabes que mi vida ha cambiado, o mejor dicho por el momento lo que ha hecho es serenarse en una independencia de espíritu y una verdad que me hacían mucha falta. Encarar la verdad, es muy duro pero, al menos para mí, de un resultado bueno. La cara de la verdad para mí era ver que de nada sirve anular la propia personalidad en honor de lo que yo creía sagrado; la felicidad de mis hijos" (Rolón Barada, "Letter 37," 14 May 1971) [You already know that my life has changed, or rather for the moment what has happened is that it has become serene in an independence of spirit and truth that I very much needed. Facing the truth is very difficult, but at least for me, it has had a good effect. The face of truth for me was to see that it is no use annulling one's own personality in honor of what I once believed sacred; the happiness of my children]. Once Laforet had achieved the possibility of perpetual solitude, she no longer longed for it. Unfortunately, this perpetual possibility did not allow her to permanently recover her prematrimonial ontological state. Existential being may not be preconditioned, but in Carmen Laforet's case it was cumulative and irreversible. Although Laforet continued to rework the second novel *Al volver la esquina* (published posthumously in 2004) of a planned trilogy, *Tres pasos fuera del tiempo* and other projected novels, she never recovered the relatively carefree, uninhibited Carmen Laforet who wrote *Nada*.

Carmen Martín Gaite was perhaps the first postwar Spanish woman writer-thinker to recognize in a more sustained and public way the centrality of solitude in women's (especially creative women's) formation of a self from her own consciousness as a socially independent and autonomous being. Her theory is rooted in a biographical circumstance (something common to many Spanish feminist thinkers). In 1980, after moving into an apartment in New York where she was going to teach classes at Barnard College, she found herself completely alone for the first time in her life with no need to report to anyone, "ni sentir[se] interferida por requerimientos o problemas de seres humanos vinculados [a ella]" [nor feel imposed upon by the needs or problems of human beings related to her] (*Desde la ventana* 10). However, she missed those ties "porque la independencia siempre ha sido arma de dos filos para la mujer" [because independence has always been a double-edged sword for women]. In that situation she consciously proposed to "resistir a pie quieto la soledad en aquella habitación recién estrenada y carente de todo recuerdo, de conquistarla para [sí misma] a base de tesón y de mimo" [stalwartly accept the solitude of that new space that held no memories and to conquer it through tenacity and coddling] (10). (This passage reminds us of Emilia Pardo Bazán's observation about the horror Spanish women feel when they face solitude.) At this period in her life, recently separated from her husband and alone in New York, Martín Gaite read Virginia Woolf's *A Room of One's Own*, a foundational text for the development of Spanish feminist thought in the 1980s and 1990s.

Martín Gaite proposes that "[n]o hay ninguna innovación posible en el campo del pensamiento que no se lleve a cabo desde dentro y enfrentándose a palo seco con la soledad. Porque solamente aceptándola, acabará dando fruto" [philosophical innovation is impossible unless it is carried out within and confronting solitude head on. Because in the mere act of accepting solitude, it will bear fruit] (*Desde* 48). She recognized that this assertion is equally true for women and men, but she points out a fundamental difference between writers of the two sexes. She notes that men enter into the solitary state from the "bullicio mundanal" [worldly hubbub] while women, who have less access to public life, continue to be tempted by the world, which represents liberation for them. Although solitude is more complex for women than for men, when all is said and done, solitude is an absolute requirement for the creative woman. In addition to Virginia Woolf and some North American theorists, Martín Gaite considers several Spanish women writers in relation to the topic of solitude. For example, she notes that for nineteenth-century poet Rosalía de Castro "la soledad nunca le pareció una condena, sino una gracia que le permitía de vez en cuando escaparse de su circunstancia personal [de madre y esposa] para entablar diálogos con la luna, condolerse de la miseria de sus paisanos o ponerse a soñar con el hombre-musa" (86) [solitude never seemed like a curse but rather a blessing that allowed her to escape her personal circumstances from time to time and to engage in dialogues with the moon, sympathize with the misery of her countrymen, or to dream of a male muse]. According to Martín Gaite, Rosalía de Castro believed that solitude permits us to better understand ourselves and facilitates the creation of worlds that do not exist. Martín Gaite adds to this observation that "la espoleta de este empeño la dispara el deseo de escapar de la realidad y desobedecer sus leyes rigurosas, atreviéndose a sustituirlas por otras de cuño propio" (49) [the desire to escape reality, to disobey rigorous laws, and to dare to substitute them for others of her own making is the spark for this undertaking].

Martín Gaite pointed to Santa Teresa as an example of a woman writer who accepted solitude to face the social obstacles she had to overcome when she wrote: "Santa Teresa ejemplifica ese camino emprendido audazmente partiendo de cero y cuya exploración pone en cuestión y en juego la propia vida" (*Desde la ventana* 49) [Saint Teresa exemplifies this road audaciously undertaken from zero and whose exploration questions life itself and puts it into play]. Martín Gaite returns to the notion of solitude in several lectures reproduced in *Pido la palabra* [May I have a word]. Her theory of narrative as telling a story to someone, the essential need for an interlocutor, arises from the writer's radical solitude: "«Para vivir la vida como una novela, basta con que cuentes lo que te pasa o lo que desearías que te pasara. Si no tienes a quién contárselo, cuéntalo para ti; yo también estaba solo.» En este caso «sola»" (*Pido* 327) [In order to live life like a novel, it is enough to tell what is happening to you or what you would like to happen to you. If you don't have anyone to tell it to, tell it to yourself; I too was alone. In this case "alone as a woman"]. According to Martín Gaite, solitude should be accepted proudly and voluntarily (327). She finds in isolation, introspection, and dreaming the essential conditions for women who write. On all these points she appears in synch with ideas that Carmen Laforet expressed less formally in her correspondence.

Although Martín Gaite and Montserrat Roig were writing their feminist works at approximately the same time (the early years of the transition to democracy), Martín Gaite rejected the label of "feminist," while Montserrat Roig, openly feminist and political, denounced the assertion by a un unnamed anti-Franco male writer that "*la mujer no tiene, como el hombre, este poder—o este defecto—de quedar «alma sola», de desprenderse, de salir de ella misma—como lo tiene el hombre—. Y no hay nada de tan femenino como el alma, desnuda y sola. En la mujer, alma y cuerpo se involucran, se reclaman, no se pueden descompartir: su vida es unitaria*" (*Tiempo de mujer* 151, emphasis in the original) [that women, unlike men, do not have the power—or the defect—of remaining "a lone soul," of becoming unattached, of coming out of herself in the same way men do. And there is nothing as feminine as the bare, lone soul. Body and soul are intertwined in women; they require each other; they cannot be separated; their life is unitary]. Roig employs strategies similar to those of other Spanish feminist writers, including Martín Gaite and Rosa Chacel, to analyze women's position vis-à-vis solitude. For example, like María Zambrano and many modern male philosophers, she critiques the absurd scholastic distinction between body and soul, and like Concepción Arenal and Emilia Pardo Bazán, she asks "porqué las mujeres no podemos quedarnos *almas solas, salir de nosotras mismas*. Cuáles son las causas de esa *imposibilidad*" (152; emphasis in original) [why can't women be *lone souls and arise from ourselves*. What are the causes of this *impossibility?*]. Her answer is like those of Carmen Laforet and Virginia Woolf, whom she cites: "[p]ara crear, hay que tener un cierto distanciamiento de la vida cotidiana, no estar atada a los problemas concretos de la organización doméstica" (153) [in order to create, one must have a certain distance from daily life, not be tied to concrete problems of domestic organization].

However, in contrast to all the earlier writers, Roig attributes to feminism the fact that women have begun to "desarrollar en el mundo de la imaginación sus propios aspectos de marginalidad y hoy ya es posible elaborar literariamente aquella necesidad oscura a la que se refería Sábato: su propio drama, la desdicha y la soledad" (159) [develop their own marginalization in the world of the imagination, and today it is possible to elaborate literarily that dark necessity that Sábato mentioned: one's own drama, unhappiness, and solitude or loneliness]. Here solitude has two meanings: (1) it represents the space and time necessary for creation, and (2) it is a state of mind that is a theme of that creation. Like Emilia Pardo Bazán, Roig wonders if women are afraid "a volar sólo como mujeres" [to fly only as women], but she carries the theme to a more universally human terrain: "miedo a la muerte y el terror ante la soledad, ¿no son acaso tan fuertes como el miedo a ser una misma?" (162) [are not fear of death and terror in the face of solitude as powerful as the fear to be oneself?]. This rhetorical question reminds us that Rosa Chacel attributed her freedom to do her artistic and philosophical work to her husband's protecting her from "la crueldad y del desorden del mundo" (165) [the cruelty and disorder of the world] and that Carmen Martín Gaite "afirma que la situación femenina de encierro, opresión y sosiego, es idónea para escribir" (165) [affirms that women's seclusion, oppression, and tranquility are ideal for writing]. Roig published her article in 1977 before Martín Gaite lived for a year in New York, and therefore before Martín Gaite wrote the essays analyzed above.

The new generations of women feminists who have addressed the topic of solitude approach it more as a lifestyle choice than as an ontological position, although solitude as an existential condition does not disappear completely from recent Spanish feminist theory. In this new phase, single women, a theme broached by Gloria Fuertes in poetry rather than in theoretical essays, achieve a central place in Spanish women's writing.[18] Rosa Montero, like Rosa Chacel, remarks that her love of solitude stems from a long, sickly childhood: "Seguramente el haber tenido la suerte desde pequeña—producto de una enfermedad que la mantuvo cuatro años en casa—de haber leído como una descosida, fuese el motivo de sentirse no integrada en la sociedad de niñas de cocinitas y muñecos" ("Rosa Montero" 8) [Surely having had the luck from early on to have read voraciously—because of an illness that kept me at home for four years—was the reason I did not feel part of the little girls' world of dolls and miniature kitchens]. Montero never wished to marry; as a child she did not play with dolls or pretend to be a mother. Now Spanish feminists do not vacillate when faced with solitude, as did Carmen Martín Gaite for whom solitude was an "arma de doble filo" [two-edged sword]. Many Spanish feminists of the 1990s onward openly embrace singlehood and the solitary state as positive conditions:

> La soledad es absolutamente necesaria. Yo creo que para las mujeres más. Hemos sido educadas de una manera más castrante que ellos, pero todos tenemos que aprender a estar

solos. Sentirte adulto, tener una idea de lo que eres y un mínimo control de tu vida. La soledad es buena para llevarte bien contigo misma, para tratarte bien, para aguantarte, y luego . . . para no hipotecarte. Si no sabemos vivir con nosotras mismas vamos a pagar unos precios desorbitantes, vamos a tener unas relaciones antropofágicas solamente por el miedo a la soledad. Me parece que no se lo puede una permitir (y uno tampoco), el ir perdiendo el culo buscando unas relaciones baratas y a veces canallas, solamente por no estar sola. La solución no es saber resignarse, sino saber descubrirla. Es fundamental su aprendizaje, sobre todo para las mujeres. ("Rosa Montero" 9)

[Solitude is absolutely essential. I believe even more so for women. We have been educated in a more castrating manner than men, but we all have to learn to be alone. To feel ourselves as adults, to have an idea of who we are with at least a minimum amount of control over our lives. Solitude is good for learning to get along with yourself, treat yourself well, put up with yourself, and then . . . to not mortgage yourself. If we don't know how to live with ourselves we will pay an exorbitant price; we will have self-destructive relations out of fear of solitude (loneliness). Women (and men) cannot lose their self-respect in cheap and even vicious relations, just to avoid being alone. The solution is not to know how to resign oneself, but to know how to discover the solution. It is a fundamental apprenticeship, above all for women.]

Montero does not reject forming part of a couple, but she believes that one should only enter a relationship as a whole person, and in this way she affirms from a social vantage point what Rosa Chacel theorized from an ontological position.

This line of thought culminates in Carmen Alborch's *Solas* of 1999. Alborch (1947–), a career woman for her entire adult life, is completely sure of herself. She holds a doctorate in law and is a tenured professor in mercantile law at the University of Valencia, where she has been dean of the law school. She has also held posts as the Valencian government's general cultural director and as director of the Valencian Institute for Modern Art. She was the Spanish minister of culture from

1993 to 1996, and more recently she was a socialist representative to Congress and president of the Congress's regulatory commission for state radio and television outlets. Although she has been married and has had partners, she has never lost her identity as an independent woman. For Alborch, solitude is a way of life, although she subtitled *Solas* "Gozos y sombras de una manera de vivir" [Pleasures and pains of a way of life], and she calls her generation "la cosecha del 68" [the 1968 vintage] that has lived immersed in "serias contradicciones derivadas de la educación y del momento histórico que nos tocó vivir" (11) [serious contradictions derived from the education and historical moment in which we live]. In placing the emphasis on living alone rather than on solitude as an existential state, she moves the negative associations that *soledad* can conjure ("loneliness" in English) onto positive terrain. She points out that "being alone" does not mean being a "solitary person" or being unaccompanied. She recognizes the network of social and emotional support she enjoys through family and friends that allows her autonomy.

Alborch begins *Solas* with a theoretical meditation on solitude, followed by a social history of Western women and the reasons for their lack of autonomy. The book ends in the present with a kind of self-help guide for women who by choice or circumstances (divorce, for example) find themselves alone. Even in the first section of the book, in which she considers the solitary state from a philosophical point of view, she divides the approaches into philosophical and sociological. She observes that "sociológicamente, la soledad aparece como efecto del individualismo motor de las sociedades modernas occidentales, que establecen al individuo, con sus propios derechos y libertades, como objeto superior al grupo" (18) [sociologically, solitude appears as a consequence of the individualism that undergirds modern Western societies, which establish the individual with his or her own rights and liberties as superior to the group]. On the other hand, in "las sociedades comunitarias [one supposes Spain to be among them] . . . el sentimiento de soledad sólo surge cuando el individuo—siempre subordinado en sus derechos a los del grupo, la familia, el clan, el pueblo o la tribu—se aleja y abandona la colectividad de la que forma parte, que rechaza cualquier iniciativa emanada de la libertad individual como intrínsecamente perversa" (18) [communitarian societies, the feeling of loneliness only arises when the individual—always subordinated to the rights of the group, family, clan, village, or tribe—moves away and abandons the collectivity of which he or she is a part and rejects any initiative arising from individual liberty as intrinsically perverse].

Alborch finds that many women are alone because they are out of step with the society in which they live. On this point, she coincides with Rosa Chacel, who posits that women begin to acquire autonomy and identity precisely when they rebel against the dominant culture. Although Alborch does not cite Chacel, she does mention Simone Weil, the French existentialist thinker "para quien la soledad absoluta significaba la posesión de la verdad del mundo" (15) [for whom absolute solitude meant the possession of the truth of the world]. Alborch asserts that solitude is inherent in the human condition; the solitary state arises when we are born due to the rupture with the embryonic contact with the mother. According to Alborch, solitude is not so much a concept as "un estado de ánimo, un sentimiento, además de una circunstancia personal determinada" (16) [a state of mind, a feeling, besides a particular personal circumstance]. For Alborch, solitude comprises two fundamental characteristics: the lack of communication and durability, which "conduce a la ansiedad dolorosa de alguien que reclama infructuosamente el auxilio de quien alivie su sufrimiento" (16) [leads to the painful anxiety of someone who uselessly demands help from someone to alleviate their suffering]. These states can lead to "formas enfermizas de soledad" (18) [pathological forms of solitude or loneliness].

Throughout the book, Alborch emphasizes the importance for the human being of relating to others, "por ser la persona un animal esencialmente social" (20) [because the person is essentially a social animal]. For Alborch there is no "plenitud sin la relación con los otros, y de ellos buscamos el reconocimiento, la cooperación, la competencia, la imitación incluso, como antídotas contra la soledad. La existencia precisa de la mirada del otro. Nunca logramos gozar de nosotros mismos sin el concurso del otro, y hasta Crusoe precisó de la compañía de Viernes como testigo de su solitaria peripecia" (20) [plenitude without a relationship with others, and in them we seek recognition, cooperation, competition, even imitation as antidotes to solitude/loneliness. Existence requires the gaze of the other. We can never enjoy ourselves without the backing of another, and even Crusoe needed Friday's company as witness to his solitary adventure]. Alborch employs the example of Robinson Crusoe and Friday in a completely different way than Elizabeth Cady Stanton, who concentrates on Robinson Crusoe's solitude and diminishes his companion Friday's role. If Rousseau were anathema to Emilia Pardo Bazán for his theory on the social contract, Alborch agrees with Rousseau about the need for a "permanent negotiation" with others. Like Rosa Chacel, Alborch focuses this "negotiation" on love relations, and also like Chacel, she argues for the reinvention of love through a "nuevo equilibrio, el amor realmente recíproco, que . . . exige y crea la igualdad de los que se aman de manera que el hombre testimonie su amor a una mujer tratándola como a una persona humana total, no como si fuera una meta" (23) [a new equilibrium, a genuinely reciprocal love that demands and creates the equality of those who love one another so that the man manifests his love for the woman treating her as a complete human person, not as though she were a goal]. In Alborch's view, marriage as it is now constituted is an obstacle to this arrangement, so much so that both men and women are shunning the institution: "Los cambios sociales, demográficos y económicos han traído a las mujeres (y también a los hombres) una mayor libertad individual para vivir y actuar independientemente de la familia tradicional. Ahora ya no queremos sentirnos atrapados en el esquema familiar. Queremos espacio, queremos ser libres para lo que deseamos ser" (27–28) [The social, demographic, and economic changes have brought women (and men as well) greater individual liberty to live and act independently of the traditional family. Now we no longer want to feel ourselves trapped in a family structure. We want space; we want to be free to be what we want]. For this reason, both married and single people can experience solitude or aloneness.

Alborch notes that throughout Western history the model for single women has changed, but for the most part the unmarried woman has been a negative figure. She is a person who does not fit into any social category (as evidenced in the scornful term "solterona" [old maid]: "La soltera es el antimodelo de la mujer ideal" (48) [the old maid is the negative model of the ideal woman]. However, Alborch does not consider the female saints as unmarried women who acted in a solitary fashion. Well-known poet and novelist Ana Rossetti (1950–) has told me of the importance that the female saints' stories held for her when she read them as a young girl. These valiant, active women filled her imagination with possibilities unavailable to her in any other aspect of her life in the small, rural Andalusian village where she grew up during the Franco dictatorship. Carmen Martín Gaite found in Santa Teresa's prose the "oscilante historia de la mujer ante la letra escrita. . . . aceptación de la soledad, mirada cauta y concreta, búsqueda de interlocutor, pasión incomprendida y desobediencia a los modelos propuestos" (*Desde* 49) [oscillating history of a woman face to face with the written word. . . . accepting solitude, cautious and deliberate gaze, search for an interlocutor, misunderstood passion, and disobedience to proposed models]. However, it is not likely that the majority of the Spanish girls who read stories of female saints in school could overcome their environment and think of the saintly martyrs as role models as did Rossetti.[19]

In Alborch's chapter titled "Solas y solos: Una nueva categoría social" [Women alone and men alone: A new social category], Alborch moves from the historical to the legal and sociological aspects of the present day in which concepts "como autonomía, independencia, identidad, individualidad o emancipación se relacionan estrechamente con las mujeres solas, aunque no exclusivamente con ellas" (90) [like autonomy, independence, identity, individuality, and emancipation are closely associated with women who live alone, but not exclusively to them]. Alborch points out that, although civil status has changed, a problem of terminology persists. The Anglo-American term "single" has a broader meaning than *soltera* in Spanish, and there is no precise translation for "single" in Spanish (91). Thus Alborch prefers "mujeres individuales" or "mujeres singulares" (91–92), because these terms do not indicate a woman's civil status. She observes that most Spanish women are not like the character Tía Tula in Miguel de Unamuno's novel *La tía Tula*, who fiercely defends her single (unmarried) state:

> ni tampoco todas buscan persistentemente la libertad entendida como ausencia o rechazo a cualquier tipo de compromiso. Hay mujeres que viven inmersas en la renovación cultural y son partícipes de un fenómeno social que rompe esquemas. Mujeres que sin «glorificar» su estado demuestran que vivir sin pareja es una alternativa legítima y positiva que, por otro lado, no necesariamente ha de ser definitivo. (92)

[nor do all women search persistently for liberty, understood as absence or rejection of any kind of commitment. There are women who live immersed in cultural renewal and participate in social phenomena that break old schemes. Women who without "glorifying" their state demonstrate that living without a partner is a legitimate and positive alternative that, on the other hand, is not necessarily definitive.]

Alborch divides single women into various subcategories: "*voluntarias temporales solas*," "*involuntarias temporales solas*," "*voluntarias estables solas*," and "*involuntarias estables solas*" (95, 96; Alborch's emphasis) [temporarily voluntarily alone, temporarily involuntarily alone, permanently voluntarily alone, permanently involuntarily alone]. Although these classifications may seem rather pseudoscientific, in an important way they emphasize woman's will; even when the single state is not voluntary, Alborch endows the woman with will or agency, rather than helplessness. For Alborch, and this is the book's central theme, "[l]a soledad es necesaria a la hora de construir un mundo interior rico e intenso y para mantener desde el propio equilibrio las relaciones interpersonales" (97) [solitude is necessary for constructing a rich and intense interior world and for maintaining interpersonal relations from one's own equilibrium]. This concept echoes the notion of "personality" that Concepción Arenal, Carmen Laforet, and others elaborated (see chapter 2). In addition, Alborch's notion of relations between the sexes resonates with the sexual intersubjectivity Rosa Chacel posits. For example, Alborch affirms that "en las mujeres habría que fomentar su independencia y en los hombres, su capacidad para asumir una interdependencia madura y equilibrada, sin anhelos de fusión permanente porque somos completos, si no más bien con la firme voluntad común de alcanzar la mayor plenitud posible" (104) [it is important to foment independence in women and the capacity to assume mature and balanced interdependence in men. This should be accomplished without the desire to permanently fuse, because we are each complete, but rather with the firm common resolve to achieve the greatest possible fulfillment]. In developing her theory of interpersonal relations, Alborch does not mention Chacel's similar notion. Perhaps she was unaware of it; unfortunately, the writers of the Republican era and those who went into exile after the Civil War are still not well known to contemporary Spanish feminists, who often draw on foreign feminist thinkers such as Virginia Woolf, Simone de Beauvoir, Betty Friedan, and Luce Irigaray, among a long list of others.[20]

Like Carmen Martín Gaite in *Desde la ventana*, Alborch postulates a fundamental difference between men and women in electing a solitary life. Referring to males who do not marry, Alborch observes that men are considered inherently to bear responsibility and to belong to the public sphere; thus they can deliberately elect solitude, an act considered a noble sacrifice so that they can fulfill their creative vocation (107). Once again she calls on Rousseau and the social contract:

aun siendo conscientes de que el poder no se cede o se comparte sin resistencias, y de las nuevas argucias o estrategias que pueden inventar quienes lo detentan, a las mujeres nos gustaría poder hablar con posibilidades de éxito y verosimilitud de un nuevo contrato social entre hombres y mujeres que llevara a compartir los derechos y las responsabilidades en las esferas públicas y privadas, a sabiendas también de las dificultades que un pacto así puede tener cuando una de las partes ocupa todavía posiciones de subordinación, lo que la lleva a rechazar y denunciar constantemente todo lo que sea un impedimento para la igualdad. (110)

[even being conscious that power is not ceded or shared without resistance, and of the new tricks and strategies people can invent to retain it, we women would like to consider the possibility of success and verisimilitude of a new social contract between men and women that would result in sharing rights and responsibilities in the public and private spheres, knowing full well the difficulties such a pact can have when one of the parties still occupies a subordinate position in which that party must constantly reject and denounce what is impeding equality.]

Alborch's book was exceptionally popular in Spain and elsewhere. It was translated into seven other languages and has sold more than 300,000 copies. Iker González-Allende attributes the book's success to the originality and novelty of the theme: "por primera vez se dedicaba en España una monografía a analizar la soledad femenina, llegando a reivindicarla desde postulados feministas. De esta manera, numerosas mujeres y también algunos hombres vieron en la obra una" [For the first time in Spain a monograph was devoted to analyzing female solitude, and defending it from a feminist perspective. In this way many women and also some men found one in this work].

CHAPTER 2

Personality

Solitude and personality are intimately linked together. Without solitude, it is nearly impossible for personality to form. Given the challenges for Spanish women's achieving solitude, they are equally challenged in forging a true individual personality. The twenty-second edition of the *Diccionario de la lengua española* indicates that the word *personalidad* derives from *personal* and offers the following definitions of the term:

> Diferencia individual que constituye a cada persona y la distingue de otra. // 2. Conjunto de características o cualidades originales que destacan en algunas personas. *Andrés un escritor con personalidad.* // 3. Persona de relieve, que destaca en una actividad o en un ambiente social. *Al acto asistieron el gobernador y otras personalidades.* // 4. Inclinación o aversión que se tiene a una persona, con preferencia o exclusión de las demás. // 5. Dicho o escrito que se contrae a determinadas personas, en ofensa o perjuicio de las mismas. (*Diccionario de la Real Academia de la Lengua*)

> [Individual difference that constitutes each person and distinguishes that person from another. // 2. A group of characteristics or original qualities that are salient in some persons. *Andrew, a writer with personality.* // 3. A person of note who stands out in an activity or social ambience. *The governor and several other personalities attended the event.* // 4. Preference

for or aversion to a person, to the exclusion of others. // 5. An offensive or prejudicial saying or piece of writing about certain persons.]¹

Personal is defined as "Perteneciente o relativo a la persona. // 2. Propio o particular de ella" [Belonging to or relative to a person. // 2. Belonging to or referring to that person.] In one way or another these definitions emphasize the person or his or her personality as observed from outside. Above all they point to what is different, distinguishing, and original as qualities that compose a personality from someone else's perspective. The Spanish women writers who have theorized about the person or personality employ this aspect of the concept of personality to elaborate theories of women that give them a greater opportunity to be a distinct person, compared to men who traditionally have been the differentiated and orginal human beings. However, most of the thinkers addressed in this chapter go beyond mere individual differences to understand personality as a set of complex interactions between the person's interior and exterior selves. The way nineteenth-century thinker Concepción Arenal employs the term comes close to the Real Academia's definition—individual differences that distinguish one person from another. For twentieth-century writers such as Zambrano and Martín Gaite, the term *personalidad* has a more complex meaning. In key writings by these authors, the complex of characteristics that the *Diccionario de la lengua* mentions is understood as an exterior manifestation of an interior nature, or as a lack of correspondence between the interior and the exterior.

Concepción Arenal, the first Spanish feminist in whose work I have found the concept of *personalidad*, employs the term in the first sense offered by the 2001 *Diccionario de la lengua*—characteristics that mark individual difference—although in her analysis, personality is not a given or as natural as the Royal Academy's definition suggests. However, many women's journals published in the decades before Arenal's seminal *La mujer del porvenir* (written in 1861 and published in 1869) included the term *vergel* in their title. According to Christine Arkinstall, who has conducted impressive research on these journals,

> The concept of independent husbanded land encapsulated in the word *vergel*, a garden or orchard, also connotes, however, a more open space of luxuriant diversity. Exceeding the limits of the garden, or *pensil*, which informed the title of the

so-called *Pensiles* published between 1845 and 1859, *vergel* challenges an overly ordered environment to situate itself between domestication and wilderness. The liminal position characterizes the writing of its female contributors, who couch their demands for emancipation through nature imagery. ("A Feminist Press" 113)

Thus the way was prepared for Arenal's notion of women's capacity for achieving an independent and unique personality, a concept that developed over the course of her writings.

Interestingly, Arenal does not employ the term *personalidad* in her first book on women, *La mujer del porvenir*, and the word only occurs once in the next, *La mujer de su casa* (1881): "¿Quién no se persuade de lo mucho que retrae de prestar auxilio directo ni indirecto a toda reforma ventajosa para la mujer, la sospecha, vaga unas veces, otras determinada, de que peligra la virtud de toda la que aspire a tener personalidad, y que, sin estar bajo la tutela del marido, sin ser eternamente menor, no puede hacer buena casada" (*La emancipación* 61) [Who doubts that direct or indirect support for reforms that would help women is limited by the sometimes vague, sometimes clear suspicion that women who aspire to have a personality are in danger, and without being under the tutelage of her husband, without being an eternal minor, she cannot be a good wife]. By 1992, however, in "La educación de la mujer" [Women's education], the speech Arenal sent to the Congreso Pedagógico of 1892, the concept of personality becomes central to her notion of womanhood. In that speech Arenal assumes that personality is acquired and can be obtained through effort and above all by means of education. She begins with the premise that "[l]a educación procura formar el carácter, hacer del *sujeto* una *persona* con cualidades *esenciales generales*, de que no podrá prescindir *nunca* y necesitará siempre si ha de ser como debe" [education attempts to form character, to make the *subject* a *person* with *essential general* qualities, which he or she can *never* shed and will always need if he or she is to be as he or she ought to be]. And Arenal indicates that education can strengthen "al que falta carácter, personalidad, aquello que es esencial para todo hombre" [he/she who lacks character, personality, that which is essential to every person].

Arenal believes that women should receive even more education than men because they are confronted with more social threats such as frivolity, slavery, and prostitution; therefore "necesita mucha virtud . . . fuerza, mucho carácter, mucha personalidad. La mujer, para ser persona, ha menester hoy y probablemente siempre (porque hay condiciones naturales que no pueden cambiarse), para tener personalidad . . . necesita ser *más persona* que el hombre . . ." (*La emancipación* 63; emphasis in original) [she needs a great deal of virtue . . . strength, much character, much personality. The woman, to be a person today and probably forever (because natural conditions cannot change) needs to be *more of a person* than the man]. Here Arenal employs the word *persona* in a similar way to María Zambrano in the twentieth century. Arenal reasons that education can form character, can convert a man or a woman into a person who "no tiene sexo; es el cumplimiento del deber, sea el que quiera; la reclamación de un derecho, sea el que fuere; la dignidad, que puede tenerse en todas las situaciones; la benevolencia, que si está en el ánimo, halla siempre medio de manifestarse de algún modo" (*La emancipación* 197–98) [has no sex; she fulfills a duty, whatever it might be; reclaims a right, whichever it might be; dignity, which one can have in all situations; benevolence, which if it is in the spirit, always finds a way to manifest itself in some way]. For Arenal "una sólida personalidad" (*La emancipación* 65) [a solid personality] is the best way to get out of the eternal circle in which women are not respected because they are not respectable, and they are not respectable because they are not respected. To have personality is the basis for all women's good actions: "la buena esposa y la buena madre es una ilusión si se presciende de la *buena persona*, y la buena persona es ilusoria si se presciende de la personalidad" (*La emancipación* 66; emphasis in original) [the good wife and the good mother are illusions if one does not take into account the *good person*, and the good person is illusory if one does not take personality into account]. If the woman is limited only to being a wife and a mother,

> equivale a decirle que por sí no puede ser nada, y aniquilar en ella su *yo* moral e intelectual, preparándola con absurdos deprimentes a la gran lucha de la vida, lucha que no supriman, antes la hacen más terrible los mismos que la privan de fuerzas para sostenerla: cualquiera habrá notado que los que menos consideran a las mujeres son los que más se oponen a que se las ponga en condiciones de ser personas, y es natural. (67)

> [it is the same as telling her that on her own she cannot be anything, and to destroy her moral and intellectual *self*, pre-

paring her with depressing absurdities for life's great struggle, a struggle that these absurdities do not remove; rather they make the struggle more formidable because they take away the strength that sustains her. Anyone must have noticed that those who least take women into consideration are those that most oppose women's being placed in the conditions that would allow her to be a person, and that is understandable].

According to Arenal, a woman must affirm her personality totally apart from her civil status, be she single, married, or a widow. Her duties, her rights, and her dignity do not depend on anyone else. Having personality is a prior condition to a woman's being a good wife and mother. Only the woman with character, with personality, can be useful to society as a mother and wife or as a single woman doing charity work. For Arenal, the person is someone who works; one cannot be a person if one does not work. He or she who eats and does not work is a thing and not a person.[2] María Laffitte, Condesa de Campo Alange (1902–1986), makes an interesting contrast between Arenal's and Ortega y Gasset's concept of person. In referring to love, Ortega asserts that a woman's soul is more concentric, more joined to herself, more elastic.[3] Campo Alange quotes Ortega: "Un alma muy unificada supone un régimen muy unitario del entender. Diríase que el alma femenina tiende a vivir con un único eje atencional que en cada época de su vida está puesto en una sola cosa" (*La secreta guerra* 119) [A very unified soul indicates a very unitary method of understanding. One could say that the feminine soul tends to live with a single axis of attention that in each period of her life is focused on only one thing]. Campo Alange points out that while Arenal and Ortega seem to refer to the same limited view in women, in fact Ortega's statement indicates that he believes it is a fixed quality of women as a gender, while Arenal attributes it to women's socially prescribed role and education.

Although, as I indicated above, Arenal emphasizes characteristics associated with the external view of the person, a section of her 1892 speech points toward the internal realm, which Spanish feminist thinkers of the twentieth century will emphasize. In an interesting use of language, Arenal converts the concept of *persona* into a state of consciousness: "La persona es una actividad consciente y útil; todo lo demás son cosas que, según las circunstancias, podrán ser más o menos perjudiciales, pero que lo son siempre para sí y para los demás, porque en el combate de la vida no hay neutralidad posible; hay que decidirse por el bien o por el mal"

(*La emancipación* 69) [Being a person is a conscious and useful activity; everything else, depending on the circumstances, can be more or less prejudicial, but they are always prejudicial for themselves and for others, because in life's battle neutrality is not possible; one must decide between good and evil]. The distinction between "conscious activity" and "thing" is reminiscent of the phenomenology and existentialism that influenced María Zambrano's thought, but unfortunately Arenal died the following year and thus did not have an opportunity to develop this suggestive line of reasoning. Opinions about the essential and fixed nature of women persisted well into the new century: "«hi ha en la dòna una cosa permanent, fixa, invariable: y aquesta es la necessitat d'estimar»" (Miquel d'Espluges. *La paz interior en la vida cristiana de la mujer*, qtd. in Dolors Monserdà de Maciá. *Estudi Feminista: Orientacions pera la Dòna Catalana* 25) [there is something permanent, fixed, and invariable in women, and that must necessarily be taken into consideration].

In another foreshadowing of Zambrano's existential sense of "personalidad," free-thinker and Mason Rosario de Acuña (1851–1924) employed the term *personalidad* in a similar way to Arenal—a whole, autonomous self.[4] In an article from 1883 on country women's work, Acuña relates personality to satisfying work. Just as in existentialism, the sense of self arises from the regard of the other: "desde el instante en que se rodean seres que esperan algo de ti, mujer, ya tienes en tu frente una corona regia, y en tus manos un cetro omnipotente; ya no puedes, no, en manera alguna ser escarnecida como inútil, ni presentada como fútil joya, y tu personalidad altísima, conceptuada como la parte media del género humano, es una personalidad tan imprescindible, tan necesaria en el concurso racional que, sin ti fuera la tierra un desierto y no sería el hombre un rey" (*Obras reunidas* I, 698) [woman, from the minute you are surrounded by beings who want something from you, you have a royal crown on your head, and an omnipotent scepter in your hand; you can no longer be put down as useless or be presented as a useless jewel and your lofty personality, conceived as half of the human species, is an indispensable personality, so necessary to the rational competition that without you the Earth would be a desert and man would not be king].

In her speech "Consecuencias de la degeneración femenina" [Consequences of female degeneration] from 1888, Acuña prefaces her remarks with the customary gratitude to those who have invited her to speak, thus allowing her to "levantar [su] personalidad, ¡solitaria arista que los vientos sociales empujan al vacío del no ser!, hasta una altura de prestigio en que, a través de las rutinas que intentan denigrarme, veo surgir un auditorio en cuya inteligencia hallan eco mis palabras; y en cuyo corazón, no encallecido por la ruin vanidad, repercute con vibraciones de ternura el ritmo de mi corazón" (*Obras selectas* III, 506) [raise up her personality, a solitary arris that the social winds push into the void of nonbeing! up to a height of prestige that through the routines that attempt to diminish me, I see surge forth an audience in whose intelligence my words are echoed and in whose heart, not silenced by vile vanity, reverberates with the tender vibrations the rhythm of my heart]. She further notes that when standing before this group her whole being is renewed as though her audience's souls emitted a vigor that condensed in her own, obliging her to fight not for herself but for them, as though she possessed the ability to reproduce what they are thinking. Acuña's often florid style soars when she considers how her personality is enhanced by standing before the group at the Fomento de Artes: "Medid por todo lo expuesto cuán profunda será mi gratitud, al sentirme subir desde la realidad de mi pequeñez hasta la altura de vuestra valía; desde el ciclo estéril y hueco donde rueda mi personalidad, hasta la órbita luminosa y fecunda donde giran las huestes civilizadoras; desde el fondo de un hogar desconocido, hasta el santuario donde se escriben con letras inmortales el nombre de los genios" (507) [Measure by all I have said how profound will be my gratitude, on feeling myself rise from the reality of my smallness up to the height of your worth; from the sterile and hollow cycle where my personality roams up to the luminous and fecund orbit where the civilizing hordes circulate; from the depths of an unknown home to the sanctuary where the names of the geniuses are written with immortal letters].

In a change to the position regarding women's remaining in the home that she had voiced six years earlier in 1882, and now echoing Arenal's preoccupation with women's confinement to the home in *La mujer de su casa*, in an 1888 speech to the women's Masonic Lodge Hijas del Progreso, Acuña indicates that personality is something that can be lost when married women are limited to the domestic sphere. The home, she avers, becomes a grave. The home is a sacred temple that should be a monument to its greatness, but instead it is a coffin where the woman's personality unravels and destroys the last vigor of her intelligence. If the violence of her indignation allows hatred to penetrate her, she may dedicate herself to a more desperate calling, selling her body and attracting the scorn of decent people. Again foreshadowing María

Zambrano's concept of *persona*, Acuña evokes women's complete and autonomous self with the same term: "¿Qué razón sana, qué imaginación convenientemente cultivada, qué inteligencia libre de prejuicios impuestos hará caso de ese vulgar, ignorante concepto que se arroja como arma de aniquilada contundencia cuando se está defendiendo la alteza del intelecto femenino, exponiendo al manifiesto aquel nuevo mundo donde la mujer está reconocida como persona?" ("Discurso" 507) [What sane reason, what carefully cultivated imagination, what intellect free of imposed prejudices would pay attention to that vulgar and ignorant concept that hurls itself like a weapon of spent force when it is defending the elevation of female intellect, making manifest that new world where women are recognized as persons?]. Like Concepción Arenal, Acuña draws on Krausist concepts (especially the notion of human beings' perfectibility) and vocabulary to forge her arguments: "el eterno femenino, en su misión de sintetizar la vida, cuando acciona en el mundo intelectual, tampoco inicia la creación, sino que condensa, recoge, acumula, conforma, reúne, armoniza y abarca, hasta dejar un todo cumplido, capaz de transmitir con su riqueza de cohesiones los rasgos de la perfectabilidad" (507) [the eternal feminine, in its mission to synthesize life, when it acts in the intellectual world, does not initiate creation, but rather condenses, collects, accumulates, conforms, brings together, harmonizes, and covers, leaving a completed whole capable of transmitting the characteristics of perfectibility with its cohesive richness].

Monserdà de Macià considers women's loss of personality from a historical viewpoint, giving Christianity credit for endowing women with personality. She measures how far women have come since the pre-Christian era, when women were considered a mere instrument of pleasure, to Christian times when "Jesús la recull abatiduda, postergada, anulada, sols atesa pêls homes d'aquella època com a mer instrument de plaher y l'alça, la malteix, la dignifica, i retorna la personalitat perduda y la entrega al Christianisme pera que contribui ella seva obra de redempció" (*Estudi* 63) [Jesus rescues her beleaguered, prostrated, annulled by the men of that period who used her as a mere instrument of pleasure and raises her up and dignifies her, returning her lost personality to her and turns her over to Christianity to contribute her redemptive work].

Spanish feminist and free-thinker Belén de Sárraga (1873–1951) takes a much more secular approach in linking to the legal realm the existential notion of personality that we have seen in Arenal and, to an extent, in Acuña:

El hombre hoy día tiene una personalidad jurídica, que no ha alcanzado la mujer; el hombre manda, la mujer ruega; el hombre se impone; la mujer suplica; el hombre castiga, la mujer llora; pero cuando la mujer que llora es madre y esposa la que ruega, la debilidad de la mujer ha vencido: el hombre más autoritario se abate. . . . Esa influencia es absolutamente imposible de cambiarla y hay que aceptarla, buena o mala. (*Conferencias* 23)

[Today men have a judicial personality, which women have not attained. Men command; women beg. Men impose themselves; women supplicate. Men punish; women cry. But when the woman cries it is the wife and mother who begs. Women's weakness has prevailed; the most authoritarian man backs off. . . . It is absolutely impossible to change this influence, and whether good or bad, it must be accepted.]

As María Martínez Sierra will do in her 1932 *Nuevas cartas a las mujeres de España*, Sárraga speaks of full personhood in terms of citizenship: "Pero no es, señores, que la mujer sea de constitución inferior a la del hombre; no es que la Naturaleza no le haya dado dotes grandes, de valía a la mujer: es que a mujer tal como hoy existe, no es tipo natural de esposa, es que la mujer es un tipo humano enfermo y enfermo por el misticismo religioso, de exceso de sentimentalismo, enfermo de hipertrofía natural! . . . Curemos a la enferma y tendremos entonces la ciudadana" (*Conferencias* 24) [But it is not, gentlemen, that women are of inferior constitution to men; it is not that nature has not given women great and valuable powers: it is that woman, as such, does not exist today. She is not a natural wife; woman is a sick human type, ill with religious mysticism, an excess of sentimentalism, ill with natural hypertrophy!! . . . Let's cure the sick woman and then we will have a citizen]. Sárraga, however, is not arguing for woman as individual, as did Emilia Pardo Bazán or even Concepción Arenal, whose sense of the female self was usually formed in relation to others. Sárraga goes much further in denominating the woman's self as part of a social whole: "¿por qué no han nacido el hombre y la mujer para entenderse, para juntarse, formar el individuo social, que crea el hogar y que, dando hijos al mundo, da hijos para la patria y grandes triunfos a la mujer?" (*Conferencias* 25) [Why have men and women not been born to understand one another, to come together to form a social individual who creates a home and who, giving children to the world, produces sons for the country and great triumphs for women?]. Foreshadowing Zambrano's ideas on women and the soul, Sárraga cites the example of the famous Christian Council, which debated whether women have a soul.

In the 1920s, when Spanish feminists began to organize in earnest with groups such as ANME (Asociación Nacional de Mujeres Españolas) and saw some of their goals, such as equality under the law, the franchise, and right to divorce realized under the Second Spanish Republic (1931–1939), Hildegart Rodríguez (1914–1933), a precocious feminist, employed the term "personalidad" when writing of her relationship with her mother, Aurora Rodríguez Carballeira. Hildegart's was a special situation, because her struggle to attain a personality did not take place in a patriarchal milieu but in matriarchal circumstances. Her mother had decided to have a girl child as a single mother and to raise her in a totally scientific way to produce a new intellectual, thinking, writing woman who would be prepared to reform society according to her mother's eugenics principles.

It all turned out just as the mother had planned. From an early age Hildegart wrote books and gave lectures on eugenics, sex, and love. She even became involved in Spanish politics. However, Hildgart's mother did not permit Hildegart independence. The mother always considered Hildegart an extension of herself. At age eighteen Hildegart attempted to liberate herself from her mother and write on topics that interested her (Hildegart). Hildegart even fell in love and wished to live apart from her mother. The mother could not accept her creation's rebellion, and she killed her daughter. Hildegart's use of the word *personalidad* in some of her writings reminds us of her life circumstances:

> La madre, que es capaz de todos los sacrificios para beneficiar al ser querido, no puede apartarse de éste. Ya no basta para ser madre con la acción de la naturaleza, hace falta ser muy culta, mucho más que una mujer corriente, porque aquella cultura habrá de polarizarse en el nuevo ser . . . [el matrimonio] herido de muerte por la institución del divorcio no puede ofrecer ya, ninguna posibilidad . . . hoy no existe más que la apariencia, es un bello fantasma, pero privado de personalidad. (qtd. in Carmen Domingo 84)[5]

[The mother, who is capable of any sacrifice to benefit the loved one, cannot separate from him or her. It is not enough to be a mother doing the natural things; it is necessary to be very cultured, much more than a common woman, because that culture will become polarized in the new being . . . [a marriage] dealt a death blow by the institution of divorce can no longer offer any possibility . . . today only the appearance of a beautiful phantom, bereft of personality, exists.]

It seems that Hildegart, like Concepción Arenal, understood the concept of personality as a force. Hildegart also introduced the notion of mask ("beautiful phantom"), which she distinguishes from a supposedly more authentic personality. As we will see in the coming pages, Carmen Martín Gaite fuses the concepts of mask and personality that Hildegart opposes in a dichotomy that suggests the opposition between interior and exterior developed by later thinkers such as Rosa Chacel and María Zambrano.

From her earliest feminist writings, María Martínez Sierra's theory of personality emphasized the interior person. Recall that she cherished the solitude in which the person could find him- or herself (especially herself). In *Nuevas cartas a las mujeres de España* she develops these ideas most fully in a chapter titled "Nunca la libertad ha destruido una virtud" [Never has liberty destroyed a virtue], which is cast in a utopian mode. The new family organization that she envisions will be based on absolute independence, individuality, and respect for personality. In this new arrangement in which one person does not dominate over another, she asks, what will become of love and virtue? These are indestructible; thus the title asserting that freedom has never destroyed a virtue. The second half of the article elaborates how this independence and full personality will allow women whose husbands have withdrawn their affection and redirected it elsewhere to leave their husbands and live on their own (in fact, Martínez Sierra's own personal situation). No woman, she observes, should have to endure living with infidelity. If the woman chooses to live separately from her husband, she will have an even better relationship with her children, who will live with her. In Martínez Sierra's utopian society, adolescent children would go to live in communities of their peers, where they would be free of "gregario egoísmo familiar" [gregarious family egotism], and they will be prepared "mediante la inevitable lucha entre iguales, a alcanzar el supremo triunfo individualista, la afirmación, el perfeccionamiento, el desenvolvimiento pleno de su personalidad" (130) [to achieve the supreme individualistic triumph—the affirmation, perfection, and full development of their personality by means of the inevitable struggle among equals].

Rosa Chacel was the first Spanish feminist writer to fully elaborate the idea of an interaction between the interior and the exterior of a person that Concepción Arenal suggested in one of her last writings and that Hildegart also hinted at in the 1920s. At the beginning of the 1930s Chacel introduced into Spanish feminist thought the concept of an interior and an exterior being that can be differentiated from one another. In this dichotomy, Chacel privileges the interior being as the more important. This division of the self will be important in Spanish feminist thought during the remainder of the twentieth century when it comes to defining the personality. In her first feminist essay, "Esquema de los problemas prácticos y actuales del amor" from 1931, Chacel theorizes that social change originates in the person's interior. Chacel counters Carl Jung's assertion that political events—wars and revolutions—of the first decades of the twentieth century had caused changes and tensions between men and women, arguing just the opposite. According to her, first the internal change occurs and this internal change then gives rise to social changes:

> No es que la acomodación a un medio con su gradual proceso de conquista vaya creando un reducto anímico resultante de determinada combinación de sensaciones y resistencias, labor primaria, elemental en lo psíquico, sino al contrario, que el alma saturada de su medio, tranquilamente vencedora de todas las hostilidades naturales, anula en sí toda vida de relación tradicional y se queda frente a frente con su soledad. El conflicto se crea de esta autocontemplación. ("Esquema" 157)

[It is not that the accommodation to a circumstance with its gradual process of conquest creates a feeling that comes from a certain combination of sensations and resistances, primary, elemental psychic work; rather it is the contrary. The soul saturated with its surroundings, tranquilly having overcome all the natural hostilities, annuls within itself all traditional relational life and remains face to face with its solitude. The conflict arises from this self-contemplation.]

Chacel proposes the idea of women's individuality (a concept related to personality) that will arise in other feminist thinkers in the post–Civil War era. She responds that "[u]na de las cosas que con mayor evidencia pueden demostrarnos la adhesión de la mujer al mundo espiritual, a la cultura, es precisamente su primera manifestación de rebeldía a ella" ("Esquema"140) [one of the things that provides greatest proof that women participate in the spiritual world, in culture, is precisely the first sign of her rebellion against it]. In other words, the rebellious woman distances herself from the culture that surrounds her. As I noted in chapter 1, Chacel countered Georg Simmel, who denied women an individual spirit, and she employed Max Scheler's concept of an "absolute individual" to formulate her own idea of a being's identity (man or woman). Chacel does not distinguish between men and women in the formation of being, and she employs the term *hombre* as "human being" as was the custom in philosophical essays until recently.

Fifteen years later, in 1946, María Zambrano echoed some of Chacel's ideas in the review she wrote of Gustavo Pittaluga's *Grandeza y servidumbre de la mujer*, and in *Persona y democracia*, written in 1956, Zambrano developed her concept of *persona*, which although it is not an expressly feminist concept, can be linked to her feminist thought. For example, one of the central points of *Persona y democracia* is the distinction between individual and person, a distinction that was already present in schematic form in the 1946 review, where Zambrano does make specific reference to women:

> Y es que hay un problema pavoroso que el autor [Gustavo Pittaluga] ha soslayado: ¿puede la mujer ser 'individuo' en la medida en que lo es el hombre? ¿Puede tener una vocación además de la vocación genérica sin contradecirla? ¿Puede una mujer, en suma, realizar la suprema y sagrada vocación de la Mujer siendo además una mujer atraída por una vocación determinada?¿Puede unir en su ser la vocación de la Mujer con una de esas vocaciones que han absorbido y hecho la grandeza de algunos hombres: Filosofía, Poesía, ciencia, es

decir, puede crear la Mujer sin dejar de serlo? (*La aventura* 202–3; upper cases in original)

[There is a dreadful problem that the author (Pittaluga) has overlooked: can a woman be an "individual" in the same way that a man can? Can she have a vocation in addition to her gender vocation without contradicting it? Can a woman, in sum, realize the supreme vocation of woman and also be a woman attracted to a particular vocation? Can she unite in her being the vocation of the woman with one of these vocations—philosophy, poetry, science—that have absorbed and made some men great: that is to say, can a woman create without ceasing to be a woman?]

Juan Fernando Ortega Muñoz observes that by the end of the decade of the 1940s, Zambrano had stopped writing essays specifically about women and had begun writing about persons (*La aventura* 57). Perhaps she arrived at this position thanks to Gustavo Pittaluga's suggestion in *Grandeza y servidumbre de la mujer* that society was growing closer to eliminating gender distinctions.

Although she does not employ the term *personalidad*, Zambrano's concept of *persona* coincides in many ways with what other authors call *personalidad* in the social sense of an individual entity separated from others by salient distinguishing characteristics. (The Real Academia reminds us of the etymological connection between *persona* and *personalidad*.) It is possible that the concept of person that María Zambrano defines in *Persona y democracia* was influenced by the French existentialists, with whom she came into contact in the mid-1940s when she lived in Paris (there is a section on Sartre's notion of nothingness in *El hombre y lo divino* from 1955).[6] However, long before she might have read Sartre's *Being and Nothingness*, Zambrano would have known Miguel de Unamuno's ideas on personality (Unamuno, himself an exile from Miguel Primo de Rivera's dictatorship in the 1920s, was an extremely important reference for Spanish Civil War exiles.)

Since Unamuno could also have been a source of inspiration for Carmen Martín Gaite in her essays on personality in the 1960s, here I will sidetrack briefly to outline what Unamuno offered on the subject (although without any feminist intentions). As Antonio Sánchez Barbudo indicates, for Unamuno "[e]l problema de la personalidad lo provocaba el contraste entre lo íntimo y lo externo de la persona, de su persona" ("El misterio" 175) [the problem of the personality was provoked by the contrast between the interior and the exterior of the person, his persona]. The "problem" of personality for Unamuno was related directly with his desire to continue existing after physical death. He spells out this desire in the comments he made in 1932 when his play *El otro* debuted: "*El otro* me ha brotado de la obsesión, mejor que preocupación, por el misterio—no problema—de la personalidad; del sentimiento congojoso de nuestra identidad y continuidad individual y personal" (qtd. in Sánchez Barbudo 176) [*El otro* sprang from the obsession, or rather the preoccupation, with the mystery—no, problem—of personality; the anguished sense of our identity and individual and personal continuation]. Thinkers such as María Zambrano and Carmen Martíin Gaite understood personality as "individual and personal identity," but without Unamuno's anguish and the desire for a continuation of life after death. They were still focused on securing a dignified place for women in this life, much less on what might follow.

For Unamuno there is a profound and permanent self that is the most authentic, and another superficial self that is changing. The latter self emerges when "los diversos conceptos que de cada uno de nosotros se forjan los prójimos que nos tratan vienen a caer sobre nuestro espíritu y acaban por envolverlo en una especie de caparazón. . . . Antes de hacer o decir algo reflexiona si es lo que de él esperaban los demás, para seguir siendo como los demás le creen se hace traición a sí mismo; es insincero" (qtd. in Sánchez Barbudo 177) [the diverse concepts that others who deal with us forge about us fall upon our spirit and wrap it up in a kind of shell. . . . Before doing or saying something, the person reflects on what others expect of him or her, in order to continue being what the others expect, betraying him or herself; it is insincere]. According to Unamuno, this inner self cannot be known; he argues that it is impossible to undo the superficial self to reach the true self. On this point, Spanish feminist thinkers such as Chacel, Zambrano, and Martín Gaite, although they depart from the same dichotomy between interior and exterior, do not despair about the possibility of overcoming the exterior person imposed by others to discover the authentic interior self.

The concept of otherness had already begun to appear in Zambrano's work as early as 1928, in a series of articles for *El Liberal* where she first employed the term *persona*, especially in relation to women. Thinking about women's personality formation gave Zambrano existential insights that coincided with those elaborated by Jean Paul Sartre some years later. In these articles Zambrano reflects on women's potential to become a sociopolitical entity, a citizen, which includes an interior dimension: "[s]e trata, pues, sólo de ser fiel a sí mismo, limpio espejo de la interior realidad" (*Aventura* 80) [it is only a matter of being faithful to oneself, a clear mirror of the interior reality]. Here Zambrano prefigures the Sartrean notion of bad faith, according to which the person denies that he or she is free to choose and presents a false view of the self. Zambrano characterizes women as a class that has systematically denied its true nature and succumbed to bad faith:

> No es la falta de potencia intelectual, dotes organizadoras, lo que nos inquieta en la mujer, sino resistencia a actuar de modo distinto a cómo lo hizo en su antiguo puesto, con las antiguas armas, que fueron su «grandeza y servidumbre». Es la actitud de la mujer, siempre pronta a naufragar en lo doméstico, a adscribirse a perpetuidad a unos lares con exclusión absoluta; es su ausencia de la vida ciudadana lo que nos preocupa a quienes esperamos con impaciencia la plena «entrada de la mujer en el imperio de la dignidad». (*Aventura* 89)

> [We are not concerned about women's lack of intellectual power or organizational abilities but rather resistance to acting differently from the way they formerly did with the same old arms that were her "greatness and servitude." It is women's attitude, always ready to run aground in the domestic sphere, to subscribe in perpetuity exclusively to that realm; it is the absence of citizenly life that worries those of us who wait impatiently for women's full entrance into the empire of dignity.]

Although in these early articles Zambrano highlights the legal inequality of women in Spain, she does not believe that changing external conditions will solve Spanish women's problems. Rather, women must tend to "el cultivo y cuidado de su espíritu" (*Aventura* 91–92) [cultivating and caring for their spirit], an idea that will reappear in a more universal way in her concept of "person" in 1956.

Zambrano's notion of "person" was already taking shape in these early articles. Like Sartrean being, the person is formed in relation to the other. In the *El Liberal* articles, a woman's personhood arises from interaction with men. As women develop their individual personalities, confrontations with men occur that can be resolved by sharing the spiritual, cultural realm: "La mujer camina en su evolución, adquiere personalidad día por día. . . . lucha y se esfuerza, aborda de frente los problemas, da la cara a la vida" (*Aventura* 103) [Women are evolving, day by day acquiring personality. . . . they fight and make an effort; they confront their problems head on, and face life]. Men resist this new impulse on women's part, and the ensuing conflict "se nos hace de pronto persona" (*Aventura* 103) [suddenly makes us a person]. A woman becomes a person by cultivating her interior self and through her interaction with the other. By the time Zambrano wrote *Persona y democracia*, the interior takes precedence (an important difference from Sartre).

In *Horizonte del liberalismo*, published two years after the *El liberal* articles, Zambrano meditates on the meaning of the individual, which in *Persona y democracia* she will contrast to "person." Now the contact between the interior of the human being and the exterior (the other) is not focused on men and women but on the ungendered individual and his/her confrontation with life, a confrontation with a political dimension that forms part of spiritual (cultural) work: "Política es reforma, creación, revolución siempre, por tanto: Lucha—conjunción—entre el individuo y la vida. Y así, del predominio o dirección de uno de estos factores—la vida también reforma al individuo—nacen las diversas concepciones de la política, que no serán sólo de la política—nada espiritual existe aislado—sino de la totalidad de la vida" (*Horizonte* 204) [Politics are always reform, creation, and revolution, and therefore a fight—conjunction—between the individual and life. And thus the diverse conceptions of politics (which are not only political, since nothing spiritual exists in isolation, but rather the totality of life) are born from the predomination or direction of one of these factors (life also reforms the individual)]. Here Zambrano introduces the notion of consciousness; for her politics involve historical consciousness, and for Zambrano history is a dramatic dialogue between human beings and the universe. Human beings are conscious of being other to everything else, which, as Sartre would articulate most fully thirteen years later in *Being and Nothingness*, is the crux of his (her) existential situation: "En el hecho mismo de su existencia ya tiene la duda, el problema, el poder ser y, por tanto, no ser" (231) [In the fact itself of their existence they have the doubt, the problem, of being able to be and, therefore, of not being]. It is important to remember that Zambrano arrived at these midcareer positions about personhood thanks to her early thinking about women's selfhood that then became universalized.

Zambrano's notion of the individual includes freedom, foretelling Sartre's central concept of the human being as necessarily free. She postulates that to move forward, one must have faith, which creates a "zona segura" [secure zone], a "tierra firme" [dry land], that in turn allows the individual to choose, "tener libertad en suma" (233) [in sum, to have liberty]. As Sartre would theorize in *Being and Nothingness*, Zambrano posits one's freedom as always linked to that of the other:

> Y así vemos que en la raíz misma del problema de la libertad—que es el del individuo y el mundo—encontramos la contradicción, la paradoja. . . . es que existen conceptos que se suponen unos a otros, y sin uno el otro no tiene sentido. (¿Y quizá no todos?) Tal vez ocurra del mismo modo con toda la vida humana—siempre en equilibrio inestable—y nada tendría sentido en su soledad, sino en conjunción—armonía—de contrarios. (233–34)

> [And thus we see that at the very root of the problem of liberty (which is that of the individual and the world), we find the contradiction; the paradox. . . . is that concepts exist based on one and another, and without one the other makes no sense. (And perhaps all?) Perhaps the same is the case with all human life—always in an unstable equilibrium—and nothing would make sense by itself, only in conjunction—harmony—of opposites.]

Zambrano critiques the absolute individual for negating his or her connection to others; she believes it is ultimately impossible to exist in isolation: "Tampoco el individuo, por fuerte que sea, puede existir aislado: necesita para tener sentido sentirse vinculado a algo, referirse a algo, llevar a alquien tras de sí. Es una figura—no un punto—pero incompleta en su actualidad" (253) [Nor can the individual, however strong he or she might be, exist alone: he or she needs to feel like he or she connects to something, refers to something, carries someone along with them. It is a figure—not a point—but incomplete in its present form].

Zambrano's concept of *persona* reached its fullest expression in *Persona y democracia* after the long gestation period that began with the 1928 *El Liberal* articles on women. The mature version of "person," which transcends gender and refers to human beings as a universal, constitutes a complex dialectic between the individual (interior) and society (the other, the exterior), but ultimately the interior prevails: "El lugar del 'individuo' es la sociedad (individuo y sociedad aparecen simultáneamente), pero el lugar de la persona es un íntimo espacio. . . . Sólo lo es eso desconocido y sin nombre, que es soledad y libertad" (*Persona* 124) [The individual's place is society (individual and society appear simultaneously), but the person's place is an intimate space. . . . It is only the unknown thing without a name, which is solitude and liberty]. The essential condition of the human being is to feel him- or herself enclosed: "Solemos tener la imagen inmediata de nuestra persona como una persona como una fortaleza en cuyo interior estamos encerrados, nos sentimos ser un « sí mismo . . . incomunicable, hermético, del que a veces querríamos escapar o abrir a alguien al amigo, a la persona a quien se ama, o a la comunidad. La persona vive en soledad y, por lo mismo, a mayor intensidad de vida personal" (17) [We tend to have an immediate image of our person as a fortress in whose interior we are locked up; we feel ourselves to be an incommunicable, hermetic "self," from which sometimes we would like to escape or open up to someone, a friend, a person whom we love, or the community. The person lives in solitude, and for that reason, in greater intensity of personal life]. Although Zambrano affirms that the person's interior can connect with the other, the process begins and ends in the interior. The interior of the person seeks the exterior, seeks to come forth from itself in order to relate to the other, to society.[7]

Without employing the specific Sartrean terms, Zambrano attempts to unify the amorphous interior *en soi* and the socially interactive *pour soi*. If the other's regard, as Sartre argues, determines how I see myself, the reverse is also true: "La cuestión es que frente a cualquier sujeto de la acción habría que preguntarse, ¿quién es? ¿Es una persona real, con su sustancia propia, o es solamente el personaje inventado, máscara de un delirio? Si es este último estamos tratando entonces con alguien que es otro; otro no ya para mí, o para los demás, sino *para sí mismo*. Su verdadera persona está sojuzgada, yace víctima del personaje que lo sustituye" (79, italics in the original) [The question is, when confronted with the subject of an action, one would have to ask oneself, who is it? Is it a real person, with his/her own substance, or is it only an invented personage, a mask born of delirium? If the latter, we are dealing with someone that is other; other not for me, or for others, but *for themselves*. Their true persona is subjected, is a victim of the personage that substitutes for it]. Bad faith works both ways. History creates *personajes*—deforms *persona*.

As she did in her essay on Unamuno and Ortega from 1949, in *Persona y democracia* Zambrano establishes a dichotomy between *persona* and *personaje* or *enmascarado*. The *personaje* emerges when human beings allow themselves to be deformed by history, but Zambrano argues that love and dreams can dissolve the *personaje* and return the person to authentic being: "Y puesto que la esperanza se expresa en sueños surge el de que algún día no sea el protagonista de la historia este pobre niño atormentado, ni ese pobre hombre, ni este fantasma agobiado, ni ese monstruo, sino simplemente el hombre mismo, sin máscaras y con una carga apropiada a sus fuerzas. . . . Que la persona sea la máxima realidad y no el personaje" (79) [And since hope is expressed in dreams, a dream occurs that one day the poor tormented child, this poor man, this exhausted phantom, this monster will not be history's protagonist, but simply the man himself, without masks and with a burden appropriate to his abilities. . . . the person is the ultimate reality and not the personage]. In this process, Zambrano also reaffirms the centrality of the interior being: "En este caso, es «sí mismo», para ser algo mejor, para ofrecerse por entero a una empresa y entregarse a la búsqueda o a la conquista de algo que ha de ser para todos; que debe servir a todos. Y esta universalidad es intimidad también" (80) [In this case, it is "itself," in order to be something better, in order to offer itself completely to an enterprise and involve itself in the search or in the conquest of something that is for everyone, that should serve all. And this universality is intimacy as well]. Bad faith is *enajenación* or *alienación* (terms that also sound Sartrean), which Zambrano defines as "no reconocerse a sí mismo, no lograr ser fiel a la propia esencial condición" (77) [not recognizing oneself, or managing to be faithful to one's own essential condition]. In Zambrano's view, freedom (the possibility of mobility and for Sartre fundamental to being) is only possible "cuando no se pesa sobre nadie; cuando no se humilla a nadie, incluido a sí mismo. . . . En cada hombre están todos los hombres" (76) [when one does not impinge on anyone else; when one does not humiliate anyone, including oneself. . . . All humans are present in each human being]. For Zambrano one cannot live as a *persona* if one is conscious of weighing on others.

According to Zambrano, the human being "está formado por un yo y una persona. La persona incluye el yo y lo trasciende" (79) [constitutes an "I" and a person. The person includes the "I" and transcends it]. The "I" could be the equivalent of Sartre's *en soi* (being for itself), but *persona* differs from Sartre's *pour soi* (being for others) in that it (the person) possesses a moral dimension. Zambrano defines the related theme of alienation (in Spanish *enajenación* or *alienación*), possibly taken from Sartre's existentialism, as "no reconocerse a sí mismo, no lograr ser fiel a la propia esencial condición" (*Persona* 77) [not recognizing oneself, not managing to be true to one's own essential condition]. There are also Sartrean echoes in Zambrano's locating the origin of the authentic self in thought: "Al pensar se hace un vacío, en el cual disponemos realmente de nuestro tiempo [mientras que] en la acción histórica es difícil que el sujeto de ella no sea el personaje que nos hemos forjado" (*Persona* 78) [Upon thinking, a vacuum is created in which we are in control of our time, while in historical actions it is difficult for its agent not be the personage we have forged]. What distinguishes Zambrano's theory of person and its mask from that of others is her uniting interior and exterior in a view of the person that always includes a moral, social consciousness (or conscience): "Reconocerse, identificarse, quiere decir hacerse uno con aquel a quien se atribuía, como en *Edipo Rey*, la culpa de la peste en la ciudad. Y no es otro, es uno mismo. Y sólo entonces la purificación se produce; la peste desaparece" (*Persona* 76) [To recognize oneself, to identify oneself, means to become one with he who attributes to himself, as did Oedipus, guilt for the city's pestilance]. Significantly, these lessons are exemplified in one of Zambrano's few literary works—*La tumba de Antigone* (1965)—in which the central female figure, Antigone, does not die in her cave/prison as in the Greek original, but comes forth as a full personality to have a major part in the dialogue.

In *Persona y democracia* Zambrano, like Sartre, places the self in a body, but unlike Sartre, she endows her "sí mismo incomunicable, hermético" with soul (the passions). Thus for Zambrano, consciousness of oneself includes the soul: "Conocerse sería poder ver los movimientos más íntimos, esenciales y, por ello mismo describirlos y dirigirlos. El conocimiento de las llamadas «pasiones», sin duda, forma parte de ello" (36) [To know oneself would be being able to see the most intimate, essential movements and by this means to describe and direct them]. In later passages of the book, *alma* and *persona* are synonymous: "El esperar es el movimiento íntimo de la interioridad, se entiende como alma o persona y es, a la vez, pasividad y actividad. . . . se trata de desprenderse del poder al mismo tiempo que se ejerce, conservando íntegra la sustancia de la propia alma, de la propia persona" (65, 70) [Hoping, understood as soul or person, is the intimate movement of interior life; it is simultaneously passivity and activity. . . . it is relinquishing power while exercising it, conserving intact the substance of one's own soul, of one's own person]. Knowing oneself is to see one's most intimate and unconscious movements, "sorprendernos en ellos: poder describirlos y dirigirlos. El conocimiento de las llamadas «pasiones»"(36) [to surprise ourselves in them: to be able to discover and direct them. Knowledge of the so-called "passions"]. Fundamental to all the passions is the passion to be, to exist: "El anhelo es la primera manifestación de la vida humana. . . . El anhelar es como la respiración del alma" (63) [Yearning is the first manifestation of human life. . . . Yearning is like the soul's breathing]. Soul (the passions in earlier writings associated with women) and *persona* are indivisible. Thus *persona* is "algo más que el individuo; es el individuo dotado de conciencia, que se sabe a sí mismo y que se entiende a sí mismo como valor supremo, como última finalidad terrestre" (103) [more than the individual; it is the individual endowed with consciousness, which knows itself and understands itself as a supreme value, as the final earthly purpose]. This consciousness forms "un medio donde convivimos" (111) [a medium that we share]. However, "[a]lgo en el ser humano escapa y trasciende la sociedad en que vive" (114) [something in the human being escapes and transcends the society in which it lives], and like Sartre, Zambrano situates this transcendence in time, in the future.

The interior of the person searches for the exterior; it wants to emerge from itself and connect with another. Echoing Hildegart's concept of "mask," Zambrano establishes a dichotomy between *persona* and *personaje*. The personage or masked being arises when the person allows him or herself to be distorted by history, but dreams can return the person to his or her being. As noted above, Zambrano asserted that "la persona [es] la máxima realidad y no el personaje" (*Persona* 70) [the person is the ultimate reality and not the personage]. As we will see, at about the same time and perhaps likewise influenced by French existentialism, Carmen Martín Gaite also locates the dichotomy between authentic and inauthentic being at the center of her concept of personality.

During the period (1940s) that the exiled Zambrano was developing her ideas on women that would lead to her treatise on "person" and a year before Simone de Beauvoir published her landmark *Le deuxième Sexe*, María Laffitte, Countess of Campo Alange, came out with *La secreta guerra de los sexos* (1948) [The secret war of the sexes] in Franco's Spain. There she addresses the hyperfemininity prescribed by the Spain of her times, although she does not point out that in Franco's Spain such femininity was legally prescribed. Campo Alange laments that when women show any personal initiative—personality—they are thought to have become masculinized "sin pensar que en gran parte es que va adquiriendo una expresión más consciente y, por lo tanto, más parecido a la de los seres conscientes que ya lo eran con anterioridad" (67) [without considering that for the most part the woman is acquiring a more conscious expression and, thus, is more akin to beings whose consciousness had already been raised]. In a chapter on the Eve/María female stereotypes, Campo Alange points out that the radical division of women into these two types dismembers women and renders them useless, condemning them to "*no ser* plenamente" (103, italics in original) [not existing in the fullest sense of the term]. Perhaps we can detect in this statement (as we did in some of Zambrano's notions) echoes of Sartrean existentialism. However, Campo Alange believes that as time passes, these stereotypes merge, take on their own form and color, and lose their character as divine mythical ideals that are inaccessible to human beings. And within men's hearts they acquire the complex human reality of a woman. It is not clear if Campo Alange is thinking in diachronic or synchronic terms when she states that women will become real in men's hearts. In a chapter called "Un ideal de la mujer en el siglo XIV" [The ideal woman in the fourteenth century], she, like María Zambrano in her essay on Heloise, is definitely thinking historically: "Queda fuera de toda duda que la formación espiritual de la mujer tiene, por lo tanto, que llegar hasta ella por medios autodidácticos. Y es por esta razón por lo que sólo en casos especialísimos logró darse forma a sí misma" (111) [Doubtless a woman's spiritual formation thus has to take place via autodidactic means].

In another essay in the same volume, Campo Alange seems to allude to the same dichotomy between authentic and inauthentic selves that Unamuno and Sartre theorized. She refers especially to the gulf between the ideal of womanhood in Romantic literature and the real woman of flesh and blood: "Todo brote de la verdadera personalidad del individuo que recogió al azar esta proyección sirve únicamente para demostrar la diferencia entre lo que creíamos haber encontrado y lo que es en realidad" (116) [Every appearance of the individual's true personality that this projection collected by chance only serves to demonstrate the difference between what we believe we have found and what it is in reality]. In her book *La mujer como mito y como ser humano* from 1961, Campo Alange points out the discomfort that this dichotomy between the ideal and real woman provokes in men: "La personalidad en la mujer es un elemento incómodo para el varón" (*Mito* 59) [Personality in a woman is an uncomfortable element for a man]. Women with "personality" complicate the male's selection of a mate, because he would prefer to avoid a woman's critical eyes. However, Campo Alange believes that a woman's personality can help build a solid lifelong relationship.

In her young adulthood, Carmen Laforet, like Hildegart (although not to such extremes), was trapped in various family and national circumstances and suffered from lack of personal liberty. Not surprisingly, her use of the term *personalidad* echoes Hildegart's. After marrying at age twenty-five during the most repressive era of the Franco regime in the 1940s, Laforet felt that her personality had been absorbed by her family, and she struggled to recover that personality when she separated from her husband in 1970. As she wrote to Bernardo Arrizabalaga and his wife Carmen shortly after separating from her husband, she felt that after twenty-four years of marriage and the birth of five children, she needed to recover her personality. In a letter to her friend Emilio Sanz de Soto, also written shortly after her marital separation, she expresses in a different way how difficult it is to find an equilibrium between being oneself and being for others: "Ya sabes que mi vida ha cambiado, o mejor dicho por el momento lo que ha hecho es serenarse en una independencia de espíritu y una verdad que me hacían mucha falta. Encarar la verdad, es muy duro pero, al menos para mí, de un resultado bueno. La cara de la verdad para mí era ver que de nada sirve anular la propia personalidad en honor de lo que yo creía sagrado; la felicidad de mis hijos" (Rolón-Barada, "Letter 135," 14 May 1971) [You know that my life has changed, or rather for the moment what has happened is that it has become serene in an independence of spirit and a truth that I really needed. To face the truth is very difficult but, at least for me, the result has been good. The face of truth for me was to see that it does no good to suppress one's own personality in honor of what I thought was sacred—my children's happiness].

If personality (or the condition of being a person) for all the other authors discussed here has a positive sense—something women wish to acquire—in Carmen Martín Gaite's work, the concept is more ambiguous. In a series of articles published in the 1960s and later included in *La búsqueda de interlocutor* (1973) [The search for an interlocutor], Martín Gaite articulated her ideas on a female being for the first time. "Personalidad y libertad" (1961) [Personality and liberty], one of her first articles on this topic, outlines the problem of authentic being without reference to gender, although she will employ the ideas she posits there as a basis for later articles that do focus on women. Just as with María Zambrano, who in *Persona y democracia* did not refer specifically to women, although her earlier work formed the basis of the book, I suspect that Martín Gaite arrived at her ideas on personality by means of her situation as a woman and by having thought of women and their social and ontological status. The central ideas of "Personalidad y libertad" form the basis of most of Martín Gaite's feminist essays in *La búsqueda* and also of her feminist books *Usos amorosos del dieciocho en España* (1972) [Love customs in eighteenth-century Spain (1991)] and *Usos amorosos de la posguerra española* (1987) [Love customs in the post Civil War (2004)].

In the 1961 essay, Martín Gaite employs the term *personalidad* to refer to something akin to the Greek concept of *persona* or mask, a facade that one presents to others and that does not necessarily correspond to the interior nature of the person. But one could also relate Martín Gaite's concept of personality to Jean Paul Sartre's notion of "bad faith," since just as in María Zambrano's case, it is possible that Martín Gaite was influenced by French existentialism.[8] Martín Gaite points out that in this construction of being, the activities that one pursues are designed to maintain an image, "dejándonos llevar hasta donde requiera su cumplimiento, sin preocuparnos de la figura que ese cumplimiento nos haga componer" (*La búsqueda* 107) [allowing ourselves to be taken wherever their fulfillment requires, without worrying about the role this fulfillment makes us assume]. She gives the example of studying in order to receive good grades to please one's parents, instead of studying for the knowledge that one can acquire. Such an approach to action creates a labeled jar without any contents. Once we have created certain expectations in others that we will conduct ourselves in a certain way, we prefer not to cause a scandal or a disappointment by acting in a manner that is not consistent with the image we have created. Nevertheless, we are not free unless we can ignore these preconceived images that provoke more and more automatic reactions. Thus for Martín Gaite, the personality and the liberty we have sought are illusory.

In "La influencia de la publicidad en las mujeres" (1965; included in *La búsqueda*) [Advertising's influence on women], as the title suggests, Martín Gaite is concerned about the external pressures that bear on women's personality formation. The first paragraph of the essay summarizes the theories of a human being's formation that she had deployed in her article on personality and freedom. Then she applies these to the specific case of commercial propaganda directed specifically at women. Martín Gaite's acute sensitivity to language uncovers the ways in which advertising takes advantage of women's feelings of insignificance and their self-perception as inferior beings to encourage them to buy products that will enhance their sense of self-worth:

> A la buena disposición femenina para recibir de otro normas por las que regirse (tendencia fácilmente comprensible si se piensa en su pobre papel de comparsa a lo largo de la sociedad patriarcal), hay que añadir la circunstancia de que nunca una mujer se ha visto tan sedienta de afirmación y diferenciación, tan obsesionada por conquistar esa «personalidad», que ha de valerle el aprecio de los demás, como en el seno de la sociedad actual, donde todos los letreros invitan al éxito, al amor y a la felicidad individual como metas absolutas y accesibles mediante recetas prácticas. (*La búsqueda* 115)

> [To women's disposition to receive from others values by which to live (a tendency that is easily understandable if one thinks about her lamentable role as an extra throughout the history of patriarchal society), we must add the fact that women have never been so hungry for affirmation and differentiation, so obsessed with acquiring this "personality" that would garner them others' appreciation, as in the heart of today's society where all the ads invite us to success, love, and individual happiness as absolute and accessible goals through practical means.]

According to Martín Gaite, those who design ads worm their way into women's empty lives by employing a confidential tone of "just you and me." They exploit women's latent desire to mimic in order to link them as closely as possible to film stars or the rich through glimpses of the interiors of their mansions (*La búsqueda* 116–17). For Martín Gaite, the most corrosive of these strategies is their emphasis on men as the only arena for women's action. In this way, commercial advertising is a powerful way to maintain the social status quo: "Resumiendo: el daño más notable que hace la publicidad a la mujer es el de colmar fraudulentamente su deseo de ser tenida en cuenta y escuchada, alejándola cada vez más de esa independencia liberadora de que tanto le habla" (*La búsqueda* 120) [Summing up: the most notable harm that advertising does to women is to fraudulently take advantage of their desire to be taken into account and to be listened to, removing them more and more from that liberating independence that everyone talks to them about].

Martín Gaite applies her concept of women's identity formation to two specific examples in the essay "De madame Bovary a Marilyn Monroe" (the article is not dated, but it may have been written in the mid-1960s when news of Marilyn Monroe's death in 1962 was fairly fresh). In this essay Martín Gaite hypothesizes that both Madame Bovary and Marilyn Monroe committed suicide because they lacked an authentic interior personality. Martín Gaite suggests that the two tried to respond to models of behavior that were imposed from without; neither one could escape from these models when they were imitating them or when they rejected them. Martín Gaite proposes that Madame Bovary's lovers did not really interest her; she merely liked the image of herself having lovers. Emma Bovary committed suicide "porque su imagen se le había roto y porque ella no era capaz de buscar su identidad en otra imagen nueva y menos falsa" (*La búqueda* 142) [because her self-image had crumbled and she was unable to find a new and less false identity]. Martín Gaite believes that the same thing happened to Marilyn Monroe when she married Arthur Miller in 1956: "su imagen se le debió romper y volver inservible" (*La búsqueda* 142) [her image must have shattered and become useless]. Again the dichotomy between interior and exterior is at the center of the problem of women's identity.

"Las mujeres liberadas" (undated[9]) [Liberated women] is directed at the problem of women's solitude, what, as I noted in chapter 1, Martín Gaite called an "arma de doble filo" in her book *Desde la ventana* (10). She asserts that solitude is absolutely necessary for the formation of a strong and authentic interior self (what other Spanish feminist thinkers called *personalidad*). If in "De madame Bovary a Marilyn Monroe,"

Martín Gaite argues that Emma Bovary's and Marilyn Monroe's inability to "aguantarse a palo seco a sí mismas" (*La búsqueda* 125) [stand being by themselves] was the reason for their not developing an authentic interior self, in "Las mujeres liberadas" she considers the need to form relations due to the very Unamunian desire to "perdurar en otro" (*La búsqueda* 130) [live on through another], gain eternal life by means of dependence on another person (usually a man). Here she assumes a very different stance on women and others. By this time, women could leave a marriage (although divorce still did not exist in Spain) and live on their own (as did Martín Gaite and Carmen Laforet after 1970). The essay notes that the married woman has always enjoyed greater esteem than the single woman, even in periods when a husband's authority seemed more absolute. In a use of the term *persona* that reminds us of María Zambrano's, Martín Gaite remarks that the married woman always "se ha sentido más persona" (*La búsqueda* 125) [has felt herself to be more of a person] than the single woman. This situation, along with other factors, attracts women to marriage. Nonetheless, Martín Gaite continues, the married woman's elevated social status does not compensate for the lack of interpersonal communication in marriage. Women who leave a marriage often enter a series of unsatisfactory relationships, because they cannot withstand solitude, which paradoxically is the only way they can achieve true independence.

Although the concept of personality has taken on different nuances in Spanish feminist thought during the more than 100 years since it was first employed by Concepción Arenal toward the end of the nineteenth century, it is interesting to note that the words *persona* and *personalidad* have been fairly constant. The word *personalidad*, except in Carmen Martín Gaite's case, is associated with the formation of one's own individual identity that bestows independence and dignity on women. However, I have not found the term in more recent Spanish feminist thinkers. Perhaps with the arrival of democracy and legal equality for women (in María Zambrano's conception, Spanish women have become legal *personas*), they no longer have to think in terms of having a *personalidad*. However, with the domination of commercial propaganda that has not abated since Carmen Martín Gaite wrote "La influencia de la publicidad en las mujeres," one has to ask if Martín Gaite's concern about advertising's influence on creating false female identities is not still valid. And the new society created by advertising can explain the presence of the third meaning of the term *personalidad* in the most recent edition of the

Diccionario de la lengua española: "Persona de relieve, que destaca en una actividad o en un ambiente social" [Person of note, who stands out in an activity or a social milieu]. Now a *personalidad* is a man or a woman who is recognized by almost everyone thanks to the media.

CHAPTER 3

Social Class

Compared to feminist thought in other European countries and in the United States, Spanish feminist theory is uniquely tinged with social class consciousness. This was especially true in the late nineteenth century and most of the twentieth century, when Spain was finally beginning to catch up economically and socially with the industrializing nations. Even in 1981, Victoria Sendón de León would write that "esta historia del feminismo, esta lucha, esta disidencia, esta práctica política están insertadas—quién lo duda—en una sociedad de clases" (*Sobre diosas* 31) [there can be no doubt that this history of feminism, this struggle, this dissidence, this political practice is enmeshed in a class society]. Well into the twentieth century, a feudal landholding system continued to reign in important parts of the country such as Andalusia, and modern industry that fosters a strong middle class had only taken root in the Basque provinces and Catalonia. Thus the marriage of the rise of the middle class and feminist activism that took place much earlier in the Anglo-American world arrived later in Spain and came with a distinct class consciousness. By the late nineteenth century, when the Spanish middle class reached a critical mass, Spanish feminist writing burgeoned and often took into account social and economic distinctions—working class; lower, middle, and upper-middle class—when analyzing women's situation in Spain. Jo Labanyi points out how complex the shift in the class structure in late nineteenth-century Spain was for gender roles: "Regardless of who benefitted, the key issue here is that 'the social' became constructed as a female area, since it meant the extension to the public sphere of the ideology of domesticity. This blurred the public/private division, not only because female 'improvers' entered the public sphere, but also because the stress on 'family values' was an attempt to 'privatize' the public arena of class relations" (85–86). And Maria Aurèlia Capmany notes that the variety of forces that make up Hispanic countries offers what might seem an incongruous panorama: "Sin duda alguna, las primeras reinvindicaciones feministas aparecerán en los núcleos urbanos, allí donde la revolución industrial haya empujado a la mujer de la clase media a preguntarse sobre su propio destino, en el ámbito de la sociedad inestable en la que vive" (*El feminismo* 23) [Without any doubt, the first feminist stirrings appeared in the urban centers where the industrial revolution caused the middle-class woman to question her destiny in the unstable society in which she lived]. However, Capmany further opines that the most tenacious feminists are found in the agricultural sector, where women have not lived the complete alienation, the radical marginalization, that the bourgeois woman has experienced. Thus she argues strenuously against the prevailing notion that Spanish women are passive; she claims that the obstacles blocking Spanish women's progress are the same as those that impede Anglo-Saxon feminist efforts.

The notion of social class sometimes appears in unexpected places in Spanish feminist thought (for example, in upper-class Emilia Pardo Bazán's essays on Spanish women published in the English journal *Fortnightly Review* in 1889). Even in the largely preindustrial eighteenth century one can hear echoes of class distinctions. For example, in his *Defensa de las mujeres*, Benito Jerónimo Feijoo employs references to "los más ínfimos de la plebe" (328) [the lowest of the lower class] and "el vulgo" (349) [the common people]. Josefa Amar y Borbón states in the introduction to her *Discurso sobre la educación física y moral de las mujeres* [Lecture on the physical and moral education of women] that her plan for female education is for upper-class women only, because due to their acute sensibility, these women need more stimulation than do poor women. On rare instances in other sections of the *Discurso*, Amar y Borbón refers to class: "modesty, moderation, courtesy, and respect for self and others, 'de cualquier clase que sean'" (qtd. in Lewis 83) [whatever their social class may be]. Monica Bolufer notes that "From the fifteenth to the eighteenth centuries, as a response to mainstream misogyny, hundreds of dialogues, apologies, tracts, and lists of 'illustrious women,' all seeking to prove women's nobility and merit, were published in almost every European language. Works belonging to this genre were often dedicated to women of the royalty or of high rank, and represented the political, social and cultural influence of a female elite. The discussion of women's 'excellence' found its natural milieu in courtly and aristocratic circles" ("Neither Male" 390–91). Eighteenth-century feminist writers gave two reasons for women's education: (1) educated women make better mothers, and (2) women's education is a good in itself for women's greater enjoyment. The latter argument was especially employed in relation to upper-class women (see Teresa Anne Smith, 149–50).

It is clear that most efforts to advance women's situation in eighteenth-century Spain were concentrated on women of the highest social echelons. Teresa Anne Smith's list of women participating in the *junta de damas* (a women's auxiliary to the Economic Society founded in 1787) is top-heavy with noble titles (137–38). However, there was some awareness of the appearance of a middle class in eighteenth-century Spanish feminist writing. Constance Sullivan observes that by the end of the eighteenth century, Josefa Amar y Borbón registered the emergence of the middle class in *Discurso sobre la educación física y moral de las mujeres*: "the book speaks to privileged women of both the traditional nobility and the emerging middle class of wealthy merchants and the monarchy's extensive bureaucracy. Amar reveals a further sensitivity to women's varied circumstances within the classes she addresses. She is explicit in commenting that social status and the money one needed to sustain its outward appearance in an appropriate lifestyle did not always go hand in hand" ("Constructing Her Own Tradition" 147). The *junta de damas* founded an artisanal school where women could learn crafts such as embroidery to earn a livelihood. Teresa Anne Smith notes that "For the lower classes, this kind of artisanal training offered numerous advantages. On a practical level, it provided them with vocational training that could lead to economic advancement" (167). The girls even earned a modest income while taking classes.

The rise of the middle class in the Spanish nineteenth century brought thinking about women and social class more sharply into focus. According to Christine Arkinstall, as early as the liberal *trienio* (1820–1823) from January to June 1822, "the Madrid weekly *El Periódico de las Damas* (The periodical for ladies) brought together a community of bourgeois female readers and writers" ("A Feminist Press" 112). Arkinstall also notes that "[a]lthough León Amarita authored most articles (Hartzenbusch 1893, 37), they foreground women's rights, education, and contribution to the nation, and celebrate noteworthy female writers, leaders, and warriors" ("A Feminist Press" 112). The important concept of the "ángel del hogar" [angel of the house] that arose in the industrializing nineteenth century and that continued to have currency in Spain until the death of Franco in 1975 is primarily a middle-class notion. The feminist thinking of Concepción Arenal and Emilia Pardo Bazán, the two giants of Spanish feminist theory in the nineteenth century, reflects the classes from which they came (Arenal from the middle class and Pardo Bazán from the aristocracy), although in their style of argumentation both are the direct descendants of eighteenth-century enlightenment thinking about women. Both women wrote essays on Benito Jerónimo Feijoo for an essay contest in 1877, although Arenal's feminist position was strongly influenced by Krausism and Pardo Bazán's by Kant and John Stuart Mill. Thus, thanks to their Enlightenment and post-Enlightenment roots, both writers privileged reason in the formulation of their arguments. In the works that do not emphasize social class as a distinguishing feature of their feminist ideas, the authors' observations usually address the default middle class.

Although Concepción Arenal rarely mentions social class in her writings on women, in *La mujer del porvenir* she acknowledges her middle-class subject: "La mujer regularmente acomodada, que es la que nos ocupa aquí principalmente, cuando no tiene tiempo es porque lo malgasta" (231) [We are primarily concerned here with the fairly well off woman, who if she does not have time, it is because she misspends it].[1] In one of the rare passages of *La mujer del porvenir* in which she addresses social class, Arenal compares upper-class women to middle- and lower-class women on governing a household, an activity she believes is not nearly as difficult a task as women tend to portray it. Upper-class women, she opines, do not govern or oversee their homes. That occupation is left to middle- and lower-class women, although the latter work long hours just to make ends meet. In a similar vein, Alejandro San Martín writes in 1883 that "en la mujer no hay clase media, sino dos lejanas categorías sociales: la mujer de dinero y la pobre, como en los tiempos del feudalismo; y con la dolorosa particularidad de que la señorita nacida y educada en la clase media es mucho más pobre y desvalida por sí misma que la muchacha del pueblo" (qtd. in Mary Nash, *Mujer, familia y trabajo* 342) [there is no middle class where women are concerned, only two widely divergent social classes: the rich woman and the poor woman, just as in feudal times. The painful difference is that the girl born and educated in the middle class is poorer and more helpless than the country girl].[2] As Martínez Veiga points out, there are no middle-class women because women born into that social grouping are alone, as is the case with widows and orphans; they become part of the poorest sector of women. He notes that working-class women who are left on their own can look for work, which gives them an advantage over middle-class women in the same situation.

Strikingly different from the earlier sparse references to social class in Spanish feminist writing is Emilia Pardo Bazán's "The Women of Spain," an essay on Spanish women published in the British journal *The Fortnightly Review* in 1889, which is structured around social class categories—"the aristocratic class," "the middle class," and "the populace of the towns and of the country" (886).[3] Pardo Bazán devoted about an equal number of pages to each of the three classes, which she considers somewhat stereotypically. For example, she opines that Queen Isabel II "is a pure Spanish type . . . what Taine would call a 'representative type'" (886).[4] Pardo Bazán does, however, try to overcome the stereotypes and introduce nuances into her discussion. Given that Pardo Bazán herself was an aristocrat (a countess), it is not surprising that her analysis is ordered from the top down. She begins her survey of the three classes with the royal family and the aristocracy. While she admits that aristocratic women may often appear to lead frivolous lives, she attempts to rescue these women from this general view by pointing out that a number of noble women "live in modest retirement . . . devote themselves to their homes and superintend in person the education of their children; not a few occupy their time in charity and devotions and some manifest a praiseworthy interest in literary, artistic, or scientific questions" (888).[5]

Pardo Bazán's nationalism peeps through in her assessment of noble women's education, which she believes is deficient. Their education is too superficial and foreign (all the governesses and teachers come from France, Germany, or England). The countess's preference for national customs is also registered in her praise of the traditional Spanish female type: "The woman of middle height, slight and rounded form, undulating and languid or swift and stately movements; black, expressive eyes fringed with long lashes, somewhat colourless lips, dark complexion and hair of jet" (891). She laments the increasing numbers of blondes (albeit "a great part of them . . . only by the help of dyes" 891) in Madrid. She also decries aristocratic women's adopting foreign dress, because "dull colours, tailor-made garments of English production, long waterproofs and cloaks" do not flatter the Spanish figure. Here the *chulas* of the lower classes, who dress in traditional Spanish style, fare much better, especially in their use of the Spanish mantilla, which upper-class women have abandoned except during Holy Week. Pardo Bazán notes that the mantilla used to be a staple of women's dress at the bullfights, but it has now been replaced by hats. In fact, she bemoans that women hardly attend the bullfights anymore, preferring horse races. This switch is especially true of middle-class Spanish women, who do not have the stomach for the national spectacle.

As Margarita Nelken will do in her *La condición social de la mujer en España* (1919), Pardo Bazán reserves her greatest scorn for Spanish women of the middle class, albeit for different reasons. Pardo Bazán first defines what she means by middle class, because "[i]ts boundaries are so ill-defined that it embraces on the one hand the wife of the rich banker, who is middle class only because she is not of the aristocracy; and, on the other, the wife of the telegraph clerk or sub-lieutenant, who belongs to it only because she cannot be classed among the common people" (892). She decides that the easiest way to distinguish a middle-class woman is by her dress, her employing a servant, and her home's including a drawing room in which to receive guests. Her husband must not make his living by his hands (much better he be a lowly office worker, who makes 50 pounds a year, than a watchmaker or silversmith, who makes 200 or 400 pounds). Pardo Bazán observes that this prejudice against manual labor is an impediment to middle-class women's earning their own living, relegating them to waiting eternally for a husband to rescue them from penury. The working-class woman (what Pardo Bazán calls "the woman of the people" 893), however, "considers it her duty to gain her living" (893). Thus the middle-class woman, compared to the working-class woman, lacks personality. She is trained from the earliest age to suppress her natural self and remain passive just as eligible men prefer their wives to be, although Pardo Bazán points out that in recent times, men do want their wives to be able to read and write: "This system of education in which half shades prevail, and in which solidity and depth are regarded as improper, has the inevitable result of limiting, checking, and narrowing women, dwarfing their natural growth, and keeping them in continual childhood" (894). Further keeping the middle-class woman from distinction is her tendency to imitate the aristocracy, which reveals "a want of independence and energy" (898).

In a transition passage between the section on middle-class women and the analysis of working-class women, Pardo Bazán focuses on the convent as one place where the three classes "are intermixed and live in common" (898). The section on "the common people" draws most heavily on prevailing ideas about national character: "the purest national types, moral and physical, are to be found amongst the commonalty and specially amongst the women" (899).[6] However, these types are not all cut of one cloth; Pardo Bazán asserts that there are at least "ten or twelve widely different popular female types" (899), including the *ouvrière* [factory worker] of Catalonia, the *chula* [lower-class girl] of Madrid, and the Andalusian *cigarrera* [tobacco-factory worker]. If these three are marked by character traits such as working hard, impulsiveness, and *gracia* [charm], women from the Basque provinces are "industrious, and grave . . . completely impervious to the tender passion" (902). She ends her analysis of the working-class woman with the observation that Galician peasant women in her native province assume immeasurable burdens, toiling in the fields to keep their families fed: "The mistress has been emancipated by a liberator, eternal, merciless, and deaf—Necessity" (904). As Maryellen Bieder notes, Galician peasant women achieve equality with men as field workers, but "it is an emancipation of desperation, not the emancipation through education envisioned by middle-class reformers" ("Women, Literature" 41). In her well-studied speech on women's education delivered at the 1892 Congreso Pedagógico, class is not a central focus, although Pardo Bazán does note that "La cultura, hoy por hoy, se circunscribe a ciertas clases sociales" ("La educación" 88) [Increasingly, culture is limited to certain social classes]. She would like to see culture extended to a larger number of people: "Lo único que creo se debe en justicia a la mujer, es la desaparición de la incapacidad congénita, con que la sociedad la hiere. Iguálense las condiciones, y la libre evolución hará lo demás" (88) [To do justice to women, at least the congenital incapacity that society visits on them could be eliminated. Make the conditions equal and the free evolution will do the rest].

Just as industrialization and urbanization were gaining ground in late nineteenth-century Spain and perhaps as a reaction to it, Rosario Acuña chose to focus a series of 1885 articles on women of the countryside. By her observations and recommendations, one can infer that she was thinking particularly about women in northern Spain, who were often mistresses of small farms that required them to do a certain amount of agricultural work. These women are not on the lowest rung of the social order; they have maids to assist them with the household chores: "Haceos traer vuestras criadas de las más ásperas y retiradas sierras" (88) [Have them bring your maids from the rockiest and most remote mountains]. Acuña counsels the landed country woman to train these mountain women, who may have been shepherdesses, in such a manner that they will not be envious of the leisure their mistress gains through their labor. The mistress should also instruct the shepherdess-cum-maid in charitable giving. By showing them love and good will, their rude manners will be transformed into gentility infused with good sentiments to form a new class structure based on knowledge—"las ilustradas y las ignorantes" (764) [the knowledgeable and the ignorant]. Behind this advice one can hear a possible dialogue with Concepción Arenal's *La mujer de su casa* published just three years earlier. Unlike the city woman whom Arenal exhorts to leave her home to perform charity work, Acuña finds ways for the country woman to instruct and perform charity in her home. The country woman, she notes, can perform a series of agricultural chores essentially without leaving her property:

> ¿Y al realizar tales actos se rebajaría en algo la hermosa y casta dignidad de la mujer? ¿Quedarían abandonados su hogar y sus hijos? ¿Se olvidaría de sus deberes de esposa? Lejos de suceder esto, el hogar volvería a sentir ese calor de la virtud que ya le va faltando, los hijos no se verían tan olvidados como al presente, y sus deberes de esposa, cumplidos sin esos distingos de conveniencia con que en la actualidad se aceptan, llegarían a colocarla a la altura de verdadera compañera del hombre. (668–69)

> [And in carrying out these tasks, would she in any way tarnish the beautiful and chaste dignity of women? Would her home and children be abandoned? Would she forget her duties as a wife? Far from it; the home would once again feel the warmth of virtue that has become scarce, her children would not be so abandoned as they presently are, and her duties as a wife would be carried out without these shortcuts that are currently in vogue, and she would be placed in the position of true companion of the man.]

In an even more direct reaffirmation of the *mujer de su casa* that Arenal attempts to undermine, Acuña, while echoing the Krausist notion of perfection to which Arenal also appealed, states plainly that "la ruta, para vosotras, no sale del hogar; en él se desenvuelve, en él se descubren las belllezas de sus paisajes, la amenidad de su contornos; en el hogar tenéis vuestro camino hacia el porvenir" [another echo of an Arenal title—*La mujer del porvenir*] (770) [your path does not leave the home; it unfolds in it; in the home it discovers the beauty of its landscapes, the pleasantness of its surroundings; in the home you have your road to the future].

If social class was for the most part (except for Emilia Pardo Bazán's essay on Spanish women) a secondary consideration in nineteenth-century Spanish feminist thought, in the more firmly industrialized early twentieth century, it became much more important. Thanks to Spain's neutrality during World War I, Spanish industry received a strong boost, and many more women entered the workforce. Women's new role outside the home gave them increased economic benefits and public consciousness that resulted in a belated first-wave feminism with an acute awareness of class distinctions. In addition, new political ideologies spawned by the industrial revolution—socialism, Marxism, anarchism—sharpened class consciousness and created conflicts for some feminist thinkers. Some leftist thinkers, such as anarchist Federica Montseny, whom one would expect to be more interested in the intersection of gender and class, were double militants who advocated for a political ideology as well as for feminist causes. As I noted in the introduction, Mireia Bofill pointed out the intertwining of political ideology and feminist thinking in Spain. She especially emphasizes that Spanish feminism cannot prosper without taking the general political struggle into account and opines that many Spanish feminists are torn between "the general political struggle" and "women's issues," which they attempt to combine in some fashion.

In the pre–Civil War era, many Spanish feminists were identified with one or another of the leftist parties and militated to varying degrees within them—Margarita Nelken, first with the Socialist Party and later with the Communist Party; María Martínez Sierra with the Socialist Party (at least in the 1920s and 1930s); Federica Montseny with anarchism. Thus Spanish feminist theorists often felt the need to prioritize their several interests. In Montseny's case, for example, what she considered universal human concerns took precedence over issues she deemed to more narrowly pertain to women. María Martínez Sierra, while not directly addressing the division between more universal political militancy and feminist militancy, devoted most of her essays to feminist matters.

From the early twentieth century onward, class is an important feature of Spanish feminist theory, especially in Catalonia, where the middle class is most developed. In a 1903 lecture at the Centro Obrero [Workers' Center] in Barcelona, anarchist journalist José Prat comments that

> Si la mujer pertenece a la clase alta, es un simple objeto de lujo con derechos muy restringidos. Se la educa e instruye muy superficialmente. Lectura, escritura, un poco de historia y de geografía, pintura, un par de idiomas, música, baile, algo de bordado y de corte y una gran dosis de religión. De aquí no pasa. Con esto ya está en camino de brillar en los salones de contratación de matrimonios. Se le enseña el arte de cautivar al macho, que no al hombre, con su belleza natural y con los perifollos de la última moda. Se le perdonará que olvide lo poco que aprendió en el colegio, pero no se le perdonará que deje de vestir a la última moda. (qtd. in Nash, *Mujer, familia* 79)

> [If a woman belongs to the upper class, she is simply a luxury item with very limited rights. She is educated very superficially. Reading, writing, a little history and geography, painting, a couple of languages, music, dance, some embroidery and garment fitting, and a large dose of religion. It does not go beyond that. With this she is on the way to shine in the salons where marriages are contracted. She is taught to captivate the male, not the man, with her natural beauty and the finery of the latest fashion. She is pardoned for having forgotten the little she learned at school, but she would never be excused for not having dressed in the latest fashion.]

Women's confessors, Prat continues, take charge of the thinking and moral side of her life; they are adept at keeping her in the dark about everything she should know. She cannot freely reveal her inner feelings; she just has to wait for a man to choose her and take her to the altar, even if he is not to her liking. It is for that reason that adultery is so common among the upper classes. Prat also laments that women of means do not control their own finances, cannot practice a number of professions reserved for men, and are not expected to have well-informed opinions of their own. If they want to be artists or actresses, they are banished from their families. If they become nuns, they are dispossessed of their worldly goods and exposed to sexual assault by priests.

However grim and confined the life of the upper-class woman may be, Prat paints the working-class woman's situation as even worse ("tristísima" 82 [extremely sad]). From a very early age, she works in a shop or doing household chores. Her limbs are not yet fully formed; she should be out in the air and sunlight, but her parents out of necessity or egotism do not allow her to continue her education and place her in a sewing or knitting factory, where her lungs and sight are ruined and where she is subject to the sexual advances of brutal bosses. Marriage might seem like an exit from this horrific life, but it harbors dangers too—a husband who views her wages as a means to keep up his drinking habit, problematic pregnancies, being left for a younger, less worn-out woman. These working women have no concept of their rights, only of their duties to be submissive and resigned. In 1932 Catalan writer and philosopher Josep Capdevila painted a slightly different picture of the working-class marriage: "En esta familia honesta, humilde, trabajadora, sin vicios, fuerte y numerosa, habría de verse el refugio de la cultura latina y cristiana, de la flor de la civiización ante el descalabro de la familia burguesa" (qtd. in Nash, *Mujer* 202) [We should see in this honest, humble, hard-working, strong, numerous family without vices the refuge for Latin and Christian culture, the flower of civilization, in the face of the disastrous bourgeois family]. His ultimate aim is to argue against the liberal, bourgeois state: "Pero, el individuo obrero, aislado, decidme ¿qué libertad posee? Sin embargo, los defensores del liberalismo económico, cuando hablan del individuo sólo se acuerdan del individuo rico, burgués y opresor, y no del pobre, del obrero, del oprimido. Emparentada con la economía liberal está la ley del divorcio, con el consiguiente descalabro de la familia" (Nash, *Mujer* 203) [However, what liberty does the isolated working-class individual have? Nevertheless when the defender of economic liberalism talks about the individual, he is only thinking about the rich, bourgeois, oppressive individual and not the poor, oppressed worker. The liberal economy is related to the divorce law with its attendant damage to the family]. For Capdevila divorce means that young women of the working class can be seduced by money without any commitment on the middle-class man's part. His recommendation to remedy this situation is to establish family subsidies that allow working-class families to remain together.

Dolors Monserdà de Maciá believes that the upper and middle classes have a responsibility to set an example for working-class women: "Los estudis socials ensenyarán a la dama rica o ala senyora acomodada, la manera de cooperar a aquest millorament de la dòna obrera plantejat ab feliç èxit als Estats Units, a Bèlgica, a Anglaterra, Alemánia, França y Suiça, pere medi d'un eficaç protectorat moral, econòmich, intelectual; protectorat d'acció, de fets d'obrers ab la creació d' *Escoles menagers*, y de Comerç, pera dependentes, ab la formació de sindicats, gremis, lligues de compradores, salons de venda, cooperatives, borses de travail, etc." (*Etudi* 27) [Social studies will show rich or well-off women the way to contribute to the betterment of the working-class woman by means of the successful efforts to form a moral, economic, intellectual protectorate like those in the United States, Belgium, England, Germany, France, and Switzerland via the creation of managers' and commercial schools, syndicates, unions, buyers' leagues, showrooms, cooperatives, travel grants, etc.]. She has a strong sense of the duty of upper-class women toward working-class women, who can be completely worn out by the long workday and low pay that barely covers the cost of staying alive day to day. As a remedy for this dire situation, she suggests that well-off women space out the sewing they need to have done, so that the workload is more evenly distributed.

As is evident in Capdevila's assessment, by the early twentieth century the term used to refer to the middle class has shifted to "bourgeois," a practice already evident in Margarita Nelken's and Carmen de Burgos's respective *La condición social de la mujer* (1919) [The social condition of women] and *La mujer moderna y sus derechos* (1927) [The modern woman and her rights], in which they distinguish between the bourgeois woman and the working-class woman. One of Margarita Nelken's most important contributions to the history of Spanish feminist theory is her complete intersection of the categories of gender and class. Nelken found it impossible to consider women's issues apart from social class; she believed that feminism in Spain was inextricably intertwined with class affiliations. According to Mary Lee Bretz, "[t]he conflict between gender and class and the complex interactions between these two categories, which sometimes overlap and sometimes compete with each other, constitute a major focus of *The Social Condition of Women in Spain*, informed by feminist and socialist concerns and addressed to women readers and to workers; the text struggles to create bonds between these two groups without conflating them" (106). Nelken believed that working-class women, who were already equal to men in that they work, are naturally feminists. A working-class woman has a "mentalidad más sana y espontánea, ignorante de los prejuicios y de los convencionalismos, se encuentra, implícitamente, al misimo nivel social que su hermano o su marido" (*La condición social* 36) [a healthier and more spontaneous mentality; she is implicitly on the same social level as her brother or her husband because she is unaware of social prejudices and conventions]; thus her battle is limited to fighting for equal salaries and obtaining protective legislation and workers' unions that will put her on an equal footing with male workers. Nelken believed that middle-class women had a steeper hill to climb because they were combating prejudices, "un ambiente mezquino" [a mean-spirited ambience] that created a real obstacle course in the march toward liberation: "Su libertad de trabajo va siempre precedida de una emancipación moral, penosísima las más de las veces; de ahí la necesidad de la lucha, la solidaridad intuitiva con las que, en otros países, supieron ya unirse a éstas, de imitarlas" (36) [Their freedom to work is always preceded by an often painful moral emancipation; thus the need for struggle and an intuitive solidarity with and imitation of women in other countries who have already achieved this emancipation].

Nelken's analysis of the middle-class woman, which occupies an entire chapter of *La condición social de la mujer en España*, follows a Marxist line in its foundations in economics: "la cuestión feminista en España es . . . una cuestión puramente económica" (49) [the feminist question in Spain is . . . purely economic]. She avers that economics bedevil the middle-class woman most of all, because she has to find a husband to support her; her expected lifestyle is a true economic burden on the middle-class married man. The upper-class woman of means has little difficulty finding a husband, or if she does not find one, she can support herself. In the working class, since money is not an issue, there is greater freedom when choosing a marriage partner, and in fact marriage benefits a working man, because a wife can save him a lot of money on household work and paid sex. Nelken points out that middle-class women in some other countries do work and bring money into the household, but that is not the norm in Spain. She insinuates that marriage for middle-class women is a form of prostitution, since women's work is so disparaged and ill-paid that women's only options are to sell their bodies to strangers or to a husband: "La única diferencia es que, en el matrimonio, el agarradero es definitivo y que, una vez conseguido el comprador, la mujer no se preocupa ya, en compensación, de seguirle agradando" (51) [The only difference is that in marriage the hold is definitive and once a buyer has been found, the woman no longer feels it necessary to continue pleasing him as a compensation]. Nelken concludes her chapter on middle-class women vitriolically, calling Spanish women of this class "el mayor *peso muerto de la nación* y al mismo tiempo, lo que hay en ella más enérgico y más valiente" (56, emphasis in original) [the nation's greatest *dead weight*, and at the same time, what is most energetic and brave in the nation].

If Nelken's major feminist essay *La condición social* centers on social class and work, Carmen de Burgos's parallel volume *La mujer moderna y sus derechos*, published several years later, focuses on women's legal standing, an aspect of feminism that levels the playing field for all social classes, at least in theory if not in practice. Even though equal rights before the law might suppose there is no need to consider differences in social class, in her introductory history of feminism, Burgos recognizes class distinctions in some parts of her book. In outlining the various types of feminism in her first chapter, the first two categories are "El Feminismo Obrero" [Working-class feminism] and "El Feminismo Burgués" [Bourgeois feminism], which appear before "El Feminismo Mundano" [Worldly feminism], "El Feminismo Profesional" [Professional feminism], "Feminismo Cristiano" [Christian feminism], "Feminismo Revolucionario" [Revolutionary feminism], and "Feminismo Independiente" [Independent feminism] (66). She points out that feminism first arose among women of the lower classes ("mujeres del pueblo") because they were the most affected by economic problems, especially in the cities. She then declares that the middle class lagged behind in raising the feminist flag due to its resistance to work, an important focus of feminist activity. She points out that vanity precluded acceptance of middle-class women's working. Middle-class daughters were brought up idle and given to luxurious ostentation. If the head of the household died, the women in the family were suddenly thrown into a penury from which they could not escape via work. Even though she does not specify that she is thinking expressly of Spain, she must be, because in England and the United States, early (first-wave) feminism was a middle-class phenomenon. And in Spain it was the aristocratic women who fostered an early feminism in the eighteenth century. Of course, little was known of this legacy until fairly recently, thanks to the work of scholars such as Mónica Bolufer, Betsy Franklin Lewis, and Catherine Jaffe. Thus Burgos's misperception is understandable. Burgos does address the aristocracy, calling its feminism "mundano" [worldly]. Aristocratic women, she avers, took advantage of feminism not to fight for work and responsibility, but rather to escape from forced seclusion.

They wanted to be able to leave the house, travel alone, or take part in sports, activities that were considered men's realm. Theirs was an emancipation via gesture—wearing makeup, hairstyles, and clothes of their own choosing. Burgos believes that these aristocratic feminist manifestations are more authentic than traditional aristocratic women's activities such as charity work and social clubs. Burgos rues the fact that the different facets of feminism (many of them with class origins) are often at cross-purposes when they should be working together for the common good. This fragmentation and infighting are repeated in the late twentieth- and early twenty-first-century democratic era in Spain, now along ideological grounds (equality feminism versus difference feminism) rather than on the basis of class distinctions (see chapters 5 and 6).

Notions of class permeate other feminist theory topics across the chronological divide I have established. For example, some Spanish feminist theorists prefer to view humanity in terms of social class rather than polarized into male and female sexes. The institution of marriage offers Margarita Nelken the opportunity to privilege class over sex. Nelken considered middle-class marriage as a kind of prostitution, in which the woman sells herself to the man, who then becomes equally entrapped in a burdensome situation. She points out that the middle-class woman does not expect to work and usually does not, while the man is enslaved to the consumerist needs of his wife and children ("para el hombre de la clase media, el matrimonio significa verdaderamente una carga, y una carga que muchos no se atreven a sobrellevar" (50) [marriage is a real burden for the middle-class man, a burden that many do not dare to take on]. Middle-class women are educated to enter into this vile arrangement: "el matrimonio burgués se envilece desde un principio por culpa de la mujer que se vende legítimamente con no menos astucia, y a veces hasta no mayor hipocresía que una ramera" (51) [bourgeois marriage is tarnished from the beginning because women are guilty of legally selling themselves with the same astuteness and sometimes with the same hypocrisy as a prostitute].

Interestingly, two of the most overtly feminist thinkers of the Franco era—María Laffitte and Lilí Álvarez—were aristocrats (both had the title of countess). It is entirely possible that they were able to overcome Francoist censorship and publish their openly feminist texts, such as Lafitte's *La secreta guerra de los sexos* [The secret war of the sexes] and *La mujer como mito y como ser humano* [Woman as myth and as a human being], and Álvarez's *Feminismo y religión* [Feminism and religion], due to their elevated social status. In addition, both women were careful to avoid issues of social class, which, given that the working-class and middle-class intellectuals were the backbone of the defeated Second Spanish Republic, might have raised even more red flags than the gender topics they do address in their feminist works. Thus the story of social class as a topic of Spanish feminist theory, like other feminist topics, went underground in the novel, which routinely represented the lives of women of all social classes during the 1940s, 1950s, and 1960s.

Social class as an important aspect of Spanish feminist thinking resurfaces in the 1970s. Spain has never really ceased to be a class-conscious society. The Civil War, which in many ways was a class struggle, and the Franco regime, which privileged the aristocracy and upper middle class, prolonged old class structures. It was left for the democracy initiated in 1975 to attempt to address the lingering class strife, a situation that colored the women's movement during the transition to democracy. During the Franco dictatorship, working-class allegiances to the banned Socialist and Communist Parties survived in the underground, where a small residue of Republican-era feminist ideology continued as part of clandestine party activity. When the underground surfaced in 1976, the old allegiances created conditions for schisms in Spanish feminism as early as 1979. For example, the emerging equality feminism would be allied with the Socialist Party. And Lidia Falcón employs the Marxist notion of social class to formulate women as a separate social class alongside the traditional lower-, middle-, and upper-class categories.

When overt feminist activity and writing resumed in Spain in the 1970s and social class once again assumed a prominent place, the double militancy that caused some conflict before and during the Civil War years resurfaced. Double militancy was a divisive issue in the 1970s after the long oppression of both women and leftist political parties allied with the working class. In an attempt to overcome the theoretical dichotomy between gender and class, Lidia Falcón argued in *Mujer y sociedad* that women are a separate social class. In an interview she granted some five years after the book was published, she stated that in the conflict between the class struggle and women's liberation "[n]osotros consideramos que la mujer es una clase oprimida, por lo tanto, entra dentro de la problemática de la lucha de clases evidentemente y hasta que la problemática ésta no se haya resuelto, tampoco se resolverá la de la mujer. Para mí, no tiene importancia una cosa que otra, tiene la misma. La lucha debe llevarse al mismo nivel y además no es imposible" (Levine and Waldman 71) [we believe that women are an oppressed class, and therefore they clearly enter into the problematics of the class struggle, and until it has been resolved, women's situation will not be resolved. As far as I am concerned neither is more important than the other; they carry the same weight. The struggles should each be taken to the same level, and besides this is not impossible]. Carmen Alcalde saw women's struggle as the overriding one, and like Falcón, she viewed women as a social class whose interests should take precedence over all others: "para mí es más importante la lucha de la mujer. Para mí, es la primera lucha de clases que existe. . . . es más importante, la lucha de sexos, la lucha sexista. Mientras esto no se solucione la mujer seguirá colaborando con los partidos, con sus presidentes y directivas" (Levine and Waldman 33) [for me the women's cause is the most important. For me, it was the first class struggle to ever exist. . . . the battle of the sexes, the sexist battle is more important. As long as that issue remains unsolved, women will continue to collaborate with the political parties, with their precedents and directives]. As I indicated above, Alcalde argues that neither political parties nor working-class women have time for feminist militancy. But like Margarita Nelken, she sees an intimate connection between women's concerns and social class. She notes, for example, that contraceptives are necessarily a matter of social class, because middle-class women have access to them and working-class women do not (this was in the 1970s).

In 1931 Rosa Chacel observed the tendency in contemporary gender theory (especially Georg Simmel's) to radically divide the sexes and thus "feminize" women. In the 1970s Charo Ema similarly complained that the Communist Party "feminized" women by talking to them mostly about the high cost of living: "les hablaban en unos términos demasiado femeninos" (Levine and Waldman 51) [they spoke to women in terms that were too exclusively feminine]. Ema, who represented the Asociación de Mujeres Universitarias, an association of university-educated, middle-class women founded in 1953, also highlights class conflicts and Spanish feminism. Working-class women of the Communist Party, she says, considered the university women "pequeñas burguesas," [petites bourgeoises] while the university women found working-class women too wedded to party ideology. She points out that within the Communist Party *machismo* still ruled, and that sexual liberation and equality of the sexes were anathema:

No puedes decir muchas cosas porque el Partido está diciendo las contrarias; no puedes ir allí hablando de la libertad sexual cuando el Partido no está hablando de eso ni le interesa que hables de eso, porque ahora lo que hay que discutir es la recogida de basuras, y la recogida de basuras para mí es un problema del hombre y de la mujer y de todos, ¿no? No es únicamente el problema de la mujer, porque si sigue siendo el problema de la mujer, seguimos en las mismas. (Levine and Waldman 60)

[You can't talk about certain topics because the Party is talking about other topics; you can't go there talking about sexual liberation when the Party isn't talking about it nor is the Party interested in your talking about it, because the topic for discussion is garbage collection, and for me garbage collection is a problem for men and women and everyone, right? It is not just a women's problem, because if it continues to be a women's problem, we are going to be stuck in the same old rut.]

Acknowledging her debt to Margarita Nelken and her attributing special circumstances to women in Spain is Maria Aurelia Capmany, who declares that "La situación de la mujer en España se halla inserta en las condiciones políticas y sociales de su historia" (*La dona* 272) [Women's situation in Spain is inserted into the political and social conditions of its history]. Rather than divisions according to social class per se, Capmany points out a dichotomy between women of the country and the city and variations by region. She reminds us that Spanish feminism was limited to a small minority of men and women who resided in large cities. The great majority of women still lived in rural areas and in small towns. However, Capmany points out that there were important regional differences: "La actitud de la mujer gallega, de la mujer catalana y de la mujer andaluza no es sólo diferente porque estas regiones han sufrido con menor o mayor ímpetu las consecuencias de una revolución industrial" (272) [Galician, Catalan, and Andalusian women's attitudes are different not only because these regions have suffered the consequences of the industrial revolution with greater or lesser force]. She points out that Federico García Lorca's *La casa de Bernarda Alba* [*The house of Bernarda Alba*], set in rural Andalusia, would seem exotic to a woman from the

Catalan or Galician countryside. She quotes Margarita Nelken on the fact that Spanish feminism does not have a very long history and that it is a reflection of feminisms elsewhere spurred to an extent by pressing economic needs. In turn the economic motive should be the mechanism by which Spanish feminism can achieve the legal gains made by women elsewhere. She agrees with Nelken that modern Spanish women, while in no way inferior to women in other countries, have been stymied by the weight of centuries of repression. In her later book *De profesión mujer*, Capmany asserts that "El talón de Aquiles del Feminismo, más que su error, consiste en estar vinculado a la clase que le dio origen—la burguesía" (356) [Feminism's Achilles's heel—rather than its error—is to be linked to the class in which it originated—the bourgeoisie]. Thus, she concludes, feminism's motivation is tied to the weaknesses of liberalism.

In 1981 Lidia Falcón published the most radical and extensive study of Spanish women and social class in her *La razón feminista: La mujer como clase social y económica. El modo de producción doméstico* [Woman as a social and economic class. The mode of domestic production]. In that voluminous and thoroughly researched book, Falcón argues that women as a group share many characteristics that traditionally have been associated with other social-class groupings such as the proletariat and the middle class, except that the kinds of work women do (procreation and domestic labor) go unrecognized, because they are not economically remunerated. Echoing arguments that we have seen articulated by María Zambrano and Rosa Chacel, Falcón points out that, according to Marx, "«el hombre ha empezado a vivir su historia social»," but "La mujer sigue viviendo su historia natural. . . . La hembra humana no es persona si es sexo y fábrica de seres humanos" (29, 31) ["men have begun to live their social history," but "women continue living natural history. . . . The human female is not a person, but rather sex and a factory of human beings"]. Because they are occupied with their reproductive role, for the most part women are left out of productive labors, or when they perform such labors, it is from the margins where they are exploited to the maximum: "La religión, la política, la filosofía, la educación, el psicoanálisis, han sido inventados por el hombre, para teorizar la explotación de clase de mujer, y convencerla de que así *debe ser*" (32; emphasis in original) [Religion, politics, philosophy, education, and psychoanalysis were invented by men in order to theorize the exploitation of women as a class and to convince them that it *had to be* that way]. Falcón points out that arguments from nature, about what is natural, have always been employed to justify domination of one class over another (just as Aristotle reasoned the need for slavery).

Although in focusing on the concept of social class when referring to women as a group Falcón is working within a Marxist framework, she also argues forcefully against Marx's having left women out of his analysis: "Pero no percibe que este análisis, como las consecuencias que inevitablemente se desprenden de él, de la dialéctica del desarrollo materialista de la historia, no hace referencia a la mujer. Las clases que se comportan en su lucha como Marx define, están compuestas sólo por hombres" (41) [However, he does not perceive that this analysis and the consequences that devolve from it, from the dialectic of the material development of history, makes no reference to women. The classes, as they act in their struggle as Marx defines it, are composed only of men]. For Marxists and the bourgeoisie alike, all human beings are equal, and the class struggle is the same for male beings as for female beings. The nature of the work that women and men do determines whether women can enter into social history. Falcón proposes that, rather than changing the kind of work women perform in society, reproduction and domestic labor be recognized alongside remunerated work outside the home. Falcón borrows the Marxist term "alienation," normally only applied to the impoverishment of the male working class, to describe women who are in the same kind of relationship with their husbands as men are with their industrial employers: "Es el hombre—aunque sea obrero explotado a su vez por el patrono—que se beneficia del trabajo de la mujer por el que paga la mínima cuota: La comida, y muchas veces lo obtiene gratuitamente" (47) [It is the man—although he be a worker who is also exploited by the boss—who benefits from women's work for which he pays a very small wage—food—and he often gets women's work for free].

Falcón continues the line of argument initiated by Feijoo and sustained by Arenal, Pardo Bazán, Nelken, Burgos, and others that the law rather than biology is at the root of women's servitude: "La lucha de clases es una explicación política, económica y filosófica, no biológica" (297) [The class struggle is a political, economic, and philosophical explanation, not a biological one], but she adds the important dimension of class. She does not abandon the traditional notion of class according to social strata—working class, bourgeoisie, and upper class—when formulating a new division between men (dominant class) and women (subordinate class). In fact, the older class divisions reinforce her arguments about women's exploitation. For example, she points out that women of all classes are the first victims of a bourgeois ideology that exalts the individual and the division of labor between the sexes. She opines that leftist discourse is not any better, although leftist ideologues use terms such as "cooperation" between the sexes rather than "obedience" of women to men: "La tal «cooperación» en el trabajo, lleva a una división «natural» de funciones que «naturalmente» destina al hombre a las tareas de gobierno y a la mujer a las tareas domésticas" (325) [Such "cooperation" in the workplace carries a "natural" division in functions that "naturally" designates men for the tasks of government and women for domestic chores]. She also places in quotation marks the supposed "power" that women have through their domestic role to influence their husbands who are acting in the public sphere and to educate their children. For all the "power" they may have in this sense, women still own a very small portion of the world's material resources and occupy very few leadership positions.

Falcón distinguishes between the bourgeoisie, to which only a very few women belonged in the 1980s—Barbara Hutton, Elizabeth Arden, Helena Rubinstein, and Joan Crawford—and the petit bourgeoisie, which includes hundreds of thousands, if not millions, of notions and meat vendors, fish mongers, clothes cleaners, dressmakers, hairdressers, and vegetable sellers. Importantly, she also recognizes differences between countries. At the end of her book, she uses the example of Chile, although recognizing that the Chilean situation differs from that of other national entities. She notes that in Chile men of the revolutionary left preferred to do without women's support rather than give them autonomy and powers of organization. She notes that Spanish leftists, on the other hand, were sufficiently strong that they could manipulate women for their own purposes: "En la guerra civil los campos se delimitaron perfectamente. Los burgueses dispusieron de sus mujeres, y los revolucionarios de las suyas. En la conflagración las mujeres de los socialistas, de los anarquistas sobre todo y de los comunistas, aprestaron su esfuerzo, su apoyo, su lucha, su trabajo y hasta su vida, en defensa de los intereses de sus hombres" (597) [During the Civil War, the two sides were perfectly delimited. The bourgeoisie ordered their women and the revolutionaries ordered theirs. In the conflagration, Socialist, Anarchist, and, above all, Communist women lent their efforts, their support, their struggle, their work, and even their life in defense of men's interests].

Once again echoing María Zambrano's notion of individual, women for Falcón are not individuals in the same way that men are. Men affirm themselves through their work, practical production in the objective world, the elaboration of inorganic nature through which nature appears as his work and reality, while women are tied to the species, conditioned by it, separated from their own individuality, and not allowed to affirm themselves as gendered beings as men are through the work that transforms inorganic nature. Women do not work; that is, they do not transform inorganic nature. They only transform themselves periodically and fatally into a new organic nature identified with all nature that surrounds them, unable to dominate that nature (48, 49): "En ella vence la especie sobre el individuo, mientras el hombre va separándose de la especie y afirmándose como ser genérico mediante el trabajo que transforma la naturaleza y la somete a su voluntad" (48) [In it the species conquers the individual; while men are separating themselves from the species and affirming themselves as gendered beings through the work that transforms nature and submits it to their will]. The Marxists, Falcón avers, do not theorize about women's being as a problem to be solved: "Ni ellos [los marxistas] ni los comentaristas posteriores advirtieron que admitiendo que el destino de *todas* las mujeres es el mismo, sin distinción por clase social, estaban defininiendo las condiciones de la clase mujer" (56; italics in original) [Neither the Marxists nor later theorists noticed that in admitting that the destiny of *all* women is the same, without distinction of social class, they were defining the conditions of women as a class]. On these basic premises, Falcón reviews a large number of twentieth-century theoreticians, including Charles Fourier, Sigmund Freud, and Dhoquois, who like Marx fail to take women into proper consideration as an entity separate from men, considering them to be in a pure state of nature.

Following the Marxist dictum that it is not man's consciousness that determines his being, but the contrary, that the social being determines consciousness, Falcón analyzes the structure of women as a social class. Women live in a world apart, which is governed by different laws, which are the abstract Idea, Goodness, Beauty, Justice, and Religion (all with a capital letter). Thus woman is not material; her body, which enslaves her, is spirit, and her "social development," if it can be called that, is the reign of Tenderness, Inconstancy, the Sublime, and Sacrifice. Falcón further argues that because women are still closely linked to the material, they do not have their own social development; they are pure Idea. Consistent with the types of argumentation we have seen in Spanish feminist theorizing from at least the early eighteenth century in Father

Feijoo, Falcón provides a history of thinking about women to prove her point about the way women have been viewed as ideals rather than as social beings.

Falcón also follows Father Feijoo and Concepción Arenal in their style of argumentation when she summarizes the ideas of others and points out the flaws in their thinking. She particularly employs this style of argumentation in her chapters designed to prove that women indeed should be considered a social class. She affirms that any study of modes of production must begin with a definition and analysis of class, a concept she believes is based on class struggle. Thus, only in considering class struggle can she confirm women as a social class: "Sólo a partir de su cualificación como clase, del lugar que ocupa en la producción de bienes, y del trabajo excedente que le es sustraído por la clase antagónica, podremos conocer el modo de producción doméstico y por ende las relaciones de producción con la clase antagónica" (112) [Only deriving from her qualification as a class, from the place she occupies in the production of goods, and the work that is exacted of her by the opposing class, can we know the mode of domestic production and therefore the relations of production with the opposing class]. In coordination with this postulate, Falcón also asserts that "Es preciso por tanto entender que el acento ha de ponerse en *la división social del trabajo, en el lugar que ocupan los individuos en la producción*. Lugar condicionada por las relaciones de producción que se establecen" (117) [It is necessary therefore to understand that the accent should be placed on *the social division of work, on the place that individuals occupy in production*. A place conditioned by the relations of production that are established].

Falcón is able to overcome the traditional (and Marxist) exclusion of the types of work women do when considering social class by redefining the nature of work: "*la actividad con la cual el ser humano obtiene los medios para mantenerse, reproducirse y desarrollarse*" (127; emphasis in the original) [the activity with which human beings obtain the means to support themselves, reproduce, and develop]. Citing the dictionary definition of "work" as "el «esfuerzo humano aplicado a la producción de riqueza»" (127) [human effort applied to the production of wealth], Falcón asserts that work is absolutely essential to all three of these basic human activities—supporting oneself, reproducing oneself, and developing oneself. She understands "riqueza" [wealth] in the broadest sense of human, material, cultural, and artistic wealth. Riffing on Marta Harnecker's assertion that human work is the basis of all social life, Falcón claims that the human being is the basis of every society and that human beings are impossible without female reproduction. She points out that the nine months of gestation and years of lactation that women's bodies invest in reproducing are not taken into account when calculating human expenditure of energy and productive work. Falcón notes that even Marxist theorists consider the reproduction of the workforce to somehow be free (135). Couching reproduction in Marxist terms, Falcón inserts the time and effort involved in reproducing the species into the economic equation:

> la aseveración de Marx de que cada modo de producción posee su ley de población es errónea. Las leyes de la reproducción son las determinantes de las leyes de la producción. La forma y el modo en que se realiza la producción humana y todos los ítems que le son inherentes: la larga gestación de nueve meses, el parto doloroso y peligroso, tantas veces mortal, la larga inversión de la madre en la nueva cría, su tardanza en desarrollarse, en adquirir el suficiente aprendizaje, la costosa inversión de tiempo, de salud y de trabajo de la madre en la producción de nuevas criaturas, el despilfarro de vidas femeninas que cuesta la reproducción, todo ello constituye *los determinantes del modo de producción*. (138; emphasis in original)

> [Marx's assertion that each mode of production possesses its law of population is erroneous. The laws of reproduction determine the laws of production. The form and mode in which human production is carried out and all the items that are inherent to it—the long nine-month gestation, the painful and dangerous birth, which is so often fatal, the mother's long investment in the newborn, its delayed development in acquiring sufficient apprenticeship, the costly investment of time, health and work that reproduction requires, all constitute *the determinants of the mode of production*.]

Thus, for Falcón, the laws of reproduction are primary and determine the laws of production, because reproduction governs the development of productive forces. She further observes that the reproductive function that women contribute to production is never remunerated, even though production depends entirely on reproduction; the more reproduction, the more production. She puts forth the radical idea that "La reproducción es el proceso de trabajo fundamental. Las fuerzas de trabajo determinantes son por tanto las mujeres. El desarrollo de las fuerzas de trabajo humanas, el aumento de la población, es el determinante en el desarrollo de una sociedad y en los cambios que ésta pueda sufrir" (165) [Reproduction is a process of fundamental work. Therefore, the determining workforce is women. The development of the human workforce, the increase in population, determines the development of society and the changes that it can undergo]. Women are the exploited class (253), for Falcón "*la única clase dominada y explotada de las comunidades domésticas*" (255; emphasis in original) [the only dominated and exploited class among the domestic communities].

That Falcón's ideas about women as a social class were hotly debated at the time they were made public is evidenced by Charo Ema, who declared in 1974 that

> Yo creo que para entrar en un trabajo clandestino hace falta estar muy convencida, realmente, y estar muy de acuerdo, incluso todas. Nosotras no estamos de acuerdo todas, ni siquiera si la mujer tiene un conflicto con el hombre de lucha de clases. Hemos discutido mucho con Lidia Falcón si la mujer es una clase o si no es una clase, en qué medida la mujer proletaria y la mujer burguesa tienen puntos de contacto, en qué medida la familia es el problema principal. (Levine and Waldman 58)

> [I believe that in order to enter into clandestine work it is necessary for everyone to be really and truly convinced and to be completely in agreement. We are not all in agreement, not even on the question of whether women are in a class struggle with men. We have discussed a great deal with Lidia Falcón about whether women are a class or are not a class, to what degree the working-class woman and the bourgeois woman have anything in common, and to what degree the family is the principle problem.]

In *Sobre diosas, amazonas y vestales*, Victoria Sendón de León registers her profound disagreement with the idea of women as a social class: "No es el lugar de la mujer en la producción lo que la incluye en la misma clase,

¡sólo nos faltaba ser clase! ¡qué ordinariez! Es la pluralidad de sus marcas enraizadas en la ausencia y la diferencia las que la hacen precisamente inclasificable, pura posibilidad!" (119) [Women's place within production is not what includes her in the same class. We certainly don't need to be a class! How vulgar! It is the plurality of her boundaries rooted in absence and difference that makes her unclassifiable, pure possibility].

By contrast, Carmen Rodríguez asserts that the truly exploited sector of Spanish society in the Franco era was the man; she opines that married women live as parasites on man's work (here Rodríquez echoes arguments made by Margarita Nelken in her 1919 *La condición social de la mujer en España*, probably without knowing Nelken's work). She is thinking of middle-class women, who have ample domestic servants in the home and thus have few responsibilities besides going to the hairdresser three times a week, overseeing the maids, and meeting friends for *tertulias* and card games: "Pues estas esposas de estos señores, que quizá han hecho hasta una carrera universitaria o que podrían hacer cualquier tipo de trabajo comercial o en una agencia, no sé, no se plantea en ningún momento que están viviendo los dos esclavizados, aunque de diferente modo. Por otra parte, ¿cómo convencerle al hombre de que es un esclavo?" (Levine and Waldman 143) [Well these wives of these men, who may even have a university degree or could do any kind of commercial work or be employed in an agency—I don't know—no one ever points out that both of them (husband and wife) are enslaved, although in a different way. On the other hand, how can we convince the man that he is a slave?]. The man is not conscious of his enslavement; he has a false sense of power and domination, because he exercises economic control. Work, for Rodríguez, is, as it was for Martinez Sierra, Burgos, and Nelken, a matter of individual dignity—an existential issue—but also a matter of equality for both sexes: "se trata de una esclavitud mutua. El hombre es un esclavo de su trabajo, la mujer es una esclava de su dependencia y de su mente. Ella esclaviza a su marido, pero a la vez, la sociedad o el marido la esclavizan a ella como individuo" (145) [it is a mutual enslavement. The man is a slave to his work; the woman is a slave to her dependence and her mind. She enslaves her husband, but at the same time, society or the husband enslaves her as an individual].

Social class has been less of a focus in democratic Spain, perhaps because with the Europeanization and Americanization of Spain in the last forty years, class consciousness has been diluted and replaced by a sense that in democracy, class distinctions are anachronistic. In a democracy everyone—men and women alike—is expected to contribute to the common good through some kind of work. Social class, as we have seen, is closely associated with whether or not the person works, and if she does, what kind of work he/she performs. In chapter 4 I take up the issue of work as a fundamental concept of Spanish feminist theory.

CHAPTER 4

Work

As is evident in the denouement of the last chapter, closely associated with social class is work, a topic that spans the entire corpus of Spanish feminist thinking from the eighteenth century to the present day. The importance of work to the modern woman is highlighted in F. Scott Fitzgerald's comment about his wife Zelda Sayre Fitzgerald, who at the end of her life was interned in a sanitarium: "She realized too late that work was dignity" (qtd. in Liesl Schillinger, 18). Carmen Martín Gaite suggests a similar malady—idleness—in Madame Bovary and Marilyn Monroe, both of whom committed suicide, Martín Gaite believes, because their self-worth derived solely from their femininity—rather than from anything productive (see "De madame Bovary a Marilyn Monroe"). Maria Aurèlia Capmany notes the intersection of class and work especially from the nineteenth century on. She observes that working-class women have always worked, but that the problem of work for the middle-class woman arises in the nineteenth century. The industrialization of that century produced middle-class women with limited means who were not raised with the expectation of having to work, but whose precarious economic situation might require it. She also notes that the lower middle class (*petit bourgeoisie*), especially prevalent in commercially oriented Catalonia, was more amenable to women's working than the higher strata of that class grouping. The very notion of work, especially as it relates to women, is difficult to define, because the nonpaid work women do in the household or in the fields often does not count in statistical tables. Cristina Borderías, Cristina Carrasco, and

Carmen Alemany assess this difficulty in the "Prólogo" to *Las mujeres y el trabajo: Rupturas conceptuales* [Women and work: Conceptual ruptures]: "El concepto de «trabajo» mismo, como se podrá apreciar a través de las páginas de este libro, es actualmente un concepto polisémico y ambiguo, objeto en sí mismo de una larga y compleja discusión en las distinas disciplinas" (13) [The concept of "work" itself, as can be appreciated in the pages of this book, is actually a polysemic and ambiguous concept, itself a matter of a long and complex discussion in different disciplines]. As Ubaldo Martínez Veiga observes, "lo que es considerado como trabajo es, precisamente, el industrial" (9) [what is considered work, is, precisely, industrial work], and his book *Mujer, trabajo y domicilio* explores why what women do in the domestic setting is not considered work. He coins the term "no-trabajo" [non-work] for work in the domestic sphere. In Marxist terms, it is work that does not produce a saleable product, emphasizing the "outside-the-home" nature of what is considered "real" work ("salaried" and "nonsalaried" are less important characteristics in determining what is considered work than "domestic" and "nondomestic").[1] We already noted in the last chapter Lidia Falcón's attempt to circumvent the Marxist definition of work.

Without any particular consciousness that his observations are heavily weighted toward the most privileged classes, Father Feijoo opines in *Defensa de las mujeres* (1726) that women are especially suited for political work; he praises women's political sagacity, beginning with Semiramis, Queen of the Assyrians, Artemis, the two Aspasias, Agripina, Elizabeth I of England, and Isabella I of Spain. In citing the example of the women on the island of Fermosa [sic?] where women are priests with political power, he suggests that women have an aptitude for a greater role in the religious professions than they enjoyed in Christianity. However, his subtle reasoning leaves the question of women in the Christian religion up in the air, since there appears to be a conflict between divine and earthly love. Divine decree dictates women's subjection to men, although in fact women rule and must be obeyed in many places in the human realm. He notes a ridiculous example from Persia in which the belly of a deceased king's wife was crowned, because it was thought she was pregnant with a boy. Feijoo also points out that women can be consummate economic administrators, as witnessed in their management of household affairs.

Pedro Rodríguez Campomanes, as is typical of eighteenth-century thought, takes a publicly conscious view of the need for women to work. In his "Discurso sobre la educación popular de los artesanos" [Discourse on the popular education of artisans], he registers some urgency in widening the social base of workers "para ampliar la prosperidad de la nación, el trabajo femenino se erigía como indispensable. Por lo que había que sacudir la abulia de tanto tiempo e instar a las mujeres «para que no permanezcan ociosas en pueblo, ni provincia alguna sin producir utilidad al Estado»" (Folguera 24) [in order to increase the nation's prosperity, women's work was seen as indispensable. Thus it was necessary to shake off their long-standing apathy and urge women everywhere 'not to remain idle without being useful to the state']. Based on direct observation, Jovellanos insists that women perform the same kinds of work as men, and he believes that women are men's inseparable companions not only in the home, but also in the forest, on the beach, in the field, hunting, walking about, shepherding, cultivating the land, and following him in all the other exercises of life, essentially affirming women as capable of any work activity. Richard Herr asserts that Campomanes extolled women's work in coastal regions such as Galicia and Asturias, where they did everything from going out on fishing boats to weeding, planting, and harvesting crops. He also argues that in northern Spain where the conquest against the Moors began in the eighth century,

> In particular, Asturias was the home of Pelayo, a Christian leader who waged a successful battle against the Moors in Covadonga in 722. Pelayo's victory marked the beginning of the reconquest, which was fought by the subjects of Pelayo's successors in Asturias and Galicia. Spaniards like Campomanes considered themselves the descendents of Pelayo. Thus, for Campomanes the success of Spain relied on expunging Islamic practices brought to the peninsula with the invasion from North Africa in 711 and realigning Spaniards with the European practices of their past. The eradication of female idleness, an undesirable remnant of Spain's Muslim past, was essential to improving Spanish society in the future. (76)

As Rebecca Haidt notes, Campomanes extolled meaningful work for urban women, warning in his 1775 *Discurso sobre la educación popular* (Discourse on popular education) that *la ociosidad* (idleness) was especially problematic among urban working-class women (for whom domestic service was one of the largest of employment categories) and urged city women to lead "una vida activa y atareada, en lugar de la flojedad volumptuosa (p. 215)" (49) [an active and work-filled life, instead of voluptuous laziness]. Campomanes particularly recommended lace-making, button-making, fan-painting, and preparation of other artistic materials as appropriate livelihoods for idle urban women. Haidt also provides a fascinating account of eighteenth-century Spanish women who in house-to-house sales supplied *petimetras* [showy women] with the finery they required to maintain the proper public appearance (see especially her chapter 3, "Petrimetras, seamstresses, modistas [dressmakers]: clothing work and the margins of 'decency'").

Concepción Arenal and Emilia Pardo Bazán, two of the most important Spanish feminist thinkers of the nineteenth century, had in common with Father Feijoo that their early lives unfolded in Galicia, an area of Spain where women had always worked, especially in highly visible agricultural fields. According to María Aurèlia Capmany, "Sin duda alguna el comportamiento de la mujer gallega del pueblo, que ellas conocían profundamente, no les dejaba lugar a dudas sobre las facultades ante el trabajo de ambos sexos. Es notorio que tanto en Concepción Arenal, como en la condesa de Pardo Bazán jamás se plantea la duda sobre las facultades de la mujer para trabajar, para estudiar, para intervenir en la vida pública de la nación" ("Prólogo," *La condición social* 12) [Surely, their intimate knowledge of Galician village women's behavior left them no doubt as to the ability to work in both the sexes. Notoriously, neither Concepción Arenal nor the Countess Pardo Bazán ever doubted women's ability to work, to study, to intervene in the public life of the nation]. Concepción Arenal points to the example of North America, which was built on work, which in turn underpins equality (*La mujer del porvenir* 203–4). As Carmen de Burgos will do almost seventy years later, Arenal affirms women's "right to work"; she argues from the principle of equality that society cannot deny women the ability to exercise their faculties (*La mujer* 88). She confidently states that women can "ejercer toda profesión u oficio que no exija mucha fuerza física y para la que no perjudique la ternura de su corazón" (*La mujer* 79) [exercise any profession or trade that does not demand much physical strength and that does not endanger the tenderness of her heart]. She immediately retracts the statement about physical stamina, recalling the backbreaking work women undertake in the agricultural sector (something she would have observed at close hand in Galicia and Asturias). Although she hedges a bit on the equal intellectual capacities of men and women (not being able to come up with any female names to set alongside Plato, Galileo, Leibnitz, Pascal, Kant, and Cervantes), she believes nonetheless that women are perfectly capable of performing in professions such as pharmacy, law, medicine, teaching, the priesthood, clerking, as notaries, and in more ordinary work. She emphasizes that women, who are naturally more compassionate, more religious, and more chaste, are well suited for the priesthood, especially the Catholic priesthood, which requires celibacy and auricular confession. She points out that if women could be priests, all the problems of confessions made between people of the opposite sex would disappear (one wonders if her argument would be bolstered by the recent sexual abuse scandals in the Catholic Church). She believes that women's qualities—compassion, piety, emotion—especially equip them to hear confessions, since "la religión es principalmente un sentimiento" (*La mujer* 81; here Arenal is a prescient forerunner of contemporary cognitive science) [religion is principally a sentiment].[2]

Arenal further argues that in considering women capable of exercising any profession, she is thinking of the social good in general. She opines that what matters most in many professions is not knowledge, but conscience. For example, when a client is seeking a lawyer, the lawyer's rectitude is central; to avoid suits, the lawyer must inform the client as to what is possible and not possible according to the law. Doctors need to know scientific facts, but "¡ay del enfermo si no tiene conciencia también!" (*La mujer* 83) [Too bad for the poor sick person if the doctor does not also have a conscience!]. And she argues the same case for clerks and druggists. In fact, women, she avers, being more compassionate, religious, chaste, and moral are ideal for carrying out these professions, especially medicine, when it comes to treating women, the poor, and children. Interestingly, despite her earlier declaration that women should be allowed into any profession, Arenal sets some limits. For example, she does not think female doctors should perform operations. She also excludes women from the military and war, except as doctors and nurses to tend the wounded, from the profession of judge to spare them having to suppress their compassionate nature in rendering harsh sentences, and from professions in which they would have to forcefully exercise an authority incompatible with their sweet, affectionate natures. Nor does she believe women should have political rights, because politics can be militant—passionate, full of intrigues and dishonesty. She doubts that promised changes in political tactics are likely to come about. She recommends that women cling to the domestic sphere and leave the public sphere to men, advice she will radically alter in *La mujer de su casa* twenty years later.

Significantly, of the many uncompleted projects on which Arenal was working in her later years, when serious health problems threatened her life, she chose to focus her flagging energies on her feminist work before she died. She clearly felt an urgency to correct or elaborate on certain ideas that she had held earlier. The preface to *La mujer de su casa* informs us that *La mujer del porvenir* was a *boceto* [sketch] rather than a *cuadro* [painting] although in fact many of the ideas of *La mujer del porvenir* reappear in new dress. For example, she encourages women to leave the domestic sphere and participate in public life for the health of the family, because all men are influenced by women from the time they are born until they die. Thus "los hombres . . . en la medida que rebajan a las mujeres, son rebajados por ellas, material, moral e intelectualmente" (*La emancipación* 204) [when men diminish women, they are materially, morally, and intellectually diminished in turn]. A woman who leaves the home to make charitable visits to the poor or the incarcerated sees important models of what a person should not be. Arenal argues against the received wisdom that women who spend time on these activities neglect their home and family, pointing out that most women in comfortable economic circumstances have a surfeit of time that allows them to pursue idle and useless activities. This situation is physically and morally debilitating and contributes to their downfall and that of the family. Arenal believes that women's work is tedious; it does not exercise the brain. Thus women combat tedium by reading novels, which fuel their passions and lead to social ills such as adultery. Uneducated women are unhappy, and this condition deleteriously affects their children. In addition, and foreshadowing an argument Carmen de Burgos developed more extensively in the early twentieth century, Arenal contends that if women could make their own living, there would not be unhappy marriages, an argument that resurfaces in the Franco era when women were once again relegated to the home.

However, just as in *La mujer del porvenir*, the heart of her argument for women's leaving the home to perform various kinds of work is found in the social benefits that accrue to the nation as a whole. According to Arenal, other countries are more advanced, because their citizens all contribute to the public good through their work: "no es posible que el Gobierno . . . ni la legislación más completa y sabia vivifiquen a un pueblo cuando los legislados son masa pasiva, ciudadanos mecánicos, que no hacen otros movimientos que el que les imprime el resorte legal" (218) [it is not possible for a government or the most complete and wise legislation to enliven a people when those who are being governed are a passive mass, mechanical citizens, who do nothing more than what legality motivates]. Arenal puts all work on an equal footing, eliminating the distinction between men's work as important and women's work as minor. To underscore this point, Arenal employs the distinction between "spirit" and "material," which are central to María Zambrano's and Rosa Chacel's feminist thought in essays from the 1930s and 1940s that draw on Max Scheler's philosophy. In writing about men's and women's work, Arenal asserts that "El hombre no es espíritu puro, y existe bajo la forma de materia organizada" (239) [Man is not pure spirit and exists under the form of organized material]. She believed that Christianity is at fault for the low esteem in which manual work is held; she sees no difference in importance between hunting a deer (men's work) and rendering it edible (women's work). In the end, everyone—men and women—are subject to material laws. Everyone needs the physical exercise that material work provides, and those of the upper classes who do not perform work that involves the body must use a gymnasium or so some other form of non-labor exercise. (Here again class and gender distinctions coincide; when it comes to involving the mind or the body in work, Arenal insinuates that women have much in common with the working class, an argument that resurfaces in Lidia Falcón's essay *Mujer y sociedad*.) Arenal insists that mental and physical work are not opposed and that such a division of labor is a false dichotomy.

In *La mujer de su casa* an important rationale for women to work in meaningful employment is relief from boredom; Elisa Lamas makes the same argument about middle-class women's lives during the Franco era. Drawing on vocabulary that surely derives from Krausism's central notion of harmony, Arenal opines that "La inacción intelectual, y aun material, de la mujer, no puede ser la paz, porque no es la armonía; y el hombre, engañado por aparente sosiego, siente escozores y picaduras de insectos invisibles, o dormido en un oasis despierta sobre un abismo" (257) [Women's intellectual and material inactivity cannot lead to peace, because it is not harmonious; and men, deceived by the apparent calm, feel stings and bites of invisible insects, or having fallen asleep in an oasis, awake over an abyss]. Also drawing on this argument ten years later in 1891, Arenal devoted an entire essay to women's work ("El trabajo de las mujeres," published in the *Boletín de la Institución Libre de Enseñanza*). Here Arenal highlights the poor remuneration for work that women perform and the personal and social consequences of such disparity. In the style of Father Feijoo, Arenal sets out to debunk erroneous thinking, especially that women do not need very high pay, because their income is only supplementing that of a man (father, husband). She also explodes the myth that women's work is primarily in the home, an idea that completely ignores women of the working classes: "La mujer ha trabajado siempre fuera del hogar; trabajará; es preciso que trabaje, y para que esté el menor tiempo posible fuera de él, no hay más medio que mejorar su educación y las condiciones de este trabajo: si ganara en seis horas lo que gana en doce, podría estar dieciocho en casa" (86) [Women have always worked outside the home; they will work; they must work, and so that they be away from home as little as possible, it is necessary to better their education and working conditions: if women earned in six hours what they earn in twelve, they could be home for eighteen hours]. Her arguments for bettering women's working conditions outside the home continue to be bolstered by the notion that women's sphere is essentially in the home. It is impossible to know if Arenal employed the argument for fewer hours in the factory to increase the amount of time at home merely to appease those who believed women's place was in the home, or if she honestly believed it. In her own life, Arenal certainly did not adhere to this rule.[3]

While most of Emilia Pardo Bazán's feminist writings focus on the related topic of women's education, her article "La exposición de trabajos de la mujer" (1893) addresses women's work. The article reviews the exhibits of women's needlework and writing that Spain sent to the international exposition in Chicago. Although Pardo Bazán laments that the exhibits were put together in haste and therefore were not of the highest quality Spain could offer, she points out that for the first time Spain recognized women's work by including it in an international exhibition. As we saw in Pardo Bazán's writing on social class, her interest in women's work emphasizes work carried out by upper-class women. The list of contributors of needlework to the international exhibition is top-heavy with aristocratic titles. The article primarily describes items in the exhibit, but it also gave Pardo Bazán the opportunity to slip in a few opinions on women's work in general. She insinuates that the exhibition, centering as it did on handwork and writing, did not take into full account the scope of Spanish women's work. She points especially to women's presence in the fields of her native region of the northwest: "En mi país la mujer ara, cava, poda, siega, riega, hace leña" (165) [In my country women plow, dig, plant, irrigate, and chop wood].

Pardo Bazán believes that Spanish women are less involved in industrial work, although she notes that they are central to the tobacco industry (a contribution that, she laments, is absent from the exhibition). Spanish women's needlework is the most conspicuous display of women's work, a fact that allows Pardo Bazán the opportunity to remark that a lot of that kind of work is a waste of time, a sentiment that María Martínez Sierra echoed a few years later. Pardo Bazán writes that her feminine nature inclines her toward appreciating the beauty of needlework: "mi razón y mi piedad por la mujer me inspiran cierta antipatía y guerra a la labor de aguja. Pena causa imaginar la paciencia, el tiempo, el derroche de vista, las interminables horas de encierro que representan esas labores, no siempre bellas, rara vez aprovechables, y en algunas ocasiones contrarias hasta al fin útil del objeto que enriquecen" (166) [my reason and my pity for women inspire a certain antipathy and war on needlework. It is painful to imagine the patience, the time, and the wear and tear on the eyes that the interminable hours of enclosure this work entails, work that is not always beautiful and rarely useful and sometimes contrary to the purpose of the object they adorn]. Of the latter problem she gives the example of lace on sheets, which are only used when one is asleep. She also points out that the most recognized needleworkers are men, as is evidenced in the Madrid street name "calle de *Bordadores*" [Embroiderer's Street].

An interesting and unique feature of the history of women's paid work in Spain was the tobacco industry in the nineteenth century, when cigar-making became almost wholly a female enterprise, as captured in Prosper Merimée's novel *Carmen* and the opera *Carmen* by Georges Bizet (See D. J. O'Connor for a more complete accounting of representations of female tobacco workers). Early on, tobacco factory administrators learned that female hands were more dexterous in working the tobacco leaves into a fine finished product. The tobacco factories were highly regulated and work conditions particularly favorable to women. Female tobacco workers were considered whole persons in the sense outlined in chapter 2 of this book: "the female cigar maker was required to show a minimum level of educational achievement in a country where half the female population was illiterate (and the level was higher among modest classes and in certain regions)[;] there was no doubt that she would be or could easily become a figure of distinction among those working in industry, with a personality of her own" (Capel Martinez 136). In addition, the tobacco industry provided opportunities for career advancement for women, who could work their way up to administrative and supervisory posts.[4]

National consciousness of women's paid work was evident by 1900 when the first of the laws protecting women in the workplace was promulgated (see Laura Nuño Gómez 255), although as Nuño Gómez points out, "Las ínfimas condiciones laborales de las mujeres obreras no serían objetivo de esta nueva regulación" (256) [The terrible working conditions of female laborers are not the reason for these new laws]. By the 1920s when María Martínez Sierra, Margarita Nelken, and Carmen de Burgos were writing in the wake of the large numbers of Spanish women entering the labor force during World War I when the Spanish economy was expanding and prices for basic goods rose concomitantly, work holds a much more central place. María Martínez Sierra's *Feminismo, Cartas a las mujeres de España*, and *Nuevas cartas a las mujeres de España*; Margarita Nelken's *La condición social de la mujer*; and Carmen de Burgos's *La mujer moderna y sus derechos* register this new phenomenon and feminist consciousness of it. In 1920 José Francos Rodríguez sounds the new note. He argues that women's careers cannot be limited to securing a marriage partner (qtd. in Nash, *Mujer, trabajo* 105). He believes that only women's abilities, not male tyranny, should define their activities:

> ¿no están ellas manifiestas en diversas profesiones y en distintos empleos? Puede pedirse que por motivos de carácter económico, por fines que tienden a la armonía social, se estudie el modo de impedir el desequilibrio que ocasione la entrada de la mujer en la vida del trabajo. Pero ¿cerrar el camino a la independencia personal, negar el derecho que la mujer tiene a ganarse la vida? Eso no es justo ni además posible, porque el ímpetu de los acontecimientos destruirá los prejuicios y egoístas resistencias que traten de mantener el dominio masculino. (qtd. in Nash, *Mujer, trabajo* 106–107)[5]

> [Aren't they obvious in different professions and employments? Can one ask that we study the means of preventing the inequality occasioned by women's entering the workforce be studied for economic reasons or for social harmony? But

to close off the road to personal independence, to deny the right that women have of making a living? This is not just or even possible because the force of events will destroy prejudices and egotistical resistance that male dominance tries to maintain.]

In 1916 during the influx of Spanish women into the workplace thanks to positions created in the boom war years for Spain, Carme Karr de Lasarte echoes Concepción Arenal's *La mujer de su casa*. Arenal placed the larger social mission ahead of family in writing that humanity's love of fellow human beings is a noble mission for women that is just as important as maternity: "«Unicamente preparando a la mujer para hacer *sola* el camino de la existencia tendremos buenas esposas, buenas madres, buenas ciudadanas». Es necesario por todos los medios romper aquel antiguo molde de la formación femenina que no tenía otro ideal para la mujer que el matrimonio o el convento" (qtd. in Nash, *Mujer, trabajo* 97–99) ["Only in preparing women to face *alone* life's journey will we have good wives, good mothers, and good citizens." It is necessary by any means to break that old mold of educating women that had no other ideal for women outside marriage or the convent]. However, Karr's conservatism dominates in the end when she asserts that woman's social mission begins in the home.

María Martínez Sierra's arguments for women's right to work appeal even more clearly to traditional—Christian and maternal—Spanish values. In a speech delivered at a festival held to benefit "la protección al trabajo de la mujer" [protection of women's work] in 1917, Martínez Sierra argued in favor of providing work to women who need it and paying just wages for such work as "una obra cristiana, ultramoderna y feminista" (*Feminismo* 12) [a Christian, untramodern and feminist work]. She fully realized that the Spanish women in the audience might be put off by the word "feminism"; thus she attempted to give the term a charitable cast. Bourgeois women should find honest work for the less fortunate "en vez de darles un socorro como limosna; administrando su labor honradamente; librándolas de la tiranía de un intermediario explotador; hacen ustedes obra de puro feminismo, puesto que, mujeres, trabajan ustedes en favor de sus hermanas desvalidas." (*Feminismo* 12) [rather than give them assistance in the form of alms for the poor; administering their labor honorably; freeing them from the tyranny of an exploitative intermediary; you do pure feminist work, since, as women, you work to aid your helpless sisters]. She discourages Spanish women from doing their own sewing at home, urging them to hire professional seamstresses to take care of their sewing needs. She believes housewives' time would be better spent going out to do the grocery shopping rather than sitting at home sewing: "Si se pasan ustedes el día cosiendo, serán ustedes viejas a los treinta años; engordarán ustedes, cosa que les causa tan saludable horror." (*Feminismo* 169) [If you spend the day sewing, you will be old at age thirty; you will get fat, which causes you such healthy horror]. One cannot help but note that no sympathy is expressed for the professional seamstress who spends the day indoors sewing and who ages too quickly because of it.

In "Un oficio de mujer noble y desdeñado" [A noble and disdained woman's profession], Martínez Sierra laments that so many Spanish women scorn the profession of nanny. Spanish families have to seek nannies in Switzerland, Germany, or England, because Spanish girls look down on the work, preferring the job of tutor to that of nanny (another manifestation of the dichotomy between physical and mental work). Martínez Sierra argues that the scarcity of nannies in Spain means that caring for children receives a higher wage than instructing them in reading, history, and geography. In "Iniciativa laudable en favor de la mujer. Una carrera esencialmente femenina" [Laudable initiative in favor of women. An essentially female career], she is excited to learn that in Cataluña there are ten openings for female students in a school for librarians. She believes women's qualities—order, cleanliness, patience, aptitude for classification and language study—make them especially able librarians. If librarianship is essentially a middle-class profession, Martínez Sierra addresses the working-class woman in "Celia en los infiernos" [Celia in the infernos], praising a book about a wealthy woman who visits working-class residential neighborhoods and the factories where the working classes make a living. Celia's story reminds Martínez Sierra of two upper-middle-class North American women who actually went to work in factories to find out first-hand about conditions there. The book they wrote about the experience lit a fire of interest in the United States, provoking Congress to draft laws about children and women in the workplace: "El infierno, el infierno: el hambre, el frío, la angustia, la desnudez . . . , la tentación esperando a la puerta del taller a la obrera cansada y hambrienta" (*Feminismo* 157) [The inferno, the inferno: hunger, cold, anguish, nakedness . . . , the temptation waiting at the tired and hungry working woman's door].

In *Nuevas cartas a las mujeres de España*, Martínez Sierra addressed the thorny issue of women's double workday—paid employment outside the home and the endless chores inside the home—a situation that recent Spanish feminists have revisited. Martínez Sierra's solution to this situation is utopian. She notes that affordable housing is becoming scarce and, given the greater employment opportunities for women, good domestic service is also difficult to find. In addition children often work far from the family home and must live elsewhere. Thus family lifestyles must change radically. Martínez Sierra's solution is a kind of cooperative with each couple or individual living in two "amplias y ventiladas" (115) [spacious and well-ventilated] rooms with a bathroom. The entire building would be served by professionals (not maids), who would provide heat, water, cleaning, trash removal, and cooking. (The scheme is similar to today's retirement communities.) Martínez Sierra realizes that this arrangement might seem frightening to her readers, but she assures them that the "libertad personal" (117) [personal liberty] they would gain would be highly satisfying. Women with families would especially appreciate being relieved of all the tedious chores that fall to their lot, and single women would be able to relax after work rather than having to heat water for a bath, prepare a meal, and clean the house. She believes that the new housing arrangement would greatly improve human relations, especially those between men and women.

Like Margarita Nelken, Martínez Sierra employs nationalistic rationales in her feminist argumentation, although she incorporates motherhood into the equation, which Nelken does not. Martínez Sierra advocates women's education and suffrage, because educated women who vote will raise better (male) citizens:

> Y . . . figúrense ustedes que tienen un hijo, el primero, hijo de amor y de ilusión, y que sueñen ustedes para él toda la gloria del mundo y toda la felicidad, por añadidura. Le quieren ustedes héroe, santo, sabio . . . ¿No les gustaría a ustedes que ese hijo, esperanza viva, pudiera educarse en una escuela que le enseñase a ser hombre de veras, en una Universidad que formase su espíritu para nobles batallas, para gloriosos triunfos? Pues bien: esa escuela y esa Universidad pueden y deben crearlas las leyes. Si las madres españolas votasen las leyes, ¿creen ustedes que estaría la enseñanza oficial en España en el lamentable estado en que hoy se encuentra? . . . Piensen

ustedes que si la patria es como una madre para los hombres, para las mujeres es como un hijo . . . (*Feminismo* 10, 28)

[And . . . imagine that you have a son, the first, son of love and illusion, and that you dream all the glory and happiness in the world for him. You want him to be a hero, a saint, a wise man . . . Wouldn't you want this living hope, your son, to be educated in a school that would teach him to be a real man in a university that would form his spirit for noble battles and glorious triumphs? Well, the law ought to create this school and this university. If Spanish mothers voted on the laws, do you think that official education in Spain would be in the lamentable state it is today? Consider that if the state is like a mother to men, for women it is like a son . . .]

Martínez Sierra's argument is strategic. Through a concatenation of circumstances, women are the mothers of the nation. As educated citizens who acquire suffrage, they will vote for better schools and universities, which will in turn better educate their sons to become the future leaders of the nation.

Geraldine Scanlon judged the style of Martínez Sierra's arguments paternalistic ("escribe como un maestro de Escuela severo pero amable" (197) [she writes like a severe, but amiable school marm], but, of course, when Scanlon wrote her book in 1974, she still believed that María's husband Gregorio had written Martínez Sierra's feminist lectures and essays. Even when one knows the female gender of the author, the arguments can appear patronizing, but they also respond to the mentality of the day and attempt to convince traditional Spanish women (most likely from the middle class) to consider progressive measures by speaking to them in language that is comforting and familiar. Scanlon comments that "[e]l tono insípido de la propaganda feminista de Gregorio Martínez Sierra nos da una idea bastante exacta del espíritu de la mujer de clase media" (197) [the insipid tone of Gregorio Martínez Sierra's feminist propaganda gives us a fairly accurate idea of middle-class women's spirit]. Alda Blanco argues persuasively for a much more firmly feminist view of the essays María Martínez Sierra wrote under her husband's name: "But if in part the essays of 'Gregorio Martínez Sierra' register the rich complexity of the protest against the subordination of women, they also reveal the theoretical turns of a corpus of ideas that always seem to be refining and making more precise what it means to be a woman in patriarchy" (81).[6]

In *Cartas a las mujeres de España*, Martínez Sierra includes a long letter to the women of Spain on the subject of "La mujer y el trabajo" [Women and work] in which she admonishes her readers not to be frightened by the notion of work: "El trabajo no tiene de terrible más que el nombre" (*Cartas* 17) [Work has nothing bad about it except the name]. In fact, she asserts that work is "la sal de la vida y lo mejor de lo mejor que se puede encontrar en este mundo pícaro" (*Cartas* 17) [life's salt and the best of the best that you can find in this diabolical world]. Martínez Sierra argues that when facing work, women should consider it with happiness rather than resignation, thinking of the end result rather than the process. She employs the metaphor of a journey where the actual travel may be tedious—dirty and long—but the views from the window and the destination a delight. She also points out the delights of the work itself, exercising skills, creating something, feeling in charge. Repeating the historical argument so common in Spanish feminist writing, Martínez Sierra reminds her readers that since the earliest times human work has been equally divided between men and women. Women prepared the meat men hunted; men waged war, while women tended the crops; women wove cloth, made bread, constructed huts, and made drinks.

Martínez Sierra notes that when armed defense became less necessary, men began to take over some of the work women had performed. From the Middle Ages through the nineteenth century, women educated their children and carried out numerous domestic tasks. However, with the advent of machines, women's lives have radically changed; women no longer weave, knit, bake bread, or make clothes, and they have become parasites on men who labor, occasioning women's social and personal regression: "La mujer que no trabaja se corrompe, y de compañera del hombre se convierte en esclava del hombre" (*Cartas* 21) [The woman who does not work becomes corrupt, and instead of man's companion, she becomes man's slave]. Raising children is still women's purview, and women can only do that well if they are well informed. Drawing on the same Krausist notion of perfection that Concepción Arenal employed, Martínez Sierra argues that

> La Humanidad camina hacia Dios al caminar hacia su perfección: el camino de la Humanidad es la vida. De nuestras madres la recibimos hombres y mujeres, en un escalón de marcha. Hombres y mujeres tenemos obligación, al pasarla a nuestros hijos, de haberla hecho subir otro escalón al menos.

Este es el verdadero espíritu del progreso, y este progreso, todos, hombres y mujeres, tenemos el deber de traer nuestro grano de arena. (21)

[Humanity moves toward God by moving toward perfection; Humanity's road is life. We men and women receive life from our mothers in a rung of progress. We men and women have the obligation, upon passing it to our children, of making it go up at least one more step. This is the true spirit of progress, and we all, men and women, have the duty to contribute our little grain of sand to this progress.]

Useless women, she proclaims, cannot produce useful men.

Martínez Sierra continues her analysis of the value of work for women in "El derecho a trabajar" [The right to work], a title that Carmen de Burgos will echo in *La mujer moderna y sus derechos*. As in so many other Spanish feminist essays on women's work, Martínez Sierra considers the professions most suited to women. Before beginning to address this question, she feels the need to answer the fundamental feminist question "¿Es la mujer un ser humano?" (*Cartas* 26) [Are women human beings?]. For Martínez Sierra, in the eyes of God, "la mujer y el hombre son absolutamente iguales" (*Cartas* 26) [women and men are absolutely equal]. However, this equality has not translated into equal work opportunities. Martínez Sierra points out that women are not allowed to exercise the "liberal" professions such as lawyer, architect, judge, or doctor. Men work in jobs that pay high salaries, while women are relegated to mopping floors, carrying jugs of water from the well, glass blowing, plowing, or sewing. She believes that what worries men about women's working is not the type of work, but the pay involved. Like Concepción Arenal, Martínez Sierra believes that women are particularly apt for medicine; she points out that in primitive societies, medicine was practiced exclusively by women. She notes that in Spain custom rather than laws prevent women from studying for the more lucrative and prestigious professions, and she urges women to study the civil code to learn about their rights. In the letter titled "Una vida heróica. La primera mujer de los tiempos modernos que se ha doctorado en medicina" [A heroic life. The first woman of modern times to receive a doctorate in medicine] Martínez Sierra confirms women's aptitude for medicine. To make her example (a Scottish woman) more appealing to a Spanish audience, Martínez

Sierra compares the first woman to receive a doctorate in medicine to Santa Teresa.

In another letter, "Del amor a la patria. Obligaciones diversas; un solo deber" [On the love of country. Various obligations; one single duty], Martínez Sierra admonishes wealthy women to provide well-paid work for less fortunate women rather than giving them alms, a practice, she believes, that foments the laziness that dooms Spain as a nation. And in "Algunas consideraciones sobre el ejercicio de la caridad" [Some considerations on exercising charity], Martínez Sierra follows in Concepción Arenal's steps in assessing the value of charitable work. Rather than remaining at the superficial level of how to administer charity on an individual basis, Martínez Sierra assesses the need for charity as a social evil. She calls on rich women of leisure to employ their time in instructing those who are without means to support themselves; better that they should give their time and intelligence rather than their money. Martínez Sierra reinforces this message in "Caridad social. Un problema angustioso y urgente que pueden resolver facilmente las mujeres de buena voluntad" [Social charity. An anguished and urgent problem that can easily be solved by women of good will], directed especially at middle-class women, who do not pay their employees well—seamstresses, dressmakers, ironers—but give alms to others who do not work. Martínez Sierra recommends three measures to remedy this situation: (1) Echoing Concepción Arenal's *La mujer de su casa*, she opines that women are too individualistic and exclusive because they have always lived enclosed and apart from the world. She exhorts women to awaken a sense of solidarity in working women and help them understand that they are exploited. (2) Warehouses should be established to sell what working women produce at the same price as retail. By cutting out the middle person, working women could be paid a decent wage. (3) Workshops with adequate space, light, and air circulation should be established where women can perform their work. Martínez Sierra believes that working at home ("trabajo a domicilio") is not healthy.

Martínez Sierra has other recommendations for women of the middle classes who work. In "Para las que nunca se divierten" [For those women who never have any fun] she exhorts women who work as clerks, typists, or telegraph operators to seek diversion, even though there does not seem to be enough money to spend on going out. However, she points out, occasionally having a good time is beneficial medicine and no more expensive than a prescription at the pharmacy. She especially recommends that middle-class women associate in women's clubs: "Lo esencial es que tengáis un lugar «vuestro» que no sea la casa, que no sea el taller, o la oficina, o la escuela, o la tienda; un salón limpio donde podáis olvidaros una hora al día de la obligación, hablando unas con otras, leyendo periódicos o libros, según vuestra afición; haciendo algo de música, seria o ligera, según vuestra cultura y vuestro estado de ánimo; bailando si os parece" (*Cartas* 157) [The essential thing is that you have "your" place that is not the home, the factory, the office, the school, or the store; a clean room where you can forget your obligations for one hour a day, conversing with one another, reading newspapers or books, depending on your tastes; making some light or serious music, according to your upbringing and your state of mind; dancing if you wish]. In "Caridad social. La protección al trabajo de la mujer" [Social charity. Protecting women's work], Martínez Sierra continues her concern with middle-class working women, calling for a benefit exhibition of handwork to pay for a locale for the society *La Protección al Trabajo de la Mujer* [Society for the protection of women's work]. She also exhorts her readers to shop only in establishments that treat their female employees fairly: "Es preciso limitar las ganancias de algunos para que vivan todos; es preciso que para todos haya pan; es preciso que la mujer que se dispone a emplear su dinero en una compra, sepa que su dinero va a parar a manos a quienes pertenece de justicia, a las que se cansaron trabajando para crear lo que ella es menester" (*Cartas* 166) [It is necessary to limit wages so that everyone can live; it is necessary for everyone to have food; it is necessary for the woman who is going to use her money for a purchase to know that her money is going into the hands of the right person, the person who worked tirelessy to create what she needs].

Of the fourteen chapters in *La condición social de la mujer en España*, Margarita Nelken devotes four to the topic of work, more than to any other subject. In the chapter "Las carreras" [the professions], Nelken laments how few women undertake university study that would lead to careers in law, medicine, and other professions that require extensive course work. Those who do attend the university face isolation, ridicule, and scorn. Echoing ideas we have seen in Concepción Arenal, she argues that women who study at the highest levels are intellectually disciplined and thus morally stronger. And she enters into the biological arguments of her day about the relative size of women's brains, affirming that women's smaller size brain corresponds to their smaller bodies, none of which has any bearing on the brain's complexity and capacity. The differences between men's and women's mental capacity is due to the exercise the brains of each receive. Like her predecessors, Nelken draws on history and examples to prove her points, citing Santa Hildegarda, who elaborated a theory of the circulation of blood before Harvey, and Madame Curie, who collaborated with her husband in discovering radium. As I noted earlier, Nelken employs some of the same feminist reasoning that calls on motherhood and nationalism that we find in Martínez Sierra, although the tone of her writing is much less conciliatory. Mary Lee Bretz points out that "*The social condition of women in Spain* calls for radical change and expresses a strong critique of the existing social structures" (103). Thus, as Bretz observes, at the same time Nelken rhetorically employs terms such as "*maternity, motherhood, future citizens*" (111, emphasis in original), she "criticizes those who combat feminism in the name of 'motherhood' and who blindly accept certain 'feminine' occupations with no concern for the environmental hazards to the mother, the fetus, and the infant" (111–12). While Margarita Nelken's ideological framework for her feminist positions is essentially egalitarian, she is not above employing difference feminist arguments at times. For example, she points out that women's natural skill in the kitchen coincides with abilities that would make her a good laboratory scientist or pharmacist.

Despite their growing numbers in the workforce, women's wages and the types of work available to women were vastly inferior to those for men. Margarita Nelken attributes this situation to women's education, and she links work to the basic dignity of the human being: "La preparción en una carrera, o en un empleo da porvenir que responda al imperioso mandato que se presenta a todo individuo digno de bastarse a sí mismo y de ser lo más útil posible a los demás. Poco a poco, casi inconscientemente, estas muchachas van formando una conciencia nueva, una moral nueva, en la mujer española" (55) [The preparation for a career or on-the-job training provides a future that responds to the imperious mandate that every individual be able to take care of him or herself and to be as useful as possible to others. Little by little, almost unconsciously, these young girls are growing into a new consciousness, a new morality, for Spanish women].

In arguing her points about work, Margarita Nelken borrows strategies from Concepción Arenal and other nineteenth-century Spanish feminist thinkers who appeal to nationalism as a reason for women's leaving the home and engaging in the public sphere. These thinkers, including Nelken, were quite possibly attempting to make their feminist messages more amenable to their conservative, Catholic readers, who were skeptical of women's assuming any role outside the home. Work, Nelken contends, leads to economic independence for women, making unhappy abusive marriages less likely. She also argues that intellectually disciplined women will be more moral. Ultimately, the argument for the importance of work to the individual becomes an argument for the health of the nation. As I noted in the last chapter, Nelken believed that middle-class women were a dead weight on the nation. Thus, for her, work becomes the center of individual being (its very existential core) as well as the backbone of a strong nation.

Maria Aurèlia Capmany ("Prologue") reveals how important it was to her to have come across Nelken's book from 1919 when she was writing *La dona a Catalunya* in 1965. In the early years of the Franco regime, books like Nelken'a were completely erased from public memory. Capmany was surprised to realize that many of the feminist issues Nelken had addressed in *La condición social de la mujer en España* had still not been resolved: "Margarita Nelken hablaba con una prosa dúctil y eficaz, con un absoluto rigor dialéctico, con un propósito de inserción en la circunstancia histórica que resultaba—¡desgraciadamente!—terriblemente actual en 1965, como—¡por nuestros pecados!—en 1975" (17) [Margarita Nelken spoke with a flexible and effective prose, with an absolute dialectic rigor, mindful of her historical circumstances, which unfortunately turned out to be terribly appropriate in 1965 as it was (to our disgrace) in 1975]. Capmany calls it an aggressive book that denounces the tame Spanish feminism to date and argues for inserting women's issues into the general social revolution being agitated for and for the view that the social revolution cannot take place without addressing women's concerns. Capmany especially appreciates Nelken's analysis of Spanish women's situation according to their social classes. Capmany also provides a useful summary of public reaction to Nelken's book. Capmany calls the book's reception "violent." Conservative newspapers panned it, while more liberal reviewers defended it. The minister of public instruction allowed an indictment to go forward against a normal school teacher who assigned the book to her students.

Carmen de Burgos devotes one of the fourteen chapters of *La mujer moderna y sus derechos* to the right to work. As is her approach in this book as a whole, Burgos traces the history of women's work in Spain, beginning with its legitimation under Carlos III in the eighteenth century with the establishment of the tobacco factory in Seville. Even though tobacco work was a great step forward for Spanish women who wanted or needed to work, they still had many obstacles to overcome. Returning to the concept of *la mujer de su casa* that Concepción Arenal first addressed in 1881, Burgos observes that given the many objections to women's working outside the home, it is astonishing that no one complains about women's working as domestic servants, employment that requires women to completely abandon their own homes: "Criadas, asistentas, costureras, lavandoras, planchadoras a domicilio abandonaban su casa sin protesta de nadie" (133) [Maids, seamstresses, laundresses, ironers who live in abandon their own homes without anyone's protesting]. This situation, Burgos points out, is not the case with factory work, which occasions such a hue and cry. Like so many other Spanish feminist theorists, Burgos has recourse to history in making a case for women's paid work outside the home. She provides a long list of aristocratic women—Penelope, Nausicaa, Isabel I—who sewed and washed clothes (here she is mixing paid work with working in one's own home) and village women who are represented as early as Greek and Roman times as engaging in milling, weaving, and carrying goods. She points out that among the early peoples of Spain, women worked more than men. Gothic women tilled the soil, and in Saint Isidore's time women were so overworked that the Council of 1020 prohibited forcing women to make bread for the king, if they were not his servants.

Burgos points out the contradictions between the laws and the realities. In the Middle Ages women were excluded from work by law, but no one was disturbed by women's performing the most taxing agricultural work in all the regions of Spain. Even in her own time—the late nineteenth and early twentieth centuries—women were the ones who got up in the middle of the night to feed the animals (while the men slept), and women harvested the crops. Burgos points out that "no es un sentimiento de piedad por el sexo débil maltratado, ni por los niños y los hogares lo que levanta el movimiento de protesta de que la mujer vaya al taller. Lo formulan la ruina de un lado y el egoísmo de otro" (134) [it is not a sense of pity for the mistreated weaker sex, or for the children and homes that instigates the protest about women's working in a factory. It is formulated on the one hand by ruin and on the other by egotism]. Burgos argues, however, that for women factory work has advantages over domestic work, because the law legislates an eight-hour workday and inspections of workplaces ensure that they are more hygienic than houses. The fewer hours at work leave more time for the woman to administer her home and family and to relax; in addition the pay is better in factories.

Social class and marital status enter into Burgos's consideration of women's work. Like Margarita Nelken, she pays particular attention to the anomalous situation of middle-class women when it comes to work, although her attitude toward women of her own class is more sympathetic than Nelken's. Burgos finds it lamentable that middle-class women who are not expected to work sometimes must do so out of necessity, a fact they try to conceal as much as possible. Middle-class women who must work end up engaged in needlework or making candy or artificial flowers, which they can do at home away from the public gaze. While women's intellectual work (teaching, one supposes) is acceptable to middle-class mores, any kind of handwork is not, so middle-class women scrupulously hide these types of employment. This situation means that handwork is very poorly paid. In addition, handwork is time-consuming, and women who engage in it get little exercise or recreation. Married women are another group that is discouraged from working outside the home, primarily because the mother's absence can be detrimental to her children. However, Burgos has not found that the mortality rate of children of women who work is any higher than among those who do not work.

As will Rosa Chacel and María Zambrano a few years later, Burgos argues against the misogyny of Georg Simmel, who believed women's and men's labor should be rigorously divided according to the physical exertion required. Women, Burgos notes, are engaged in agriculture, fishing, masonry, and metalworking, all of which require physical strength, while men are tailors, hairdressers, and embroiderers, professions that do not require physical exertion. She also counters Simmel's idea that women do not need to be paid as much as men for the same work. She stresses that life is just as expensive for women as for men, and if a woman is head of a household and is in charge of her parents, brothers and sisters, children, and sometimes even her husband, it does not cost her less to support them than it would cost any man in the same position. In fact, she adds, everything is more difficult for a woman. She has to put up more guarantees when she wants to rent an apartment, and some utility companies require deposits from women that they do not require of men. However, women do save money when it comes to spending on tobacco, alcohol, or coffee in coffee shops, which also makes them better workers because they get more rest and have clearer minds.

Burgos argues fervently against giving women special protection in the workplace and in favor of absolute equality both in working conditions and in salary considerations: "Lo indispensable es la *igualdad*; la llamada protección perjudica a la mujer más que sus mismos enemigos. . . . El verdadero feminismo no desea privilegios" (141, 142) [What is indispensable is *equality*; so-called protection damages women more than her enemies. . . . Real feminism does not desire privileges]. For example, prohibiting women from working at night robs many women of work opportunities that they cannot afford to be denied. Burgos also believes that any protection legislated for women should be extended to men, such as the weight limit for loads carried on the head. Neither men or women, she observes, should be made to carry out work that is dangerous or destructive. Prohibitions should be based, not on gender, but on individual characteristics. With her usual infallible logic, Burgos argues that both men and women deserve to be protected and that it would be absurd to take care of girl children and not boy children: "La protección debe acompañar desde la cuna al sepulcro a los dos sexos por igual" (143) [Protection should be afforded both sexes equally from cradle to grave]. She also notes that the kinds of work that women are prohibited from doing are often not the most pernicious, but those that arouse jealousy and competition. She notes that nobody worries about women washing clothes, which claims numerous victims; ironing, which is hot and tiring; flower-making, which involves using poisonous dyes; pedaling a sewing machine, which causes heart palpitations; or working with tobacco, which causes eye problems and tuberculosis.

Burgos ends her chapter on women and work with the enlightened example of Henry Ford, who raised workers' hourly wage, established the eight-hour workday, and reduced the work week to five days, all of which produced excellent results. Instead of working less because they were making more per hour, the rested and satisfied workers produced just as much in less time. In addition, Burgos notes that the workers have more time to spend their money, which improves the national economy. Burgos believes that Ford's ideas should be extended to women, who, if better rested and paid, could similarly contribute to the national economy. In an improved national economy, there would be plenty of work for both men and women, eliminating any competition between the sexes for jobs. She concludes with a call for unity between working men and women in the quest for better working conditions because "La causa de la humanidad es sólo una" (149) [Humanity only has one purpose].

In 1939 with the conservative National Movement under the leadership of Francisco Franco having won the Civil War, Spanish women's legal and actual situation took a giant leap backward. Many of the measures regarding the family and women reverted to the Napoleonic Code installed in 1889. Women's work was redefined as domestic and bound to the home, and women's work outside the home (especially for married women) was discouraged in every way possible and was rigorously controlled by laws. Women were prohibited from taking nocturnal jobs, and they were encouraged to leave jobs they held and return home (after 1942 married women were required to leave their jobs and were to receive a dowry from the state). To help out with any household income lost by women's leaving jobs, the state provided a subsidy for families with more than a certain number of children. The wages of married women who did work could be paid directly to their husbands. Women were barred outright from some professions, such as chief administrator in state jobs (including the telephone company), diplomat, work inspector, notary, functionary in departments of justice, state lawyer, state police, or state administration of the stock market. Even a politically and religiously conservative thinker such as Mercedes Formica, who herself had received a law degree, could see the impossible nature of this legislation given the economic realities of post–Civil War Spain. In a review of Simone de Beauvoir's *Le Deuxième Sexe* (a work whose distribution in Spain was prohibited by the Church until after Franco died), Formica proclaimed that "Ya nadie puede plantear en conciencia, si una mujer debe o no trabajar. La española de este momento tiene que trabajar, se enfrenta con este imperativo, inesquivable en nuestro medio, aunque precisamente nuestro medio, por paradoja, no se caracterice por facilitar el trabajo de la mujer" (qtd. in Rosario Ruiz Franco 50) [Now no one can ethically dictate whether or not a woman works. The Spanish woman today has to work; she faces this unavoidable imperative in our situation, although paradoxically it is precisely our situation that does not facilitate women's working].

Although the militant feminism of the 1920s and 1930s that built on the work of nineteenth-century pioneers such as Concepción Arenal, Emilia Pardo Bazán, Concepción Gimeno de Flaquer, and Rosario Acuña had to wait until the 1960s to make the beginnings of a comeback, the earliest nineteenth-century feminist thinker, Concepción Arenal was not forgotten in the Franco era, perhaps due to her Catholicism. It is also true that the Franco-era writings on Arenal do not emphasize her feminist essays. For example, Juan Antonio Cabezas's *Concepción Arenal o el sentido romántico de la justicia* (1942) is essentially a biography detailing how Arenal's life intertwined with that of liberal romantics of her age.

Cabezas does not mention *La mujer del porvenir* until page 216, where he states that "No es el de Concepción un feminismo histérico, influido por las teorías que ya vienen incubando en el extranjero. Su feminismo es un «feminismo aceptable» como lo califica el padre Alarcón" (216) [Concepción's feminism is not hysterical, influenced by theories that were being incubated in foreign countries. Her feminism is an "acceptable feminism" as Father Alarcón classifies it], and on page 220, Cabezas refutes some of Arenal's feminist precepts. Other Franco-era books on Arenal include Manuel Casas Fernández's *Concepción Arenal en su aspecto pedagógico* [Concepción Arenal in her pedagogical aspect] and Jesús Fabio Fernández's *Las ideas sociales de Concepción Arenal* [Concepción Arenal's social ideas], neither one of which deals specifically with the feminist aspects of her thought.[7]

Interestingly, if paid work for women was viewed as a major goal by nineteenth- and early-twentieth-century Spanish feminists, in the Franco era such work became suspect. By 1966, when Maria Aurèlia Capmany wrote *La Dona a Catalunya*, there was definitely a new air of liberation in Spain; in this climate her chapter on work titled "El treball, una nova esclavitud?" [Work, a new slavery?] sounds a note of alarm. Capmany repeats arguments we have seen in earlier Spanish feminist thinkers, noting that women have always worked "en els camps, s'ha esdernegat rentant i tragiant coves de roba, ha portat tota mena de pesos, ha filat, ha teixit, ha fet cèramica, ha anat a vendre als mercats. . . . Naturalment sense contracte de treball" (*La dona* 171) [in the fields, they have to exert themselves washing and carrying loads of clothes, transporting all kinds of weights, have spun, knitted, done ceramics, have gone to sell in the markets. . . . naturally without a work contract]. She quotes Lidia Falcón's *Los derechos laborales de la mujer* (1963), which in turn quotes Gregorio Marañón on women's capacity for specific kinds of work, such as teaching, medicine, laboratory and office work—anything that requires patience, manual dexterity, and attention to detail. Capmany differs with Marañón because he limits his observations to middle-class women, who are a small percentage of women in Spain. She also points out that Spanish law does not distinguish between salaries for men and salaries for women, but in reality there are significant discrepancies. If Lidia Falcón considers women as a social class, Capmany contemplates womanhood as a profession in her essay "De profesión mujer" [Woman: A profession].

Although Lidia Falcón dedicates sections of *Mujer y sociedad* to women's work, especially to the legal restraints on women's working during the Franco era, she does not believe, as did some pre-War feminist thinkers, that work and economic independence will achieve true female liberation. Work is not central to Falcón's existential conception of women's independent state. She postulates that if women achieve a sense of themselves as women, economic liberation will follow. She does not believe that women have been economically oppressed, because they have never held wealth (if they do, it is because their fathers or husbands allow it): "Ella es un personaje, un ser oprimido, lo mismo economicamente que sexualmente, que personalmente. . . . Porque no ha tenido nunca poder económico, no ha tenido tampoco el poder politico. La mujer se liberará como ser humano, más tiene que liberarse en una sociedad en que no haya distinciones de clases" (72) [She is a puppet, an oppressed being, economically, sexually, and personally. . . . Because she has never had economic power, nor has she had political power. The woman will become free as a human being, but she has to become free in a society without class distinctions]. Eva Forest also argues that work in and of itself is not necessarily liberating: "El trabajo por sí solo no libera a nadie. Aunque estuvieran en igualdad de condiciones con el hombre, tampoco liberaría el trabajo" (Levine and Waldman 102) [Work in and of itself does not free anyone. Even if it were carried out in equal conditions to men's, work would not be liberating]. She even speaks of work in some societies (clearly including Spain) as a type of slavery for both men and women, although she believes women suffer a double oppression, if they work outside the home, because their work at home continues to be the same. According to Forest, for work to be liberating, it must be appropriate and satisfying.

Mireia Bofill also addresses whether work is liberating. She notes that women of around thirty years of age grow tired of staying home and develop a desire to work. Bofill believes that these women are exploited "porque esta mujer ve el trabajo como una liberación, no lo ve como la explotación por parte de la empresa donde trabaja" (Levine and Waldman 45) [because this woman sees work as liberation, not as exploitation on the part of the company where she works]. Bofill finds this situation to accrue especially in more intellectual work, while Carnen Alcalde points out that working-class women, who should be the most conscious of women's oppression, are too busy working to be conscious of anything, much less to do anything about their oppression (Levine and Waldman 32). Elisa Lamas approaches women's working from the point of view of the married woman. She notes that it is extremely rare for a Spanish man to consider women as complete human beings capable of anything beyond taking care of the home and children, and Spanish men are unwilling to share household responsibilities. She also notes that when it comes to studying for a career, if funds are limited, what funds there are go toward educating the male children, leaving the female children out. If women do manage to get a degree in order to enter a profession (for example, law or engineering), employers invariably select the male candidate over the female. A woman candidate for a position has to be ten times better than the male candidate to be a serious contender. Lamas also points out that in manual labor employment, where there is supposed to be equal pay for equal work, factory owners get around this rule by basing pay on production rates. Women who work double workdays at home and in the factory are often unable to produce as much as men who are more rested. Lamas accurately predicted in 1974 that were the political system to change, because women do work and under such lamentable conditions, the latent women's movement would surface in full force. When dictator Francisco Franco finally died in November of 1975, that is exactly what happened.

Franco-era feminist thinkers who were aligned with the revolutionary left looked to the Soviet Union and to China for models. Mireia Bofill, for example, finds that under Stalin the Soviet Union sent women back to the home and the family in order to advance economically by adopting some capitalist tendencies. In a way her argument recognizes Lidia Falcón's desire to incorporate women's work in the home and the family into the national economy, although she gives such economic appropriation of home and family a negative cast. Bofill notes that China is less rigid ideologically about women's place in the workforce than the Stalinist Soviet Union, and she is especially attracted to a model she found in a book by French feminist Claudie Broyelle, who describes small industries that women have founded in their neighborhoods, allowing them to engage in employment outside the home while remaining close to home. In a system with some similarities to María Martínez Sierra's utopian society, these industries spawn day-care centers for children, teams of people who clean houses and do other household chores for the women who work in the local industries. Day care is an especially crucial service for women who work, and according to Bofill day care occasioned an entire movement in the late Franco era, because the state was doing little about it. The Franco government did encourage industries to offer child care, but this approach (according to Bofill) had the negative side effect of making women workers more dependent on the companies they worked for and less able to negotiate with them. Bofill greatly prefers government-supported day-care centers in the neighborhoods rather than factory-sponsored child care at the plant. Lidia Falcón assures that the Franco government, despite its overt policies on women's remaining in the home, will make it possible for women to work: "Las utilizarán para trabajar porque ya se sabe que trabajan, y bien, y que son un sostén de la economía de cualquier país, muy importante. Y para que trabajen, les pondrán guarderías infantiles para que lleven los niños" (Levine and Waldman 76) [They will use them to work because they know they work, and well, and that they are an important support to the economy of any country. And so they establish childcare centers for the children so that they will work].

Carmen Rodríguez brings up the question of the married middle-class woman who does not necessarily have to work to survive (eat, have shelter, etc.), but who feels an existential need to work: "lo que yo deseaba era sentirme útil para mí misma y para los demás" [what I wanted was to feel useful to myself and to others] (Levine and Waldman 136). Her children were now in school, and she had hired help for the household chores. She saw her options as becoming a typical bourgeois woman who goes to the hairdresser, makes social calls, and goes shopping, or she could stay home and become neurotic (she feared the latter would be her course of action). She did find a job at a magazine, which was not satisfying because the editors gave her all the tasks no one else wanted to do. She worked long hours and arrived home tired, which created problems with her husband. The experience was consciousness-raising for her and for those around her. Everyone finally realized that she was working because she had a vital need to do so. When the magazine she worked for had to cut back on personnel, she was the first to be let go, but she fought the decision in the courts and eventually moved up to the world of television journalism and was able to devise some programs on women's issues. Rodriguez echoes Margarita Nelken (without acknowledging her, probably because she had not had the opportunity to read *La condición social de la mujer en España*) in stating that middle-class men are exploited (her word is "enslaved"), because they have to work very hard to support their wives (who do not work) and their families.

In the democratic era when women gained equal rights under the 1979 constitution, the topic of work receded in the Spanish feminist agenda, giving way, as we will see in the chapters that follow, to the contentious debate over equality and difference.[8] However, women's having gained equal rights in the workplace (equal opportunity, equal pay) did not always reflect reality. In 2004 Ana María Díaz Gutiérrez writes about the "engañosa paridad" [deceitful parity] for women in the workplace. In government and large corporations there is a glass ceiling for the highest and most prestigious positions that women cannot penetrate, and she worries that "estaremos entrando en un período de involución o desaceleración en el proceso de inserción de la mujer en la sociedad" (qtd. in Zecchi 103) [we will be entering into a period of involution or deceleration in the process of inserting women into society]. She insists that women must continue to demand quotas and educational reform as the most effective means of achieving equality in the workplace. She notes that women receive 59 percent of the university degrees, but their numbers are not reflected in the most prestigious and highly paid professions. Women's numbers are significant in nursing (83.3%), languages and literature (75.4%), pharmacy (72.2%), medicine (63.3%), economics and business (53.7%), and pedagogy (79.9%), but still quite low in industrial engineering (20%), civil engineering (17%), architecture (34%), physics (13.15%), and computer science (17.6%).

Women are also underrepresented in receiving doctoral degrees, and only 5% to 18% of full professors (*catedráticas*) are women (36% of assistant and associate professors are female). She concludes that there is an enormous imbalance between the numbers of women undergraduates in the universities and the number of female professors: "Las instituciones educativas . . . mantienen las actitudes estereotipadas con respecto al género existentes en la sociedad y utilizan para el estudio textos que las reproducen y difunden los roles tradicionales, con lo que las estudiantes no son suficientemente alentadas hacia una carrera profesional y continúan contemplando el trabajo fuera de casa como algo secundario en su vida" (Zecchi 115) [Educational institutions maintain stereotypical attitudes present in society with respect to gender, and they use textbooks that reproduce and disseminate traditional roles so that female students are not sufficiently encouraged to consider a professional career, and they continue to consider work outside the home as secondary in their lives]. The goal yet to be achieved is to increase the numbers of women in governing educational institutions and at the highest levels of university instruction, and promulgating labor legislation that will favor women's entering the workforce and defend women's equality in terms of work rights and salaries. She warns that without such legislation, women will be at higher risk in economic recessions (one wonders exactly how her predictions have played out in the current economic downturn that has lasted some eight years now and shows little chance of improving in the next year or two).

It is also difficult for the equality legislation to address the problem of the double workday (especially for married women and mothers). As Laura Nuño Gómez indicates, "la pauta observada por la transformación de los modelos familiares y por los nuevos roles de género anuncia una mayor implicación de los varones en el cuidado y en la educación de sus hijos o hijas. Sin embargo, la descompensada relación entre la incoporación de las mujeres al mercado laboral y de los hombres a las responsabilidades del cuidado ha provocado que el problema que representa la conciliación siga percibiéndose como un asunto de organización familiar que afecta mayoritariamente a las mujeres" (200) [the rule observed in the transformation of family models and by new gender roles suggests a major implication for men in cities and for the education of sons and daughters. Nonetheless, the uncompensated relation between the incorporation of women into the labor force and men into care-giving responsibilities has caused the conciliation to continue to be perceived as a matter of family organization that principally affects women]. The consequence of this situation for women in paid employment outside the home is that many women only work part-time.

To a large extent Spanish women's work concerns continue to differ by class, especially in the long-unregulated arena of domestic service. For example, a 1927 law dictated a minimum of twelve hours between work shifts for women employed in "fábricas, talleres y demás explotaciones y establecimientos industriales y mercantiles" (Martínez Veiga 212) [factories, workshops and other industrial and mercantile establishments], but it explicitly excludes "las mujeres dedicadas al servicio doméstico, las que realizan trabajo a domicilio y las que trabajan en talleres de familia" (212) [women dedicated to domestic services, those that work at home and those that work in family workshops]. Thus women in domestic service were subject to twenty-four-hour work shifts with practically no time for rest or recreation. They were the last to go to bed and the first to rise in the morning, and were on call for emergencies at any time of the night.[9] Martínez Veiga points out the contradictions inherent in this legal loophole. While women's labor was often overregulated in the public sector (for example, women were prohibited from working night shifts in factories), it was unregulated in the domestic sphere, where women could be asked to work at all hours of the night. Even as recently as a 1985 law that fixed a forty-hour work week for domestic service, employers were allowed to impose a "tiempo de presencia" (213) [time on call] that could be as high as sixteen hours a day.

In 1995 Victoria Camps considered the situation of women and work from the perspective of the welfare state that had been in place in Spain from the early 1980s when the Socialists gained a majority in the Spanish government. She weighs what women have gained—the right to work and many social benefits—against what society has lost, above all the care of family members. She laments that in the welfare state, family care has become dehumanized in day-care centers and homes for the elderly. She wishes to recover the "valores cálidos" [warm values] that are only found in small private social structures such as the family. In addition, the labor force cannot absorb so many women on top of the numbers of men who work. She notes that some thinkers have suggested women's part-time work as the solution to this deficit, but she does not think women should bear the burden of giving up full employment. She believes reducing the number of hours worked for everyone could solve the glut and would increase the amount of time that both men and women have to spend with family members who need their love and care: "Es de esa manera, desde abajo y desde la cotidianidad, desde donde podemos romper la estructura patriarcal de nuestras instituciones" (49) [In this way, from below and in daily life, we can break the patriarchal structure of our institutions]. As we will see in the next two chapters, her approach is a challenge to the rational-enlightenment feminism of the equality feminists, although her suggestions are also based on equality between the sexes both at home and in the workplace.

CHAPTER 5

Difference

Spanish feminist theory of the democratic period (after 1975) has been dominated by a debate between theorists who approach feminism from the point of view of legal equality between the sexes and theorists who approach feminism from a difference perspective. I understand "equality" feminists to believe that women must continue to work for a parity with men that remains elusive despite the constitution, and for specific laws guaranteeing equality in institutions such as marriage and the workplace. For equality feminists, women's reality includes less access to work, unequal wages, more responsibilities at home even if they work full-time outside the home, and restricted abortion, among other issues. Equality feminists locate their roots in the eighteenth century, when the concept of social equality culminated in the French Revolution. Some equality feminists call themselves *feministas ilustradas*, or Enlightenment feminists, after eighteenth-century philosophers such as François Poulain de la Barre, who argued for women's equality with men. Their philosophical method privileges reason or the logos as the only sure path to a more just world for women. Equality feminists also refer to Descartes, Rousseau, and Kant in their rational arguments about the role of the state and society in the lives of individual human beings. Thus, equality feminists place significant emphasis on official social institutions and the law as the means to achieve parity between the sexes. In terms of their historical roots in the Spanish feminist tradition, equality feminists in democratic Spain, such as Amelia Valcárcel and Celia Amorós, have continued the work of pre-Franco-era feminist thinkers such as Margarita

Nelken (*La condición social de la mujer en España* [1919]) and Carmen de Burgos *(La mujer moderna y sus derechos* [1927]), although they do not necessarily acknowledge their Spanish forebears. The Spanish difference feminists, on the other hand, maintain that women are essentially different from men and should not attempt to equal men in the public sphere. Rather, they should cultivate feminine roles such as motherhood and caregiving. Spanish difference feminists have relied for inspiration on the Italian difference feminists led by Luisa Muraro. In addition to the philosophical divide, the schism between Spanish equality and difference feminists includes geographical differences. The equality camp is centered primarily in Madrid and in the 1980s had links to the socialist government then in power; the difference group was centered primarily in Barcelona, which is a traditional rival to Madrid as the hegemonic city and cultural capital of Spain.

While equality feminists look to the law to right the wrongs they perceive in Spanish society, difference feminists such as Victoria Sendón de León and Milagros Rivera are more interested in women's interior realm; from a feminocentric position, they identify distinctly female qualities, which, if nurtured within a female hierarchy, would, they believe, contribute measurably to the betterment of women's lives and society as a whole. They argue strenuously against the notion of equality, which, they believe, accepts patriarchal values. Spanish difference feminists reject political action for securing rights. Philosophically, difference feminists often draw on more-recent French and Italian feminists, such as Luce Irigaray, Carla Lonzi, and Luisa Muraro, who posit a feminine self, a women's mode of existence that differs from male being in the world. Interestingly, Spanish difference feminists, especially Milagros Rivera, have discovered an ally in the work of exiled Republican philosopher María Zambrano. While Zambrano's articles on women published in 1928 in the left-leaning *El liberal* and her early long essay *Horizonte del liberalismo* (1930) could make her a source for equality feminists, her 1934 "Hacia un saber sobre el alma" [Towards a knowledge of the soul] and much of her writing in exile point toward her move to the interior realm, the "soul," which coincides with difference feminism's notion of "partir de sí" [departing from oneself].

However, the difference/equality split in Spanish feminist theory has historical roots that antedate the recent democratic era by several centuries. As I noted in the introduction to this book, Mary Nash argues that the history of Spanish feminist thought is best understood within a difference rather than an equality framework, especially given that Spanish feminism did not receive its initial impetus from a desire to achieve the vote. According to Nash, as a whole, early Spanish feminism subscribed to a proto-difference feminist position. She argues that Spanish feminism arose in the nineteenth century from the cult of difference and that "el claro predominio del discurso de la domesticidad en la configuración de los valores y modelos de feminidad en la sociedad española contemporánea" ("Experiencia" 160) [the clear predominance of the discourse of domesticity in the configuration of value and models of femininity in contemporary Spanish society] was central to Spanish women's lack of interest in achieving political parity with men (for example, as I noted earlier, there was no Spanish suffrage movement). This omission allows Nash to maintain that "[n]i siquiera el proceso de Modernización económica, cultural y política en las primeras décadas del siglo XX que conllevó una reformulación modernizadora de un nuevo prototipo femenino—la 'Mujer Nueva' o 'Mujer Moderna'—cambió el eje constitutivo del discurso tradicional de la domesticidad ya que la maternidad seguía representando la base esencial de la identidad cultural femenina" (162) [not even the process of economic, cultural, and political modernization in the first decades of the twentieth century that brought with it a modernizing reformulation of a new female prototype—the "New Woman" or the "Modern Woman"—changed the constitutive axis of the traditional discourse of domesticity since maternity continued to represent the essential base of female cultural identity].

However, Nash believes that difference feminism opened a space for feminism in a conservative, Catholic country, which eventually led to a discussion of women's equal rights: "el discurso de la domesticidad amparó en términos políticos la noción de una ciudadanía diferenciada por género, es decir, una ciudadanía política para los varones y una ciudadanía social para las mujeres" (163) [the discourse of domesticity in political matters supported the notion of a citizenship differentiated by gender; that is to say, a political citizenry for males and a social citizenry for females]. Thus, Nash observes that nineteenth-century Spanish feminists such as Concepción Arenal and Emilia Pardo Bazán argued for equal education but not for equal political rights.

Mónica Bolufer likewise believes that early Spanish feminism is of a difference orientation. She notes that in the second half of the eighteenth century, as in the rest of Europe,

> the most common tendency was the configuration of a model of difference, which presented men and women as essentially different and irreducible, claiming that among them there was no hierarchy but rather a natural complementarity. It was argued that men inclined towards action, abstract reflection, and exterior activity, while women tended towards interior life, the world of emotion, and the family, which in the eighteenth century was being redefined in more intimate and sentimental terms. This representation of social organization between the sexes attributed to men and women moral, intellectual, and physical qualities that corresponded with different functions and spaces assigned to each sex. Key to the representation of difference was the emerging culture of sensibility, particularly in sentimental literature and in popular medicine. ("New Inflections" 43)

Early Spanish feminist thinkers such as Benito Jerónimo Feijoo and Concepción Arenal found it difficult to remain on an exclusively equality track. For example, after pointing out many advantages that women have over men, Feijoo asserts that it is not his purpose to "persuadir la ventaja, sino la igualdad" (331) [to persuade his audience of women's superiority over men, but rather their equality with men]. By the time of the 1812 Constitution, the gains women had made toward equality in the eighteenth century, at least in thinking if not in fact, were reversed when liberal ideas began to take root in Spain. The 1812 Constitution does not even mention women in the liberal nation; it was taken for granted that women were not included. There was no marriage law in Spain until 1870, except for that of the Church. Adultery laws under the liberal regime (1820–1830) were particularly backward, reflecting a Golden Age honor code. (These would continue in place well into the twentieth century, as Carmen de Burgos's novelettes and *La mujer moderna y sus derechos* attest.) Education for girls also languished in the first half of the nineteenth century until the Ley Moyano of 1857 stipulated that girls should receive an education, although it dictated a curriculum designed to prepare them to be primary-school teachers. As Jo Labanyi observes of the Krausists, "Although the Institución Libre's prospectus stated that girls should be educated 'con' and 'como' their male counterparts practically all Krausists (the Institución's founder, Giner, among them) insisted that women were complementary to men (that is, equal but different) and should thus receive a specially tailored education" (83).

Concepción Arenal likewise argues for equality within difference. In *La mujer del porvenir* she asserts that women are morally superior to men because they are less impulsive, more compassionate, and more patient. Women's passions, she asserts, are less aggressive and their instincts less strong; thus women are less likely to commit crimes. In addition, women are more religious than men, and they are particularly suited for art and theater. Arenal ultimately tips more toward difference feminism by emphasizing areas in which women are different from men: "Es moralmente superior aquel que siente menos impulsos malos o los enfrene con mayor energía, aquel que haga más bien y menos mal a sus semejantes. Bondad, sensibilidad, compasión, paciencia" (*La mujer del porvenir* 67) [The one who feels fewer bad impulses or who restrains them with greater energy is morally superior; the one who does more good and less bad to his/her cohorts. Goodness, sensitivity, compassion, patience].

By 1881, however, when Arenal wrote *La mujer de su casa*, her position emboldened, and she argued fervently for women's role outside the home, albeit on different terms from those exercised by men (Arenal emphasizes women's social role as charity workers). However, based on new observations, she now retracts her earlier assertion in *La mujer del porvenir* that women are equal in intelligence to men: "Debemos declarar que hoy no abrigamos aquel íntimo convencimiento de la igualdad de inteligencia de los dos sexos, manifestado en *La mujer del porvenir*. Nuevos hechos observados y una reflexión más detenida nos han inspirado dudas que sinceramente exponemos: la infalibilidad no es cosa que razonablemente nadie deba conceder a otro ni reclamar para sí" (269) [We must now declare that today we no longer harbor that intimate conviction manifested in *La mujer del porvenir* that the sexes are equal in intelligence. New observed phenomena and a more studied reflection have inspired doubts that we sincerely reveal: infallibility is nothing that anyone can reasonably bestow on another or claim for him or herself].

Arenal now wonders if there is not a difference in the intelligence of the two sexes analogous to the more obvious differences in their physical being. Are women more spontaneous and less reflective than men? Are women less observant and more intuitive? Are women's actions of greater extension and less intensity? Are women more persevering? Are they more receptive and less creative? And finally do they have an intelligence that is comparable to men's but not equal to men's? Arenal only asks these questions, but does not answer them. She believes that there is not enough evidence to make a determination, and she refers the reader to Elizabeth Cady Stanton, Susan B. Anthony, and Matilde Joslyn Gage's *History of Woman Suffrage* for the wealth of information it contains for combating conventional errors about women's inferior condition. Her conclusion is ambiguous about women's intellectual equality to men: "Que, llegue hasta donde llegue la inteligencia de la mujer, debe procurarse que vaya hasta donde puede llegar; porque si el hombre se perfeccione cultivándola, ella no puede menos de estar sujeta a la misma ley. . . . Que las dudas respecto a la igualdad de la inteligencia de la mujer no se refieren a su aptitud para los conocimientos conunes y su aplicación" (277) [Whatever women's intelligence may achieve, it should always try to achieve as much as it can; because if men can perfect their intelligence by cultivating it, women must be subject to the same law. . . . The doubts about the equality of women's intelligence do not refer to their aptitude for common knowledge and its application].

Rosario de Acuña (1850–1923), whose flamboyant style is echoed in that of democratic-era difference feminist Victoria Sendón de León, starts from the premise that the two sexes are equal at birth. Rather than working through an argument, Acuña takes this truth to be self-evident. In an article from 1881, she avers that

> Entremos de lleno en la cuestión y, puesto que de igualdades se trata y unos quieren propinárnosla con relación al bruto y otros la subliman hasta la naturaleza del ángel, juro y perjuro, sin que en esto haya ofensa para ninguna de las dos escuelas, que tan iguales nos hicieron nuestros padres Adán y Eva, si es que existieron tan inéditos personajes, como iguales venimos siendo a través de los siglos y a pesar de sus variables alternativas. Pues, repartido por igualdad de partes entre la raza del hombre el imperio de la naturaleza, lo que a ellos les sobró de brutalidad, nos lo pusieron de astucia y, lo que a nosotras se nos dio de más en ternura, lo poseen ellos de fuerza. (166)

[Let's go right to the heart of the matter, and since we are dealing with equality, some readers might prefer me to tell it in a raw style, while others would prefer me to make it sublime like an angel. I swear and foreswear without there being any offense on the part of either of these schools of thought, which made our parents Adam and Eve, if indeed these two extraordinary personages existed, as equals across the centuries in spite of the alternative variables. Well, distributed by equality of parts between the human race and the natural realm; if men have a surfeit of brutality, we have an overabundance of sagacity, and if we are super-endowed with tenderness, men possess an excess of force.]

She rehearses some of the earlier arguments about how brain size is not important, but rather what matters is the exercise that one gives it, before entering into a rather novel argument that, like Amelia Valcárcel some one hundred years later, employs irony and hyperbole. She argues that women are equal to men and have equal influence in public matters through pillow talk. Men, who are judges, doctors, and are active in other professions, often consult their wives. The wives have learned the ins and outs of these professions in the company of their husbands.

That equality, however, according to Acuña, is cemented in difference:

> A pesar de que las leyes de la naturaleza se rigen por principios fijos y, por tanto, lo inmutable es su esencial condición; a pesar de que nunca podrán alterarse las diferencias que distinguen sin inferioridad por ninguna de ambas partes nuestros opuestos sexos, pudiera muy bien venir un lamentable periodo revolucionario que nos sumiese por largo espacio de tiempo en las más funestas consecuencias. ¡Alerta, mujeres! Nuestros emancipadores quieren para nosotras la libertad de medios, pero no os olvidéis que con ella perdemos la libertad de acción, mil veces mejor que el falso oropel de los aparentes poderes. (175)

[In spite of the fact that the laws of nature are governed by fixed principles and therefore essentially unchangeable, in spite of the fact that the differences without inferiority on the part of either one of our two sexes can be altered, a lamentable revolutionary period might arrive that could submerge us for a long time in the most unfortunate consequences. Women, wake up! Our emancipators want us to be partially liberated, but do not forget that with it we lose liberty of action; which is a thousand times better than the false flowery speech of apparent powers.]

For Acuña, some characteristics are innate (a kind of biological determinism). She hypothesizes an inborn tenderness that fills the vast empty spaces of men's brains. She admonishes her "sisters" to flee emancipation, because it would undermine the real power they exercise in their present position:

> He aquí el único ideal posible del porvenir, que nunca se llamará emancipación porque . . . solamente al esclavo se le puede manumitir, y nosotras nunca lo fuimos. El que otra cosa os haga ambicionar, os lanzará de lleno en el país de las quimeras, vestidas con el burlesco traje del ridículo, a la par que aquellos que intentan arrojarnos del pedestal donde nos colocó la naturaleza, no consiguen más que anudarse con dobles vueltas el dogal de las astucias femeninas. (179)

> [Here is the only possible future ideal, that can never be called emancipation because . . . only the slave can be freed, and we were never slaves. If you wish anything else, you will be thrown headfirst into the country of pipe dreams, dressed in the silly costume of ridicule, just as those that attempt to knock us off the pedestal where nature has placed us achieve nothing more than tying themselves up with double knots of feminine wiliness.]

As María Zambrano will argue in the 1940s, Rosario de Acuña believes that woman is passion, especially love: "La luz de sus pasiones, bastardeadas por el matiz de ilegítimas que las imprime la ley, será la que caiga en el celebro femenino, en lluvia de frases elegidas para llevar sensaciones a las alturas fantásticas" (*Antología* 99) [The light of her passions, bastardized by the taint of illegitimacy that the law places on them, is what falls on the female brain]. And in an 1885 article she argues that woman's role is to live for others (vol. 2, "Vivir por los demás," 1031–35).

In an 1888 speech at the Fomento de Artes, Acuña reiterated the differences between the sexes ("Entre los sexos de nuestra raza existe la diferencia; repito que es imposible negarla, al menos en el estado adulto" [522] [It is impossible to doubt that there exists a difference between the sexes of our race]). She points especially to the division between intellect attributed to men and feeling being women's province, although her goal was to unite these two qualities in both men and women: "igualad sus cerebros; rebajad la fatuidad del hombre; elevad la dignidad de la mujer; enseñadlos a pensar en la misma escala, a sentir en el mismo tono; educad al varón para que sea justo con la mujer, no galante. . . . Que la mujer tenga conciencia de sí misma; hacedla inteligente. Para que tenga inteligencia desarrollad su organismo con elementos iguales que aquellos que rigen la educación del hombre" (530–31) [equalize their brains; reduce men's fatuity; raise up women's dignity; teach them to think on the same scale, to feel to the same degree; educate the male to be just with women, not gallant. . . . The woman should be conscious of herself; make herself intelligent. In order for her to be intelligent, she should develop her organism with elements equal to those that govern men's education]. Her new vision is the union of men and women in a kind of apotheosis that combines vague religious iconography with a Krausist ring of earthly perfection: "la grandeza de ese ideal sublime que surge en los orientes del porvenir, levantando sobre apoteosis gloriosa al hombre y a la mujer, unidos por eterno abrazo de sus inteligencias y de sus corazones, para un solo fin de ventura humana" (533) [the greatness of this sublime ideal that arises in the east of the future, rising above the glorious apotheosis to men and to women, united in an eternal embrace of their intellects and their hearts for one sole purpose in the human enterprise]. And in a speech in 1888 delivered at the inauguration of a new women's Masonic lodge (Hijas del Progreso), she talks of *"la mujer por la mujer,* la mujer engrandecida, ilustrada, dignificada por la mujer, la mujer . . . probando sus fuerzas como ser pensante, manifestando sus condiciones como ser racional en su radio de acción pura y genuinamente femenino" (163, her italics) [*the woman for the woman,* the exhalted, enlightened, dignified woman for women, the woman proving her abilities as a thinking being, revealing her condition as a rational being in her radius of pure and genuinely feminine action].

Concepción Gimeno de Flaquer, proponent of what she calls "feminismo moderado" [moderate feminism], is likewise difficult to classify within either difference or equality feminism. In "El problema feminista" [The feminist problem], she first argues for equality: "Anhelan los feministas que el matrimonio sea la asociación de dos seres conscientes, libres e iguales; exigen la misma ley moral, civil y económica para los dos sexos, alcanzando con el triunfo de sus ideas que la mujer deje de ser moralmente menor, civilmente exclava" (*Antología* 105) [Feminists want marriage to be an association of two conscious, free, and equal beings; they demand the same moral, civil, and economic law for the two sexes, achieving with the triumph of the ideas women's emancipation from being a moral minor and civil slave]. Employing arguments that we have seen in previous feminist thinkers, Gimeno de Flaquer points out that if women are indeed inferior, as some would have it, they should not be judged as equal when punished for crimes. However, she ends her 1903 speech affirming women's difference and suggesting that women can prevail over men by employing their femininity. Why, she asks, would women want to enter a corrupt political system for which they would be blamed, if they were to participate in it through the vote? She summarizes the aims of moderate feminism as avoiding

> todo obstáculo a las manifestaciones de las facultades intelectuales de la mujer; educar esas facultades para que puedan utilizarse, teniendo en cuenta que las mentales, como las musculares, atrófianse si no se ejercitan; darle trabajo bien remunerado que la defienda de la inmoralidad, concederle la libre disposición del capital, proporcionarle empleos en Bancos, Museos, Biblioteas y Administración de Sociedades benéficas, mejorar la suerte de la obrera, suprimir la trata de blancas, dejarle ejercer profesiones literarias, artísticas y científicas, especialmente la medicina, para la que posee grandes facultades, superando al hombre en ginecología y en el tratamiento de las enfermedades de la infancia. (*Antología* 108)

[any obstacle to women's exercising their intellectual faculties, educating these faculties so that they can be used, keeping in mind the mental as well as the muscular; they atrophy if they are not exercised; to give them well remunerated work that defends them against immorality, concede them free use of capital, give them work in banks, museums, libraries, and administrative posts in charitable societies, better the working woman's lot, eliminate prostitution, allow them to exercise literary, artistic, and scientific professions, especially medicine, for those that have the ability, far better than men in gynecology and the treatment of childhood diseases.]

Notably the professions for which she believes women are especially suited have to do with women's anatomy and caring for children.

The early twentieth century saw other Spanish feminist thinkers rely on difference feminist arguments to increase the acceptance of their ever-more-daring ideas about women's place in the world. In the 1920s, María Martínez Sierra argued that feminism did not have to exclude femininity. In *Cartas a las mujeres de España* she defines a feminist as someone who is "partidaria de que la mujer debe pasar su vida lo más feliz posible, haciendo la mayor suma de bien posible, siendo lo más útil posible a la humanidad, gozando con tan perfecta naturalidad como el hombre la plenitud de sus derechos de ser humano, basta haber nacido "ser humano," y por añadidura, mujer" (14) [in favor or women's having the happiest possible life, doing the greatest possible good, being as useful as possible to humanity, enjoying with perfect naturalness, just like men, the fullness of her rights as a human being; it is enough to have been born a "human being," and also a woman]. Martínez Sierra seems to connect directly with the eighteenth century when she argues in her chapter "Algunas consideraciones acerca de la felicidad" [Some thoughts on happiness] that the human mission on earth is to be happy (see Elizabeth Franklin Lewis on the notion of happiness in the eighteenth century). She adds happiness to the Krausist prescription for perfection: "La felicidad es un deber tan absoluto como la perfección" (*Antología* 171) [Happiness is as absolute a duty as perfection]. And she notes that we cannot just sit back and wait for happiness to come to us; we have to work for it. As if she had insights into contemporary neuroscience that facial expressions can influence feelings (e.g., a smile can produce a sensation of happiness), Martínez Sierra avers that "acerquémonos al espejo y sonríamos a nuestra propia imagen. La imagen nos devolverá la sonrisa y nos obligará a sonreír de nuevo. . . . Sonríamos, pues, para que la vida nos sonría" (*Antología* 172) [let's go up to the mirror and smile at our own image. The image will return our smile and will oblige us to smile again. . . . Let's smile so that life will smile back at us]. The ideal of womanhood that Martínez Sierra depicts in the essays in her book are of the saintly martyr who suppresses any feeling of resentment or bitterness for her lot—confined to the home, putting up with crying children.

In a line of argument that is reminiscent of Father Feijoo and Concepción Arenal, among other earlier Spanish feminists, and appealing to women's sense of self, in "Poder de la belleza y deberes que impone" [The power of beauty and the duties it imposes], Martínez Sierra, avers that women are free and enjoy all the qualities associated with men—force, knowledge—but they possess an additional weapon, which is beauty. Women, she avers, have the same strength, knowledge, fortitude, language, and power as men, and she lists women's distinct qualities, including *bondad* [goodness], and then adds beauty to the equation. As Carmen de Burgos will do in her 1927 book *La mujer moderna y sus derechos*, Martínez Sierra addresses the topic of dress. For Burgos, dress is liberating (see my article "Fashion as Feminism"), but Martínez Sierra's passage on dress takes on a moral tone. She admonishes women to dress in a prudent manner that will not incite men's appetite, which they will then have to satisfy in an illicit manner. She advises women to use charity rather than bustline to capture men's hearts: "Y todas estas almas consoladas, confortadas, amparadas por ustedes, serán su imperio, y para conquistarlas no habrá sólo menester pintarse los ojos ni agrandar el escote, siguiendo el último insensato figurín de París" (*Antología* 180) [And all these consoled souls that are comforted and supported by you women will be your empire, and in order to conquer them you will not need to make up your eyes or lower your neckline, in the latest ridiculous Paris model].

Martínez Sierra also addresses the perennial Spanish feminist topic of women's education, referring to the "felicidad de la humanidad" [happiness of humanity] as a reason for women to be educated. Employing arguments that we have seen in eighteenth- and nineteenth-century Spanish feminist thinkers about women's role as educators of future generations, Martínez Sierra adds that this is divine work: "Somos obreros de una labor divina, colaaboradores con Dios en una de sus obras maestras, soñadores con Él en su divino sueño de perfección" (*Antología* 182) [We are workers in a divine labor, collaborators with God in one of his masterpieces, dreamers with Him in his divine dream of perfection]. Like Concepción Arenal's arguments, Martínez Sierra's are clearly infused with Krausist notions of human perfection. She especially recommends that women, the fountain of life, study the natural sciences, and urges them to study nature, not from books, but through observation in their own gardens or balcony flowerpots: "Así, pues, ciencia en primer lugar: ciencia maestra de la vida: Fisiología, Botánica, Historia Natural, Física, Química, Geografía en todas sus ramas, y siempre en el terreno y sobre el terreno. Realidad, ante todo (*Antología* 183) [Physiology, botany, natural history, physics, geography in all its branches, and always in the earth and upon the earth. Reality above all]. She also recommends that women study history so that they can be a force for peace: "Aprenderéis a aborrecer el privilegio—aunque tal vez pertenezcáis a las clases privilegiadas—, a detestar la guerra, a desear apasionadamente la igualdad (que no es la identidad, y otro día hablaremos de eso) (*Antología* 186) [You will learn to abhor privilege—although perhaps you belong to the privileged classes—, to detest war, to yearn passionately for equality (which is not identity; we will talk about that another day)]. Even though Martínez Sierra mentions equality here, it is clear from her many other arguments that she considers women different from men in many respects and that they have different interests and different roles in life.

Other Silver Age feminist thinkers—Margarita Nelken, Clara Campoamor, Hildegart Rodríguez, and Carmen de Burgos—fall more into the equality camp than the difference orientation, although Carmen de Burgos often straddles the two positions. For example, Anja Louis in *Women and the Law: Carmen de Burgos, an Early Feminist*, explores "where, how and why the prevailing equality feminism resisted its own politics and slid into difference feminism" (19), and in "Carmen de Burgos: Modern Spanish Woman," Maryellen Bieder notes that in *La mujer moderna y sus derechos*, Burgos "openly identifies herself with feminism, understood as 'the cause of woman's liberation, in accord with her nature,' but in a way that still acknowledges gender difference" (255). Burgos's rational style of argument, her cool level-headedness, and her ability to go straight to the heart of the matter with incontrovertible evidence align her with the long, rational, equality feminist tradition that began in Spain with Benito Jerónimo Feijoo, informed as we now know, thanks to Mónica Bolufer, by seventeenth-century radical Enlightenment thinker François Poulain de la Barre. De la Barre has more recently inspired Celia Amorós's Enlightenment (or equality) feminists of the post-Franco democratic era. In the fourth chapter of *La mujer moderna y sus derechos*, Burgos mentions what Descartes's rationalism offers feminism: "Descartes no acepta por verdadero más que lo que muestra la razón, y al querer demoler prejuicios sirve la causa femenina" (111) [Descartes does not accept as true anything except what reason can demonstrate, and in attempting to erase prejudices he served the female cause]. Burgos pointed out long before 1980s equality feminism did that Descartes's disciple François Poulain de la Barre "pide en *Educación de las Damas* y en *Igualdad de sexos*, todos los derechos de la mujer" (111) [in *Women's Education and Equality of the Sexes* asks for all rights for women].

Although Burgos argues for legal parity ("La base está en las leyes, en la proclamación de la «Igualdad de derechos» "[*La mujer* 60] [The basis is in the laws, in the proclamation of the "Equality of rights"], as Anja Louis and Maryellen Bieder note, Burgos's arguments sometimes slip over into a difference feminist position when the point she is making seems to benefit from such a maneuver. For example, on the page following the above quotation in which Burgos calls for legal equality, she declares that feminism never meant "un deseo de inversión de sexos o de funciones, y mucho menos de aspiración a la igualdad, que hace imposible la naturaleza" (61) [a desire for the inversion of the sexes or their functions, and much less the aspiration to equality, which nature makes impossible]. However, here as elsewhere, Burgos seems to distinguish between biology and the law. In chapter 2 of *La mujer moderna*, for example, she undermines the biological arguments for inequality tendered by Gregorio Marañón, Otto Weininger, and Paul Julius Moebius.

As I mentioned above, Bieder and Louis also note that Burgos's feminist stance evolved over time, beginning closer to difference feminism and ending closer to equality feminism. Even in the last work, *La mujer moderna y sus derechos*, Burgos's position is subtle, complex, and ultimately pragmatic. She may have most in common with postfeminist Spanish thinkers such as Carmen Alborch (1937–; *Solas* [Women on their own], *Libres: Ciudadanas del mundo* [Free female citizens of the world]) and Lucía Extebarria (1966–) (*La Eva futura* [The future Eve]; *En brazos de la mujer fetiche* [In the arms of the fetish woman]), who try to supersede the narrow confines of both equality and difference feminism to defend women's right to be both feminine and feminist (it would seem that Spanish feminists are constantly reinventing the wheel). However, despite Burgos's often original and eclectic positions on some feminist issues, her style of argumentation places her firmly in the Enlightenment equality feminist camp; thus I continue the discussion of Burgos's feminist thought in chapter 6.

The Franco era, beginning in the 1940s and continuing until the mid-1970s, as a period of conservative ideas about womanhood, was a fertile ground for difference feminism. It is hard to know how María Lafitte's *La secreta guerra de los sexos* [The secret war of the sexes] published in 1948 passed censorship muster, but perhaps her recourse to the age-old Spanish feminist tradition of rebutting previous texts about women served her well, especially since a large part of her key chapter "¿Qué es lo femenino?" [What is the feminine?] contains many quotations from Fray Luis de León's *La perfecta casada* [The perfect wife]. Even though Lafitte refutes Fray Luis's misogyenistic claims about women, the many quotations from the sixteenth-century text give Fray Luis's ideas a certain weight. She clearly differentiates the sexes with contrasts such as

> La mujer—dicen—es un ser intuitivo, mientras el hombre es reflexivo. . . .
>
> El sexo femenino es el afectivo, mientras el masculino es el activo. . . .
>
> La mujer es subjetiva.
>
> El hombre es objetivo.
>
> La mujer es centrípeta, gira sobre sí misma, teniendo en ella su fin.
>
> El hombre se orienta al exterior, en busca de aventuras—ciencias, comercio, guerras, arte.
>
> (*Antología* 318)
>
> [Women—they say—are intuitive beings, while men are reflective. . . .
>
> The feminine sex is affective, while the masculine is active. . . .
>
> Women are subjective.
>
> Men are objective.
>
> Women are centripetal; they rotate around themselves; they are their own end.
>
> Men are oriented toward the exterior, looking for adventure—science, commerce, wars, art.]

The title of the book and of the eponymous chapter "La secreta guerra de los sexos" underscores the difference message of the book. The difference orientation, as well as the author's noble title (Countess of Campo Alange), may well have garnered favor with the censors. The chapter on the war between the sexes has recourse to the age-old technique in Spanish feminist treatises—the reliance on history as evidence. After delineating the triumph of patriarchy in classical times, Lafitte finds that the Middle Ages and Renaissance brought improvements in women's situation, although it is not until the nineteenth century, she argues, that one sees real progress in terms of women's ability to act. However, she believes this freedom was diluted by the fact that women are limited in their actions to mimicking men. Echoing terminology learned from Max Scheler and José Ortega y Gasset (whom Rosa Chacel and María Zambrano rebutted in the 1920s and 1930s, especially their notion of culture as a male domain), Lafitte points out that since the nineteenth century men have fought ferociously to maintain their dominion over culture. The fact that women were defeated in this battle relegated motherhood to an inferior status.

With her friend Lilí Álvarez, María Lafitte founded the Seminario de Estudios Sociológicos de la Mujer (SESM) [Seminar of Sociological Studies of Women]) in 1962 to conduct feminist research. The group published several books, which they signed collectively. Álvarez was an important figure in the European sports world before she turned to feminist activity and writing during the Franco era. As the illegitimate daughter of a wealthy man, Álvarez lived her early life in the great cities of Europe and Latin America. She gained a name for herself as a skater, skier, and finalist in three Wimbledon tennis matches. She won a driving championship in Catalonia, and in 1924 she was the first Spanish woman to participate in the Olympics. Her writing career began with sports chronicles, and in Francoist Spain she turned to writing about spiritual matters. Her book *Plenitud* (1947) combines spiritualism and feminism in some of its chapters.

In "Feminismo y masculinismo" Álvarez points out that feminism and masculinism are two sides of the same coin, even though she says little about masculinism and much about feminism. Álvarez argues that we cannot understand feminism without the concept of masculinism, because "el feminismo de las mujeres no es más que la reacción tardía y consciente al masculinismo previo, peestablecido y, por eso mismo, inconsciente y potentísimo de los hombres" (*Antología* 339) [women's feminism is nothing more than the belated and conscious reaction to a prior, pre-established, and for that reason unconscious, and very powerful masculinism, on the part of men]. She also points out that women's feminism is a conscious effort, while men are not conscious of their masculinism. For Álvarez, a distinguishing feature of feminism is consciousness; while she believes that masculinism is characterized by its unconscious nature: "el masculinismo reside en la inconciencia" (340) [masculinism resides in the subconscious]. She concludes that the remedy to this situation is for men to become conscious of their masculinism. Also writing shortly before the end of the Franco era, Maria Aurèlia Capmany points out that women had been convinced by lawyers, doctors, psychiatrists, and dressmakers that they were different, thus they gave up their fight for equality: "la habían convencido de que en este su modo de ser diferente se hallaban su felicidad y su gloria" (34) [they had convinced her that her happiness and glory were located in her way of being different]. This argument found its way into the Spanish difference feminist theorists of the 1980s and 1990s.

The history of the Spanish feminist movement since the late Franco years until the mid-1990s has been well documented. Most subsequent accounts refer to María Ángeles Durán and María Teresa Gallego's now-classic chronology, which divides the movement into three phases: (1) from 1975 to 1979, when the feminist movement was created, expanded, and organized; (2) from 1979 to 1982, when "the movement was divided by strong internal disputes and divisions" (207), and (3) from 1982 to 1985, when the organized movement fragmented into "many micro-organizations all over the country" and institutions accepted "the feminist question" (207).[1] Although Durán and Gallego, like leading equality feminist Celia Amorós ("Algunos") and others, locate the open hostility between equality and difference feminists at the general meeting of the Spanish feminist movement held in Granada in May 1979, Anny Brooksbank Jones believes the schism was already evident by the time the constitution was voted on in 1978.[2] According to Brooksbank Jones, the constitutional vote itself was an occasion for differences of opinion to assert themselves:

> Radical feminists who saw party politics as irredeemably patriarchal tended to reject the [Constitution] as "machista," while most dual activists gave it qualified support. As the detailed and painstaking incorporation of constitutional principles

into law got under way, however, earlier levels of concerted activism and mobilization proved impossible to sustain. Outside of the parties too the promised coexistence began to look increasingly unrealistic, as the loss of focus encouraged the proliferation of single activist groups and a corresponding dispersal of energies. (10)

Brooksbank Jones notes, however, that at the Granada Jornadas Feministas in 1979, "the familiar distinction between single and dual activism [was] redrawn around the axes of equality and difference" (Brooksbank Jones 11). According to Durán and Gallego, at the Granada Conference Spanish feminists had not yet theorized the concepts of equality and difference as they would in the 1980s and 1990s:

> [T]here was never any attempt to arrive at a real theoretical analysis of either of these two concepts. Broadly speaking, the idea of equality was adopted by the section of double militancy that advocated the formation of a political platform demanding women's rights and liberties for women and eliminating all the barriers encountered by women. The women who advocated "difference" feminism were involved with the radical groups [those not allied with political parties who wanted to make feminist concerns a first priority beyond more general party platforms]. (213)

Because democratic-era Spanish feminism had its beginnings during the late Franco regime when many feminists were double militants who belonged to either the underground Communist or Socialist Party, feminism in early democratic Spain worked mainly through party antidictatorial, prodemocratic (or sociodemocratic) activism.[3] Thus, Spanish feminist theory of the post-Franco era continued to be informed by political ideology, although as Brooksbank Jones, following Monica Threlfall, observes, "Spanish feminists seeking political legitimacy were hampered by the absence of a strong feminist tradition, the lack of a democratic culture sympathetic to the idea of equal rights, and the disinclination of many progressive women to return to sex-segregated activities after the years of Catholic-run, single-sex schooling" (Brooksbank Jones 7).[4] The stridency of the debate and the sui generis nature of the divide between Spanish difference and equality feminists, unique among Western feminisms, can only be understood in the context of Spanish women's having to overcome forty years of institutionalized proscriptions for women under the Franco regime and its virulent repression of the Republican era's advances toward women's legal equality. The postdictatorship Spanish feminist movement's beginnings in the underground leftist resistance to the Franco regime have made an indelible mark on both equality and difference feminism. Significantly, the venue for airing the debate at several key points was the leftist journal *El Viejo Topo* [The old mole], first with a special section titled "Masculino/Femenino" in 1980, just as the recently legitimized Partido Socialista Obrero Español (PSOE) was ascending in the political landscape (leading to its victory in the 1982 elections), and again in the mid-1990s when corruption scandals ended socialist political hegemony.

Difference feminist ideas had circulated in Spain in the 1970s,[5] and a difference feminist group (LA MAR) existed briefly in 1977–1978. As I indicated earlier, difference feminists reject institutionalized politics. Mercedes de Grado notes that "[e]l ideario feminista de la diferencia originó una réplica en las filas de las militantes de corte socialista, que evolucionan en sus posiciones y empiezan a abogar por un feminismo de la igualdad que contrarreste la reinvindicación de la diferencia. Sin embargo, estos dos tipos de feminismo van perdiendo progresivamente contacto con el feminismo como movimiento de masa" (30) [difference feminist ideology initiated a replica in the socialist militant ranks whose positions evolved and began to argue for an equality feminism that undermined the difference orientation. However, these two types of feminism were progressively losing contact with feminism as a mass movement].

Victoria Sendón de León's *Sobre diosas, amazonas y vestales. Utopías para un feminismo radical* [On goddesses, Amazons, and vestal virgins: Utopias for a radical feminism], published in 1981, is characterized by the utopian nature of much difference feminist thinking. Sendón de León's book signals a break from the more temperate discussion of difference and equality that had taken place to date in Spain. Sendón de León lashes out at rational logic, one of the main tools of equality feminism. The basis of her argument is to pit reason against myth: "Se trataría de concebir la representación como estrategia política, pero no una política restrictiva de cambio de estructuras, sino una auténtica política creadora de nuevas percepciones, mitos y ritos que respalden afectivamente al mundo de la lógica y de la acción. Lo demás son reformismos ya caducos" (206) [It is a matter of conceiving representation as a political strategy—not a restrictive politics of structural change, but rather an authentic politics that creates new perceptions, myths, and rituals that affectively support the world of logic and action. The rest are worn-out reforms]. And taking on the Enlightenment directly, she avers that

> No sé si se trata de un juicio heredado del siglo de las luces, pero cuando se habla de liberación, de libertad en general, se presupone que indefectiblemente va unida a una fuerte carga de racionalización, a un triunfo de la lógica con la consiguiente destrucción de mitos y religiones. Creo que se trata de un esfuerzo inútil además de perjudicial. Inútil porque convivimos con los mitos al igual que convivimos con nuestros sueños o nuestro inconsciente. Cuando se desmitifica se hace en aras del mito de la ciencia como saber supremo; cuando se seculariza se cambian mitos de primera clase por mitos de segunda. La teoría marxista pudo llegar a ser inspiradora de una revolución por los mitos que albergaba y no por su carácter de ciencia. El mito del proletariado como clase salvadora o el mito de la futura sociedad comunista como parusia final. (206)

[I don't know if it is an idea inherited from the Enlightenment, but when we speak about liberation, liberty in general, we suppose that it is definitively tied to a strong dose of rationality, a triumph of logic with its subsequent destruction of myths and religions. I believe that it is a useless and damaging effort. Useless because we live with myths just as we live with our dreams and our unconscious. When we demythologize we undo the myth of science as supreme knowledge; when we secularize we exchange first-class myths for second-class myths. Marxist theory could inspire a revolution because of its myths and not for its scientific aspect. The myth of the proletariat as a saving class or the myth of the future communist society as a final stage].

Sendón de León rails relentlessly against reason as a motivating force for feminist thinking, and claims to follow Deleuze and Guattari in their rhyzomic mode of exposition. However, she follows a pattern of argumentation that we have seen in Spanish feminist theory from its beginnings in Father Feijoo—debunking established ideas in order to replace them with new, supposedly more valid ones. Her first chapter addresses "Las vacas sagradas" [The sacred cows]—Freud and Marx. In epistolary style, she first addresses Freud, criticizing his completely overlooking the individual, and then "don Carlos," who inspired a double militancy (socialism and feminism), in short "hechas un lío" (51) [tangled in a web]. Structuralism is no better—a mere "plato de lentejas" (74) [dish of lentils]. What can we expect, she asks, of a mode of thought that accepts, or only slightly revises Marxism and Freudism, the two large thought systems of our time? Both the right and the left are means for converting individuals into undifferentiated masses. We need a new way of thinking, and her answer is ritual; a new way of thinking would produce a new way of living: "Los mitos nos ponen en comunicación directa con el inconsciente colectivo, una memoria de la especie que aún ignoramos hasta qué punto siguen moviendo los hilos de la historia" (85) [The myths put us in direct contact with the collective unconscious, a memory of the species that we still do not know to what point they continue to move the forces of history]. She looks to notions such as discontinuity and ambiguity, which she associates with non-Western cultures for an antidote to structuralism. Instead of parallelism, antagonism, taxonomies, past, future, she poses pure present, form, gesture, play, challenge, and surprise. She believes that modern thought has lost sight of the benefits of ritual to humanity, precisely because of its focus on work and its only alternative—free time, "que tiene todo menos de libre, y de tiempo nada excepto la matemática del reloj" (211) [that has everything except freedom and of time nothing except the mathematics of a clock].

Sendón de León also briefly develops a theory of time, which shows knowledge of Gaston Bachelard's ideas on the subject. The instant is the only meaningful temporal unit, and in a quotation of Roupnel, she affirms that "'La idea que tenemos del presente es de una plenitud y de una evidencia positiva singulares. Allí nos instalamos con nuestra personalidad completa, y encontramos una identidad absoluta entre el sentimiento del presente y el sentimiento de la vida'" (93) [The idea that we have of the present is one of plenitude and of singular positive evidence. There we install our full personality, and we find an absolute identity between the sense of the present and the sense of life]. Many of these ideas echo ideas we have seen in María Zambrano, and thus it should not be surprising that Zambrano's thought was profoundly influential in some Spanish difference feminists such as Milagros Rivera and Italian difference feminists such as Luisa Muraro. However, I have not been able to find any references to Zambrano in Sendón de León. It is likely that the similarities derive from common sources such as phenomenology (the Heidegger that inspired poststructuralists and Scheler on whom Zambrano drew in her early work). Heidegger could have been an inspiration to both in their elaboration of their ideas on time. José Ortega y Gasset is also present in statements about the centrality of one's circumstances to being: "el ser humano no puede pensar, ni crear, ni siquiera vivir más allá de sus propias circunstancias y entre sus circunstancias también están las económicas, las de clase" (95) [the human being cannot think, create, or even live beyond his/her own circumstances and also among his/her circumstances are the economic ones, those of class]. And just as Zambrano did in the 1940s after sustained contact with Sartrean existentialism, Sendón de León absorbs some of Sartre's ideas into her concept of women's being in the world.

Sendón wants to start from zero, not from the radical interior of existentialism or from the radical exterior of Marxism, both originating in patriarchy. To a certain extent she adopts a standpoint philosophy: "Mi tesis es que este 'dónde estamos' como mujeres no podemos seguir interpretándolo desde esquemas que han servido para la comprensión y transformación del mundo enraizadas en el sustrato de una civilización patriarcal" (100) [My thesis is that we cannot continue to interpret this "where we are" as women as schemes that have served the understanding and transformation of the world rooted in the substratum of patriarchal civilization]. She asserts that women are the "missing link" in any revolutionary practice and that one cannot think in terms of Marxist structure and superstructure, whose hierarchy she does not accept. Instead, we must first consider the struggle between the sexes, between master and slave. Women are alienated because they live in a masculine-dominated world. For this world to be hers, she has to transform it completely, first theory ("pensamiento-estructura" [thought-structure], followed by "situación-estructura" [situation-structure], and finally "individuo-sociedad" (103) [individual-society]. Her most important affirmation is perhaps that sex takes precedence over social class in any reconsideration of social structure, because one does not belong to a sex as one belongs to a social class; one has or is a sex. As I noted in chapter 3, she soundly rejects Lidia Falcón's notion of women as a social class: "No es el lugar de la mujer en la producción lo que la incluye en una misma clase, ¡Sólo nos faltaba ser clase! ¡qué ordinariez! Es la pluralidad de sus marcas enraizadas en la ausencia y la diferencia las que la hacen precisamente inclasificable, pura posibilidad" (119) [It is not women's place in production that places her in the same class. We hardly need to be a class! How vulgar! It is precisely the plurality of her markers rooted in absence and difference that make her unclassifiable—pure possibility].

Sendón considers equality a myth, a phantom: "Quiero la diferencia. Me repugna profundamente la igualdad" (113) [I want difference. I find equality profoundly repugnant]. She denies that equality is the basis of freedom. Equality is not the end-all and be-all of humanity; it is sex: "Ser mujer o varón constituye la marca que instaura todo un código de comportamiento, sentimientos, posibilidades, formas, leyes, tiempos, espacios, hábitos y frustraciones" (115) [To be a woman or man constitutes the frame that underlies an entire code of conduct, feelings, possibilities, forms, laws, times, spaces, customs and frustrations]. She completely rejects any attempt to incorporate women into patriarchal society. Women are a mystery and an object of fear for men because they are different, and thus men have created institutions that repress that which they fear. Sendón summarizes feminism as "la fisura entre la fantasía del hombre y la realidad de mujer" (152) [the fissure between male fantasy and female reality]. She points out that empirical psychoanalysis tries to determine the *complex* designation that in and of itself indicates the polyvalence of all the connected meanings, while existential psychoanalysis tries to determine the originary election. This election, operating in front of the world and being the election of a position in the world, is totalizing, as is the complex. Since the complex precedes logic, it *elects* the attitude of the person with respect to logic and principles; it is not a matter of interrogating it with respect to logic. This election collects in a prelogical synthesis the totality of what exists and as such is the center of reference for an infinity of polyvalent significations.

Further on, Sendón de León throws the notion of equality on the trash heap with provocative, vitriolic language: "Nos ronda el fantasma de un mito o el mito de un fantasma: la igualdad [. . .] ¿Iguales en qué? [. . .] Quiero la diferencia. *Me repugna profundamente la igualdad*. [. . .] ¿A qué igualdad se refiere? [. . .] No me vale esa falacia de que la igualdad es requisito para la libertad. La libertad no crece en putrefactas aguas pantanosas" (*Sobre diosas* 112–14, qtd. in de Grado 430; emphasis is de Grados's) [A phantom of a myth hovers over us—equality . . . Equal to what? . . . I want difference. *I am profoundly repelled by equality* . . . To what equality are they referring? . . . The fallacy that equality is a requirement for liberty does not convince me. Liberty does not grow in fetid, dank waters].

As foretold in Sendón's comment, in the mid-1990s the debate between equality and difference feminism grew bitter. Perhaps the stakes were higher now that the socialist government was discredited, and legal reforms and institutions such as the Instituto de la Mujer were threatened in the wake of socialism's crumbling hegemony. Difference feminists became more disillusioned over the discrepancy between the theory of gender equality and the reality of women's lives in the day-to-day world. They also mourned a perceived loss of "feminine" qualities in Spanish life—willingness to act as caregivers, the cult of motherhood, and emphasis on home and family life. In the uncertain political climate, difference feminists probably felt more emboldened in their rejection of traditional political engagement. *El Viejo Topo* published a special issue on feminism in 1994 that reveals the deepening divide between equality and difference feminists as they increasingly defined their positions in terms of philosophical alliances. Unlike in the 1980 issue of the same journal on femininity and masculinity, now both sides of the schism were equally represented.

In her essay "Partir de sí" for the special issue of *El Viejo Topo*, Milagros Rivera prefers the expression "práctica política de la diferencia" [political practice of difference] to "feminismo de la diferencia" [difference feminism]. According to Rivera, such "practice" does not demand rights, quotas, or power within the patriarchal order; nor does it measure itself against patriarchal values ("Partir" 31); therefore the opposite of equality feminism is "desigualdad, no diferencia" ("Partir" 31) [inequality, not difference]. Rivera exhorts feminists to think the unthinkable and say the unsayable, "mirar el mundo entero y decirlo con palabras nacidas de una política que no cancele el cuerpo femenino" (31–32) [look at the whole world and say it with words born of a politics that does not cancel out the female body]. Rivera invokes a new symbolic order that echoes ideas put forth by French feminist thinkers Luce Irigaray and Hélène Cixous, as well as those of the Italian Milan Book Store and Verona Diotima groups. She especially relies on Luisa Muraro's *El orden simbólico de la madre*, although she brings the concept of the symbolic order of the mother closer to home by comparing it to María Zambrano's notion of poetic reason, a link she develops further in *El fraude de la igualdad* (1997) [The fraud of equality].

Central to achieving the new order in which women intervene freely in the world is the concept of "partir de si, el partir de lo que tenemos, que es principalmente la experiencia femenina personal" ("Partir" 53) [beginning from oneself, to begin from what we have, which is principally personal female experience]. "Partir de sí" allows for a "first-person politics" that accords ample space to female personal experience, which, Rivera believes, structuralism and certain postmodern authors thoroughly devalued. (As I note below, Spanish equality feminism is also averse to postmodernism.) A politics in the first person frees women from living a partial reality, an existence limited by the masculine sex. Rivera is against affirmative action, because a first-person politics does not enter into dialogue with the system of democratic representation. In first-person politics the key strategy is the mediation of another woman or women, whose authority the woman recognizes; the woman-to-woman relationship allows her to realize herself, to signify, and thus opens the way to a female liberty that modifies existing power relations in society. The first of these relations is the relation with the mother, the mother who taught the woman to speak, guaranteeing a concordance between words and things.

Celia Amorós's searing answer to the concept of the symbolic order of the mother appeared in 1998:

> ¿A quién beneficia este nuevo tratado de paz entre los sexos, cuyos términos, esta vez, han sido definidos por las propias mujeres, sin que se sepa qué batalla han ganado, a menos que sea la victoria 'simbólica'? ¿No habremos cambiado nuestra participación en el derecho a la primogenitura—¡oh, qué concepto tan patriarcal!—por un plato de simbólicas lentejas? Simbólicas, desde luego, porque no sé cómo se va a paliar la feminización de la pobreza desde la política de la 'diferencia sexual.' ("Feminismo" 133)

> [Who benefits from this new peace treaty between the sexes, whose terms this time have been defined by women themselves, without knowing what battle they have won, unless it is a "symbolic" victory? We have not changed our participation in the right to primogeniture—oh, what a patriarchal concept—for a symbolic dish of lentils? Symbolic, after all, because I don't know how we are going to condone the

feminization of poverty from the political perspective of "sexual difference."]

The more heated polemic between equality and difference feminists had been brewing since 1996 when *El Viejo Topo* published the Spanish version of *El final del patriarcado* [The end of patriarchy], the same year it was edited in Italian by the Milan Women's Book Store. Not only do difference feminists theorize a symbolic order of the mother, but now they declare that patriarchy as the source of female identity has ended. Celia Amorós expresses dismay at the optimistic title of the work, which at first she thought meant that systematic male domination over women's collective lives had ceased in spite of all the evidence to the contrary—the persistent feminization of poverty, rampant violence against women, the notable inequality in the distribution of domestic duties, the segregation of work on the basis of sex, and women's lack of access to positions of responsibility. Amorós was disappointed to discover that instead of talking about matters relating to women's concrete lives, "estamos hablando de lo simbólico, nada menos que de 'la política de lo simbólico'" ("La política" 64) [we are talking about the symbolic, nothing less that "the politics of the symbolic"]. Thus patriarchy has been banished by "un efecto de conjuro que emanía de la actitud despectivo de quienes han llegado a la verdadera 'toma de conciencia'" ("La política" 64) [a magic effect that emanated from the scornful attitude of those who have arrived at a real "consciousness"]. One can easily detect the aversion to postmodern philosophy in this interpretation of the linguistic orientation of a symbolic order.

In the declaration of the end of patriarchy, Amorós hears familiar Heideggerian echoes of the end of the reign of the subject "con sus pretensiones fundamentantes y sus designios objetivadores y manipuladores de un ente que ha perdido el aroma y el halo del ser en un mundo desencantado" ("La política" 64) [with its fundamental pretensions and the objectifying and manipulative designs of something that has lost the aroma and halo of a being in a disenchanted world]. Amorós dismantles one by one all the happy present and future circumstances difference feminists describe. For example, the Milan group quotes the cheery statistic that Italian women (and probably Spanish women a close second) count the highest number of women working inside and outside the home to prove that traditional domestic roles no longer constrain women's lives and have ceased to be a barrier to their having paid employment. Amorós considers that the Milan group presents this statistic as some kind of "armonía preestablecida" [preestablished harmony]. She notes that this positive interpretation of the double workday for women inspires in her a "hermeneútica de la sospecha" ("La política" 64) [a hermeneutics of suspician]. Amorós categorizes as "new stoicism" or "something akin to a slave mentality" ("La política" 67) difference feminists' view that abstract law cannot take into consideration the complexity involved in decisions women must make and that women should just ignore the patriarchy and forge something different based on their inner urges. Directly addressing the difference feminists as "inefables anunciadoras del fin del patriarcado" [ineffable announcers of the end of patriarchy], she retorts that "los muertos que ustedes matan gozan de muy buena salud" ("La política" 67) [the dead that you are killing enjoy very good health]. She further argues that the positions taken by difference feminists intentionally or unintentionally reinforce rightist political positions.

The combative tone of the equality/difference exchange of the 1990s was perhaps self-immolating, although Milagros Rivera attempted to revive the smoldering embers in her acidly titled *El fraude de la igualdad* [The fraud of equality] of 1997. While *El fraude de la igualdad*, like Rivera's article for the 1994 *El Viejo Topo* special issue, relies on concepts such as the symbolic order of the mother borrowed from Luce Irigaray and Luisa Muraro, she now more fully integrates ideas inspired by María Zambrano. She invokes Zambrano's statement from her 1945 essay "Eloisa o la existencia de la mujer" [Heoloise or women's existence] that "«La vida de la mujer es *la vida del alma*». . . . Vida misteriosa de las entrañas, que se consume sin alcanzar la objetividad. . . ." (*El fraude* 79–80) [Women's lives are "the life of the soul". . . . Mysterious life of the entrails that consumes itself without achieving its objective] to reinforce the notion of "partir de sí," which she believes is erased by the concept of equality. Like Zambrano, Rivera elaborates on the importance of language in forging the female or, in Zambrano's terms, poetic, realm. In the symbolic order of the mother, "la capacidad de transformación de la palabra aprendida de la madre. . . . la fluidez de la lengua que ella [la madre] enseña, la fortuna mudable del azar que abre la vida a la necesidad de relacionarse con los demás, sin cuya percepción y escucha no hay ni sociedad ni palabra" (*El fraude* 17, 31–32) [the capacity to transform the language learned from the mother. . . . the fluidity of the language that the mother teaches, the mutable fortune of happenstance that opens life up to the need to relate to others, without whose perception and listening there is no society or language]. On this point, she quotes Zambrano's *España, sueño y verdad* [Spain, dream and reality]: "«Y la peña se hace así entraña maternal, alma».... «El alma virginal de la palabra. Allí se da a ver algo propio de la palabra: ser como agua allí donde la realidad es como piedra»" (*El fraude* 31) [The virginal soul of the word. There one sees something particular to the word: to be like water where reality is like a rock]. Also coinciding with Zambrano, Rivera is suspicious of emphasizing language at the expense of the corporeal. Here Rivera parts company with French and Italian difference feminists, who follow Lacan in privileging language as the ultimate reality. Rivera believes that the body and language are inseparable—"o sea, unidos equilibradamente" (*El fraude* 97) [that is, united equally]. She critiques Luisa Muraro for separating the soul and the body, "cuidando en este caso el estudio de la lengua y descuidando el del cuerpo, lo cual desequilibra esa unidad que ... es la obra y el gran don de la madre" (*El fraude* 95) [in this case taking care of studying language and disregarding the body, which unsettles the unity ... is the work and the great gift of the mother].

We will continue to see how the debate between equality and difference feminists developed in the next and final chapter on equality, which like difference had a long history in Spanish feminist thought, although due to historical circumstances (mostly Franco-era censorship) it was not taken into account by democratic-era equality feminists.

CHAPTER 6

Equality

In many ways the concept of equality crisscrosses all the other topics treated in this book—solitude, personality, social class, work, and difference—but I save it for last as a summarizing subject and a topic that best brings us to the present state of feminist thinking in Spain. Equality within difference is a constant strain in Spanish feminist thought (see Stuurman 86). It is also a subject that appears in the feminist thinking of every period. Fray Jerónimo Feijoo, probably influenced by François Poulain de la Barre's *De l'égalité des deux sexes* (1673), initiated three centuries of Spanish thought on the equality of the sexes when he stated in his *Defensa de las mugeres* (1726) that "mi empeño no es persuadir la ventaja, sino la igualdad" (331) [my purpose is not to argue (women's) advantage, but (their) equality]; this despite the fact that he presented a number of ways in shich women are different from (and often better than) men. Poulain de la Barre, who actually published three treatises on the equality of women and men, is a foundational pillar on which the Spanish feminist concept of equality rests, having probably made his way into Feijoo's Benedictine monastery library via the vast circulation of texts and ideas that that organization represented in Europe, and resurfacing in the late twentieth century as an inspiration for Celia Amorós's Enlightenment or equality feminists. Feijoo is also the first Spanish feminist thinker to distinguish between inequality and lack of equality ("desigualdad") referring to physical differences (354): "Mi voto, pues, es que no hay desigualdad en las capacidades de uno y otro sexo" (384) [My vote is that there is no inequality in the capabilities of the two sexes]. However, the Benedictine monk concludes that despite the complete equality in abilities, there has to be a hierarchy to avoid chaos. Also in the eighteenth century, Inés de Joyes argued for the equality of the souls of men and women, reminding us of American feminist Elizabeth Cady Stanton's similar argument in the nineteenth century. Emilia Pardo Bazán, who could well have known of Stanton's work, which was widely circulated, argued that the soul is ungendered, and thus by nature and divine intention men and women were created equal (see Christy Presson Hyland).

The situation changed in the 1920s and 1930s when Clara Campoamor, Margarita Nelken, Victoria Kent, and María Martínez Sierra "tenían en común su concepción liberal del feminismo" (Nash, "Experiencia" 155) [had a liberal notion of feminism in common]. We do find instances of theorizing about equality in pre-Republican and Republican-era works. For example, Antonina Rodrigo, quoting María Martínez Sierra's speech "De feminismo," reminds us that "María Lejárraga cifraba el *sentido* y la *aspiración* del feminismo en la igualdad, en la creencia de que «no hay libertad donde el deber no ata por igual a los dos que soportan el yugo»" (Rodrigo 125; emphasis hers) [María Lejárraga located the sense and aspirations of feminism in equality, in the belief that "there is no freedom where duty does not bind the two who bear the yoke equally"]. Martínez Sierra further maintains that the law recognizes women as equals in the realm of responsibilities and punishments, but not when it comes to rights (*Cartas a las mujeres de España* 16). Martínez Sierra refers to the oldest Spanish traditions to buttress her arguments in favor of equal rights for women before the law: "leyes visigodos, fundamento de nuestro «españolismo», y díganme ustedes lo que encuentren en ellas. Individualismo absoluto e igualdad perfecta en derechos y deberes para el hombre y la mujer; todas las restricciones antifeministas, señores españolizantes, nos han venido de extranjís" (*Feminismo* 131) [Tell me what you find in Visigothic laws, the foundation of our "Spanishness." Absolute individualism and perfect equality in rights and duties for the man and the woman; all the antifeminist restrictions, my fellow Spaniards, have come from abroad]. Although she does not mention Rousseau, she in fact follows one of his basic precepts in the social contract when she states that "[n]o hay libertad donde no hay igualdad." (*Feminismo* 26) [there is no liberty without equality]. She does, however, cite John Stuart Mill on the necessity of "igualdad absoluta" (*Feminismo* 84) [absolute equality]. Carmen de Burgos likewise advocated absolute legal parity between men and women: "La base está en las leyes, en la proclamación de la «Igualdad de derechos»: Estudiar la manera de borrar la injusticia de la desigualdad es el fin del feminismo moderno" (*La mujer moderna* 8, 20) [The purpose of modern feminism is to study the way to erase the injustice of inequality]. Co-opting naturalistic arguments about a woman's biology determining her destiny, Burgos argues that inequality is not natural; therefore feminism wishes to reestablish the natural order. Inequality in the home, she believes, "perjudica a la familia toda" (200) [harms the entire family], and she praises women's interest in fashion, because "[l]a moda tiende a igualarlo todo" (267) [fashion tends to equalize everything].

While Mary Nash does not mention the specific arguments for gender equality I have listed here, she designates suffrage advocate Clara Campoamor "una clara postura teórica de signo igualitario" ("Experiencia" 171) [a clear theoretical position of egalitarian stripe]. Thus biological essentialism, which conceptualizes women as mothers, opens a public space for a "ciudadanía diferenciada que ignora el principio de la igualdad y de la individualidad" [a differentiated citizenship that is ignorant of the principle of equality and individuality] and allows for emancipating political projects "desde el reconocimiento de la diferencia de roles de género" (Nash, "Experiencia" 163) [from the recognition of different gender roles]. Once this transition was effected, women began to question the notion of separate spheres and to claim a role in the public arena. Equality for women was legally affirmed in the Constitution of 1931 promulgated by the Second Republic. Article 2 of the 1931 document declares that "[t]odos los españoles son iguales ante la ley" (*Constituciones* 157) [all Spaniards are equal before the law], and article 25 enumerates the areas of equality, including sexual equality: "No podrán ser fundamento de privilegio: la naturaleza, la filiación, el sexo, la clase social, la riqueza, las ideas políticas ni las creencias religiosas" (*Constituciones* 161) [Nature, kinship, sex, social class, wealth, political and religious beliefs cannot serve as the basis for privilege]. Article 43 of the 1931 Constitution further stipulates that "[e]l matrimonio se funda en la igualdad de derechos para ambos sexos y podrá disolverse por mutuo deseo o petición de cualquiera de los cónyuges." (*Constituciones* 163) [marriage is based on the equality of rights for both sexes and can be dissolved by mutual desire or by petition by either one of the partners].

According to Siep Stuurman, Poulain's ideas on sexual equality are probably "the most radically egalitarian texts published in Europe before the French Revolution. . . . Poulain is the first thinker in modern Europe to build his entire social philosophy on a universal concept of equality" (1, 2). Poulain bases his arguments for equality between men and women on observation and autonomous reason. He notes that any perceived differences between men and women are not natural but are due to "'chance, power and custom'" (qtd. in Stuurman 1), thus turning "feminism into a systematic social philosophy" (Stuurman 8). Stuurman argues that the radical Enlightenment of Poulain de la Barre provided the philosophical basis for republicanism and Freemasonry. These developments would not take place in Spain until the end of the nineteenth century, because the revolutionary spirit was quashed in Spain with the Napoleonic invasion of 1808, followed by a reactionary period of civil war and political instability in which the eighteenth-century beginnings of Spanish feminist thought did not progress until the 1840s and 1850s, and even then there were only sporadic contributions by individual authors such as Spanish-Cuban writer Gertrudis Gómez de Avellaneda. Christine Arkinstall has recently uncovered a trove of women's journals from the mid-nineteenth century that demonstrates there was much more feminist writing in this period than had heretofore been thought (see *A New History of Iberian Feminisms*, Part II, chapters 3 and 5).

Mónica Bolufer outlines two coexisting and conflicting viewpoints about the equality of the sexes in eighteenth-century Spain—one argued for the "complementarity" of the sexes, while the other "affirmed, in the name of reason, the essential equality of human beings, even while admitting that in society men and women should have different functions and responsibilities" (Bolufer, *A New History* 43). Josefa Amar y Borbón (1749–1833) argued the latter position as "the most prominent woman defender of gender equality, for whom supposed innate characteristics of femininity or masculinity were actually products of moral, intellectual, and sentimental education that moulded women and men in different ways" (Bolufer, *A New History* 43). Bolufer quotes another woman writer, Margarita Hickey (1753–1793), who wrote in her *Poesías varias* [Various poems]: "que el alma no es hombre / ni mujer, y es fijo // que en entrambos casos / su ser es el mismo" (Bolufer, *A New History* 44) [that the soul is neither male / nor female, and is fixed // so that in each case / its being is the same].

Feijoo's declaration that the privileged equality between the two sexes comes after an affirmation that many women have vices (although he hastens to attribute these to men's instigation) and a list of attributes that could be considered superior in women. Thus the call for equality between the sexes is rather ambiguous and sets the tone for similar statements by thinkers right down to the present day. For example, María Ángeles Durán notes the shades of meaning with which the 1978 Spanish Constitution imbues the notion of equality—"igualitarismo radical, igualitarismo nominal, discriminación evidente, igualdad de mercado" (*Mujeres y hombres* 299–300) [radical egalitarianism, nominal egalitarianim, evident discrimination, market equality]. Like Poulain de la Barre, Feijoo, who argues from observation and example, adheres to an equality-within-difference model. After listing women's positive qualities, he hastens to assert that "las buenas calidades que atribuyo a las mugeres, son comunes a entrambos sexos" (V, 33) [the good qualities that I attribute to women, are common to both sexes]. In chapter 4 of this study on the concept of "work," I noted Feijoo's observation that women are as suited for political work as men; women, the Benedictine friar notes, display their ability to govern economically in their domestic responsibilities.

One of Feijoo's most important contributions, however, is his defense of women's ability to reason. He counters Malebranche's *Arte de investigar la verdad* [Art of investigating the truth] (and with Malebranche all Cartesians' approach to knowledge) that affirmed women's ability to "discernir las cosas sensibles" (351) [discern things via the senses] but placed them far behind men in handling abstract ideas. Feijoo argues that if women are not good at abstract discourse, "no proviene de la desigualdad de talento, sino de la diferencia de aplicación y uso" (352) [it does not come from an inequality of talent, but from the difference of application and use]. Feijoo points out that it is erroneous to say women are intellectually inferior to men, because when comparing a field hand to a politician, men's intellectual development also differs from one man to another. If a woman had the same access as men to intellectual stimulation outside the home, her natural talents could be developed: "el no discurrir, o discurrir mal depende, no de falta de talento, sino de falta de noticias" (353) [not discoursing, or discoursing poorly is not due to a lack of talent, but to the lack of knowledge]. Feijoo employs a similar example (about variation within the sexes) to counter arguments about the size of women's heads compared to those of men. Having debunked the notion of different intellects for men and women, he turns to the matter of souls, arguing for the equality of all souls. Feijoo says that those who cite Saint Augustine on the inferiority of women's souls are wrong; he cannot find any mention of women's souls anywhere in Augustine's work. Souls, he avers, are not sexed. With razor-sharp logic Feijoo comes back to Malebranche pointing out that we simply do not know what the relationship between the mind and the soul is, just as it is not known how fire burns or snow chills.

As we have seen throughout this study, Spanish feminist theory, beginning with Feijoo, employs historical arguments. Feijoo devotes the long central section of his defense of women to historical examples of women whose lives illustrate his point that women are in no way intellectually inferior to men. He organizes his list of women intellectuals by country—Spain, France, Italy, Germany, and the Near East—concluding once again that "no hay desigualdad en las capacidades de uno, y otro sexo" (384) [there is no inequality in the capacities of one and the other sex]. Feijoo continues his essay extolling women's abilities in the plastic arts—painting and sculpture—again with a number of examples. His conclusion focuses on why, given the foregoing proofs of women's equality with men, God has allowed men to dominate women, citing *Genesis:* "*Sub viri postestate eris*" (387). Feijoo points out that there are variations in the wording of the text and that Biblical scholars have not determined the exact meaning of the passage. His second argument reminds the reader that women's subordination did not exist in the state of innocence and only came about after a sin was committed. In addition, if one of the pair in a household does not dominate, chaos would result. Unlike a political entity, such as a republic where all can have an equal vote, "entre marido, y muger, no solo sería imperfecto este modo de mandar en quanto al gobierno económico, sino imposible; porque en la multitud del Pueblo, quando haya diversidad de dictámenes, se puede decidir la dificultad por pluralidad de votos; lo que entre marido, y muger no puede suceder, porque están uno a uno: y así en caso de oponerse en el dictamen, no se puede determinar sino es uno de los dos superior" (388) [between husband and wife, in economic matters that approach would be unwieldy, even impossible; because in the multitude of the people, when there are diverse orders, you can decide the difficulty through a plurality of votes; that cannot happen between a husband and wife, and thus if they were to oppose one another in the law, one could not determine if one were superior]. So, if absolute equality does not reign in practice, it is enough for Feijoo that theoretical equality be recognized: "es utilidad bastante conocer la verdad, y desviar el error" (389) [it is enough to know the truth and avoid error]. Most modern feminist thinkers would have a hard time accepting this accommodation.

Theresa Ann Smith notes that Feijoo's arguments on female equality spurred debates in the remainder of the 1720s and in the 1730s, and by the 1740s and 1750s the Spanish intelligentsia had accepted women's rationality and thus their equality with men. Feijoo's widely circulated and widely read treatise had a palpable effect on women's lives: "As young reformers began to reimagine Spanish society and create institutions focused on improving the nation, their newfound belief in women's natural equality and potential intellectual capabilities led them to include the female sex in their blueprint for reform" (18). Feijoo's *Teatro crítico*, of which "Defensa de la mujer" was an important chapter, spawned a large readership, many other publications, and lively public debates, particularly in Madrid, where cafés and other locales for meeting and discussion proliferated. Women were allowed to participate in the Academy of Fine Arts and in *tertulias* (salons), although the debate on women's proper role in society continued throughout the 1760s and 1770s. One focus of these debates was women's membership in the prestigious Sociedades Económicas Amigos del País [Economic societies of Friends of the Country], the first of which, founded in the Basque country in 1753, was also the first to admit a woman. These influential societies were established in a number of localities as a means to formulate policies that might inform the monarchy's decisions on important state matters. According to Teresa Ann Smith, Gaspar Melchor de Jovellanos "did not see men and women as completely equal" (79), but he did weigh in (in women's favor) on the important issue regarding women's membership in the Sociedades Económicas. Jovellanos criticized societies that allowed women to attend meetings but did not grant them full equality in their statutes:

> Desengañémonos, señores; estos puntos son indivisibles: si admitimos a las señoras, no podemos negarle la plenitud de derechos que supone el título de socios. . . . las señoras deben ser admitidas con las mismas formalidades y derechos que los demás individuos; que no debe formarse de ellas clase separada; que se debe recurrir a su consejo y a su auxilio en las materias propias de su sexo, y del celo, talento y facultades de cada una; y finalmente que todo esto se debe acordar, por acta formal, y si pareciese, extender un reglamento separado, que fije esta materia para lo sucesivo. (Nieto 403, 404)

[Let's not fool ourselves, gentlemen; these points are indivisible: if we admit women, we cannot deny them the full rights that the title of members supposes. . . . the ladies should be admitted with the same formalities and rights as other individuals; they should not form a separate class; we ought to be able to consult them and employ their assistance in matters relating to their sex according to each one's abilities, talent, and faculties. And finally all of this should be sealed by a formal act and, if it seems appropriate, put down in a separate regulation that fixes it for the future.]

Although Jovellanos did not begin with the premise of absolute equality (he asserts that although women are endowed with less strength and vigor than men so that they would always be obedient, women were created as men's companions in all life's endeavors), they can certainly engage in any kind of work.

As we saw in the last chapter, in the mid-nineteenth century, Concepción Arenal, borrowing Feijoo's Enlightenment style of thinking based on observation and logical argument, continues to walk a fine line between equality and difference feminism. This is not surprising given that Arenal was one of the first feminist figures (preceded by Gertrudis Gómez de Avellaneda) to emerge after the paucity of feminist writing in the early nineteenth century. According to Christine Arkinstall, fewer journals were published in Spain in the wake of the 1808 Napoleanic invasion and ensuing civil war (See Arkinstall's contributions to *A New History of Iberian Feminisms*). National energies were redirected toward defeating the French and then to dealing with the swings in political fortunes for liberals under Fernando VII. As indicated in the last chapter, the liberal constitution of 1812 did not take women into account as equals. In fact the constitution did not bother to mention women at all. Up to 1870 there was no marriage law, except that proffered by the Church; adultery laws under the liberal regime, which adhered to an old honor code, were especially grievous. Women's education was not addressed until the Ley Moyano of 1857, and then only to prescribe an especially female curriculum. Arenal's first feminist book—*La mujer del porvenir*—was probably written in 1861 but not published until 1869, during the *sexenio revolucionario* (1868–1874), when various alternatives to the Bourbon monarchy, including a brief republic, were essayed. The book is an important albeit timid entry into arguing for women's place in the public sphere. As we saw in the previous chapter on difference, Arenal argues from a position that accepts women's (especially physical) difference from men.

Following the heavily biologically oriented climate of the mid-nineteenth century, in this early work Arenal accepts inequality in men's and women's physical condition, but she argues against biological differences as a determining factor in the way modern women and men conduct their lives. Arenal sees women's condition on a historical continuum in which women's physical differences are of decreasing importance as evolving human life becomes less physical and more spiritual and intellectual. Employing the same method of keen observation of reality that we saw in Feijoo, Arenal points out that one does not notice any difference in intellectual ability between uneducated men and women or between boys and girls of the educated classes. So she asks, "¿A qué edad empieza la superioridad intelectual del hombre?" (*La mujer del porvenir* in *La emancipación* 121–22) [At what age does the intellectual superiority of men begin?]. She answers her question with another question. Shouldn't we suspect education, if the difference between boys and girls coincides with instruction? In addition to educational inequality, Arenal also takes up legal inequality, arguing that one cannot consider morality without considering intelligence (127). She points out the absurdity of laws that judge women as inferior when it comes to rights but equal when it comes to punishment for crimes (106). She also argues for women's right to work: "[el] principio equitativo de que la sociedad no puede en justicia prohibir el ejercicio honrado de sus facultades a la mitad del género humano" (*La mujer del porvenir* 88) [the equitable principle that society cannot in justice prohibit the honest exercise of their faculties to half the human species]. Arenal's final argument for equality in this important book is that "La desigualdad de carácter (una forma de la debilidad), más daño aún que el marido hace a los hijos, pues, lejos de neutralizarla, la suman con la suya. En la voluble irreflexión de la infancia son indispensables ciertos puntos cardinales bien fijos: la fijeza les da carácter de ley, sello de verdad, porque cuando no se sostiene o se varía el mandato, los niños, y aun los hombres, miden por la facilidad el derecho de infringirle, suponiendo que no importará mucho lo que se defiende tan poco" (280) [A mother's inequality of character (a form of debility) causes more harm to the children than the husband's irascibility, because rather than neutralizing the husband's hot temper, she adds her own to his. Certain key points are fixed in children's voluble lack of reflection—a fixity that gives them the character of law, the seal of truth, because when the situation is not sustained or the command changes, children and even adults believe they have the right to break the rules, supposing that what is not well defended cannot be very important].

By the time Arenal penned her "La educación de la mujer" [Women's education] for the 1892 Congreso Pedagógico she forthrightly states that women's education should be the same as that for a man. In fact she believes that education for women is even more urgent than for men, because of the need to combat the negative effects of the Spanish legal and social systems have had on women. In an early version of affirmative action, Arenal argues that since women have been at a natural and social disadvantage, to achieve parity with men, they should receive more education. This measure would save women from wasting their lives in frivolity or, worse, slavery or prostitution. (As we saw in chapter 2 on personality, Arenal believes that women's personality is weak and must be fortified with additional education that will bring women up to the same strength of personality as men.) Lumping class and gender together, Arenal argues that there may be many inequalities in people's exterior conditions: "Los accidentes, las exterioridades, las apariencias, podrían variar; pero las condiciones esenciales que la educación perfecciona son las mismas cualquiera que sea la posición social del que las tiene" (*La emancipación* 66) [The accidents, exteriorities, the appearances, can vary; but the essential conditions that education perfects are the same whatever the social position of the one who has them]. Arenal concludes that if women have duties to perform, rights to demand, benevolence to carry out, then there should be no difference between her education and that of a man.

In a presentation for the same conference of 1892, Emilia Pardo Bazán observes that girls and boys receive equal religious education, but not equal moral education. In her argument, she makes a fundamental point about women's consciousness that foreshadows ideas María Zambrano will develop in the 1940s. Christianity, notes Pardo Bazan, dignified women, although she endows this shibboleth with a new dimension:

> El crisianismo dignificó a la mujer, pero no como piensa el vulgo, pues no es exacto que antes del cristianismo viviese la mujer en general relación de costumbres, ni que después del cristianismo y entre las mismas cristianas no haya habido mujeres tan escandalosas y depravadas como las Agripinas

y Mesalinas; ni menos se puede afirmar en presencia de los datos históricos, que la mujer, en la familia y la sociedad, fuese menos considerada bajo el paganismo que bajo el cristianismo, siendo cierto que la matrona romana será siempre en el mundo antiguo estereotipo de dignidad e influencia moral, social y política, al par que de severa virtud. La grande obra progresiva del cristianismo, en este particular, fue emancipar la conciencia de la mujer, afirmar su personalidad y su libertad moral, de la cual se deriva necesariamente la libertad práctica. No fue en la familia, sino en el interior santuario de la conciencia, donde el cristianismo emancipó a la mujer. Y si en esta parte no ha dado todo su fruto la obra divina, débese a la malicia humana, al egoísmo y a la fuerza estática de las viejas ideas, conjuradas contra la palabra de Cristo. (*La mujer española* 83–84)

[Christianity dignified women, but not in the way that common folk think, since it is not true that before Christianity women lived with relaxed customs or that after Christianity and among Christian women themselves there haven't been scandalous depraved women such as Agrippina and Messalina. Nor can it be affirmed from historical facts that women were less considered in the family and society under paganism than Christianity since it is the case that the Roman matron is the stereotype of dignity and moral, social, and political influence as well as severe virtue. The great work of progress in Christianity was to emancipate woman's consciousness, affirming her personality and her moral liberty from which she derives her practical liberty. It wasn't in the family but in the interior sanctuary of her consciousness that Christianity emancipated the woman. And if in this arena the Divine has not rendered all its fruit, it is due to human maliciousness, egotism, and the static force of old ideas, marshaled against Christ's teachings.]

And she quotes the scripture "«De hoy más no habrá entre vosotros amo ni esclavo, hombre ni mujer, sino todos hijos de mi Padre.»" (84) [From now on there will not be master or slave, man or woman, but all children of my Father]. Of course, Pardo Bazán must point out that

Christ's dictum has not been carried out in reality, and there are still slaves and a distinction between men and women among Christians.

However, it is a different story in terms of intellectual education, where serious inequalities exist: "Cuando menos, la educación religiosa parte del supuesto de que las almas son entitativamente iguales, e idéntico su valor a los ojos de Dios; mientras en la educación intelectual funda sus anomalías y desigualdades en la presunción de la inferioridad intelectual congénita de todo el sexo femenino" (85–86) [At the very least, religious education departs from the supposition that souls are equal as entities and identical in value before God's eyes; while intellectual education bases its anomalies and inequalities on the presumption of congenital intellectual inferiority of the entire female sex]. Like her predecessors Father Feijoo and Concepción Arenal, Pardo Bazán points out the incongruities in women's situation. Women are allowed to study, but not to exercise a profession. Women can write books on metaphysics, but they cannot become veterinarians. A woman can sit on the throne, but she cannot elect legislators: "La cultura, hoy por hoy, se circunscribe a ciertas clases sociales, aunque el ideal sea extenderla y comunicarla al mayor número. Lo único que creo se debe en justicia a la mujer, es la desaparición de la incapacidad congénita, con que la sociedad la hiere. Iguálense las condiciones, y la libre evolución hará lo demás" (88) [Culture today is limited to certain social classes, although the ideal would be to extend it and communicate it to the greatest number. The only thing that I think in justice is due women is the elimination of the congenital incapacity with which society wounds them. Equalize the conditions, and free evolution will do the rest]. Pardo Bazán goes on to say that women's education is only based on tradition. She believes that once some civilized nation dares to step beyond tradition to educate women as they do men and equalize the rights of the two sexes, there will be proof of women's equality. She says that this idea should not be considered a pipe dream, because it was already becoming a reality in some very advanced countries (95–96). The final words of her speech appeal to Spanish nationalism, recalling that the Catholic monarchs—Isabella and Ferdinand—were equals on the throne. (We now know that this was not the case, thanks to a recent book on Isabella, but that does not affect Pardo Bazán's argument.) Nationalism has always been an important element in Pardo Bazán's feminist argumentation: "Y si en un lema pretendiese encarnar mi ideal, sería en el lema a que se debió en tanta parte el descubrimiento de América; el lema que señaló la mayor época de prosperidad y florecimiento para España; el lema que recuerda la intervención gloriosísima de la mujer en los más altos destinos de la humanidad y en los más arduos problemas de la ciencia y de la política: el lema de la gran Isabel: *Tanto monta*" (97) [And if a slogan were to incarnate my ideal, it would be the slogan to which we in large part owe the discovery of America; the slogan that represents the greatest period of prosperity and flowering of Spain; the slogan that recalls the glorious intervention of a woman in the highest destinies of humanity and the most arduous problems of science and politics: the great Isabella's slogan: *She ascends the throne, the same as he*]. In her summary of the conference proceedings, Pardo Bazán, echoing the Krausist notion of harmony, emphasizes that "la sociedad no puede marchar a ningún estado armónico mientras no equilibre los dos platillos de la balanza humana" (*La mujer española* 105) [society cannot march toward any harmonic state that does not balance the two sides of the human scale]. (Recall that Pardo Bazán pointed out that the classes are equal in convents, and Hyland notes that Pardo Bazán argued that the soul is not gendered, and thus by nature and Divine intention, men and women were created equal.)

In her 1920 *Cartas a las mujeres de España* María Martínez Sierra refers to Elizabeth Cady Stanton's "Protestant" argument (without acknowledging Stanton) that "Ante Dios, la mujer y el hombre son absolutamente iguales" (26) [Before God, women and men are absolutely equal]. And she continues the religious argument for equality in her last letter of the collection: "Con Él vino a la tierra el sentimiento de hermandad entre todos los hombres, la noción de justicia: una para todos; la afirmación de igualdad ante el derecho y ante la ley sobre que están fundadas, teóricamente al menos, las sociedades modernas" (204) [The sense of brotherhood among men, the notion of one justice for all, the affirmation of equality before the law on which modern societies are founded came with Him].

As Maryellen Bieder has so aptly chronicled, Carmen de Burgos's feminism shifted over time from one of difference to equality by the time she wrote *La mujer moderna y sus derechos* in 1927. For example, in her early feminist essays and speeches, Burgos did not favor women's participation in politics and argued against the vote for women: "Eventually . . . Burgos was swayed by the Portuguese feminists Elzira Dantes and Ana de Castro that the time had come to demand the vote for women. In 1921 she organized the first public demonstration in favor of Parliament's taking up the issue. Later, as president of the Liga Internacional de Mujeres Ibéricas . . . she continued her fight for unrestricted voting rights that culminated in the 1931 vote" (Vollendorf 215, n5). Often calling on the kind of observation and logic that reminds us of Feijoo and Arenal ("Es un hecho evidente que las mujeres que ejercitan la fuerza superan a los hombres que no trabajan o se dedican a deportes" 37 [It is an evident fact that women who exert force are superior to men who do not work or dedicate themselves to sports]), in her 1927 *La mujer moderna* Carmen de Burgos advocates absolute legal parity between men and women: "La base está en las leyes, en la proclamación de la «Igualdad de derechos» . . . Estudiar la manera de borrar la injusticia de la desigualdad es el fin del feminismo moderno" (*La mujer moderna* 8, 20) [The basis is in the laws. the proclamation of the "Equality of rights." . . . The goal of modern feminism is to study the way to erase the injustice of inequality].

However, unlike Poulain de la Barre, who argued for absolute equality in all spheres of life, Burgos falls somewhere between the absolute equality of Poulain de la Barre and the limited equality of Locke and Feijoo. She argues for equality before the law, but not in daily life. For example, although Burgos believes that "el espíritu de nuestras leyes ha sido de igualdad" (166) [the spirit of our laws has been for equality], her idea of equality in relationships between men and women is more idealistic than legalistic: "Sólo el amor, que supera a toda ley, establece la igualdad entre los cónyugues y mantiene el hogar indisoluble" (161) [Only love, which supersedes all law, establishes equality between married people and maintains the home intact]. Thus Burgos distinguishes between legal parity and biological and social equality. When it comes to work, however, her concept of equality is more absolute. As I pointed out in chapter 4 on work, Burgos believed that if women's work is the same as men's, women should receive the same pay, and that there should not be any inequality in working conditions: "Lo indispensable es la igualdad; la llamada protección perjudica a la mujer más que sus mismos enemigos" (141) [What is indispensable is equality; the call for protection is more dangerous to women than her very enemies]. True feminism, she believes, does not want privileges. Like Arenal, she points out that "En cuanto a obligaciones sí somos iguales. La mujer paga las mismas contribuciones que los hombres. . . . ¡En Derecho penal las leyes son muy generosas para conceder la igualdad!" (212, 243) [As to obligations we are equal. Women pay the same taxes as men. . . . In penal law the laws are much more generous in bestowing equality].

In *El voto femenino y yo: Mi pecado mortal*, Campoamor points out that male liberalism does not make room for women's liberty, a situation that had not changed in Spain in more than one hundred years since the liberal movement took flight at the Cortes Constituyentes in Cádiz in 1810: "El hombre *liberal* español, que se llama de *ideas avanzadas*, en general—salvo excepciones, cuanto más reducidas más honrosísimas por reducidas—, consentía y alentaba una incomprensible dualidad ideológica en el hogar en el que parecían convivir el sentimiento liberal avanzado, republicano y laico del varón, con el ultramontano y católico militante de la mujer" (22; emphasis in original) [The liberal Spanish man who says he has advanced ideas, in general . . . consented and fomented an incomprehensible ideological duality in the home in which an advanced liberal, Republican, lay sentiment on the man's part seemed to coexist with the ultramontane and militant Catholic sentiment of the woman]. She believes that Spain cannot possibly move forward on its path toward liberty until this contradictory dual perspective on women is resolved.

Having been elected to the parliament in 1931, Campoamor worked tirelessly in favor of women's franchise. Her sharp reasoning surely influenced the favorable vote achieved in the Parliament in 1932. She points out the faulty logic of a draft version of the equality clause in the constitution, which stated that " 'No podrán ser fundamento de privilegio jurídico el nacimiento, la clase social, la riqueza, las ideas políticas y las creencias religiosas. Se reconoce *en principio*, la igualdad de derechos de los sexos" (43; emphasis in original) [Birth, social class, wealth, political ideas and religious beliefs cannot serve as the basis for juridical privilege. We recognize the equality of rights of the two sexes in principle]. Campoamor further notes that these two sentences contradict each other. The first one grants equality to all, although the equality of the sexes is left to the second sentence, which grants equal rights to the sexes in principle. She believes that sex should be included in the first sentence and that the second sentence should be eliminated. Campoamor scolds her male colleagues for the "in principle" rider to sexual equality before the law:

> Esta declaración consitituía una burda ficción de la igualdad que la mujer tenía derecho a esperar de la Constitución republicana. Era la eterna cicatería masculina, la reminiscencia de su vanidosa tutela, incapaz de abordar lealmente el problema de la dignificación de la mujer y de resolverlo

totalitariamente, cuando se veía en trance de no poder desconocerlo, una reminiscencia de diosecillo dispensador de la ley, la justicia o la merced, que en trance de desprenderse de algo que constituyó su plena y absoluta soberanía, le duele hacerlo totalmente y aspira a hacerlo poco a poco, concesión a concesión, en la graciosa y galante avenencia a la eterna demanda, a la obligada súplica femenina. (45)

[This declaration constituted a clumsy fiction about the equality that women had the right to expect of the Republican Constitution. It was the eternal masculine miserliness, a reminder of the vain tutelage, incapable of loyally broaching the problem of dignifying women and totally resolving it, when they came to the point of not being able to deny it. It was a reminder of the little god that dispenses the law, justice, and mercy, which was on the point of forming its full and absolute sovereignty; it was painful to do it completely and was looking for a way of doing it gradually, concession by concession in the gracious and gallant agreement to the eternal demand, the obliging female plea.]

She achieved her goal of making sex a condition for equality before the law in article 25 of the 1931 constitution, the final version of which read "The following may not be grounds for judicial privilege: nature, application, sex, social class, wealth, political ideas or religious beliefs." Campoamor also prevailed in other sexual equality clauses, such as the right of women to be elected to office, women's right to vote, the right of married women to retain their nationality, the right to investigate paternity, the conviction that marriage is based on equality of the sexes, and the right to divorce. She mentions, however, that a clause was attempted that would allow women to ask for divorce without giving a cause. Most members of parliament did not favor this amendment, and out of expediency, Campoamor went along with leaving the divorce legislation as it was (with the show-cause provision). She personally favored the amendment, because it was "acorde con un principio humano de ayuda preferente a seres desiguales" (49) [in accord with the human principle of giving preference to unequal beings], a version of our contemporary notion of affirmative action. To her great dismay and disappointment, Clara Campoamor, who had so avidly defended women's equality and right to vote, was defeated in her bid to continue her seat in Parliament in the 1933 elections. She refused to admit, however, that the women's vote was a significant factor in her loss.

Some Spanish feminist theorists of both the pre–Civil War period and the postdictatorial era not only argued for equal and collaborative relationships between the sexes, they lived them. For example, María Martínez Sierra worked as an equal partner with her husband on "their" creative and essayistic writing, although for many years he received all the credit for it. Federica Montseny maintained a stable relationship and parenthood with a male companion unsanctioned by marriage. Both foreground companionable relationships between the sexes in novels and essays and create female characters who work alongside their male partners. The subject resurfaces in 1970s Spanish feminist thought. Charo Ema says, for example, that she and other leftist feminists want to "hacer un feminismo aceptable para los hombres de izquierdas. . . . Queremos tratar de ser feministas pero no quedarnos solas" (Levine and Waldman 63) [practice a feminism that is acceptable to leftist men. . . . We want to try to be feminists, but we don't want to end up alone]. Relations between men and women continue to be central to Spanish feminist theory in the democratic era. Equality feminists, even in their most recent publications, struggle to find a means by which men and women can live together on genuinely equal terms and share workloads.

The difference feminists against whom the Spanish thinkers write are foreign. Empar Pineda's article "¿El mito de la femininidad cabalga de nuevo" [The myth of femininity rides again] challenges Carla Lonzi's difference feminism with arguments from Simone de Beauvoir's *El segundo sexo* against biological destiny and for a socially constructed feminine identity that relegates women to the domestic sphere. Pineda goes beyond what she considers mere equality before the law to propose "profundas transformaciones . . . para que la igualdad plena sea posible" (19) [profound transformations . . . for the fullest possible equality]. She claims not to suggest that women become like men, but rather that men should also be freed from the social constraints placed on them. These transformations include the elimination of the patriarchal family, the socialization of domestic work, and a complete restructuring of individual and collective consciousness to overcome "la ideología y la dominación machistas" (19) [machista ideology and domination].

In the second part of her article, Pineda attempts to balance her view and to understand those who find positive value in what are traditionally considered feminine traits in order to "autoafirmarse" (19) [affirm themselves]. She describes the position based on reason, now called equality feminism, as just another branch of difference feminism. She argues that equality feminism maintains the division between masculine and feminine by proposing that women adopt a masculine mode of thinking, which ends up creating the same division between the sexes maintained by difference feminism. The latter opposes a men's mode of thought based on reason to a women's style of thinking centered on intuition, sentiment, and life experiences. Pineda places her own position outside these polarities, which she believes dangerously allow for the reassertion of "posiciones pseudocientífcas" (23) [pseudoscientific positions]. She is especially averse to difference feminist emphasis on women's bodies and women's sensual pleasure. Her alternative to difference feminists' search for a women's space is a common space for men and women: "el del trabajo social, el de la acción, el de la ciencia, el del arte y la poesía, el de la economía, el de las relaciones afectivas, el de la política. . . . Querer ocupar este terreno es reinvindicar la igualdad. Que es lo que reivindico" (24 [that of social work, action, science, art and poetry, economy, affective relationships, politics. . . . Wishing to occupy this terrain is to demand equality. Which is what I demand].

Amelia Valcárcel's article "El derecho al mal" [The right to evil] in the same issue of *El Viejo Topo* ventures an even more subversive approach than Pineda's in defense of equality. She affirms women's right to be just as "immoral" as men. Unlike Pineda's, however, Valcárcel's position does not disparage rational thought. She rebels against thinkers such as Herbert Marcuse who suggest that women serve as models for social and ethical behavior in a reformation of society toward a benevolent utopia beyond reason: "se espera que las mujeres, sistemáticamente alejadas del Logos, tengan, por esta secular costumbre un discurso diverso en el que se pueda confiar" (28) [they hope that women, who are systematically separated from the Logos, can achieve a diverse discourse on which we can rely by means of this secular custom]. Valcárcel is repelled by extreme feminists who propose a utopian destruction of all that is associated with women, especially reproduction of the species: "la utopía, puede ser, más que una guía, un cul de sac" (28) [utopia can be a cul-de-sac, rather than a guide], and thus she posits equality as the only concept that can grapple effectively with women's situation. If women cannot convert men to good behavior, then women should adopt male values, eliminating the traditional values of chastity, sweetness, and nature. This line of thinking raised the ire of difference feminists who maintained that equality feminism is just another version of patriarchy.

Even though Valcárcel's essay is cast in an ironic tone, at this juncture the tenor of the equality/difference debate is still fairly cordial. Celia Amorós situates herself in a conciliatory position between Valcárcel and difference feminism. She politely poses the questions: "¿Cómo debería orientarse en la lucha el movimiento feminista? ¿Sería posible que tuviera la idea de igualdad con el hombre como criterio regulador de su teoría y de su práctica? ¿O debe afirmarse ante todo como voluntad de diferencia de lo femenino, como propuesta de alternativa de valores formulada a partir de la especificidad de la experiencia y la inserción en el mundo de las mujeres?" (132) [How should one situate oneself in the feminist movement struggle? Can it be possible to have the idea of equality with men regulating its theory and practice? Or can we consider feminine difference as a governing principle based on the experience of women in the world?]. Her more moderate stance (as compared to Valcárcel's) takes into account the difficulty of defining femininity. She notes the challenge of separating the truly feminine from what is now called "feminine" after centuries of oppression and marginalization.

Amorós draws on Giulia Adinolfi's notion of "subcultura femenina" [female subculture] as an important means of distinguishing between essentialist biological determinants and what is socially constructed.[1] Amorós worries that the discourse of difference feminism is on a path of self-destruction, if its values—"la dulzura, la ternura, y la emocionalidad" (*Hacia* 134) [sweetnesss, tenderness, and emotionality]—cannot become universal and transcendent in the way male values have been throughout history. She points out that the values associated with the feminine realm were invented by men. In addition, she finds difference discourse too ambiguous and suggests that "[e]l discurso ilustrado de la igualdad tiene la ventaja indudable de librarse de las ambigüedades, de ser directamente incisivo e irrenunciablemente reivindicativo, de tener un punto de referencia polémico claro al manejar en la discusión de términos precisos como los de superioridad e inferioridad para establecer las impugnaciones de las definiciones patriarcales" (*Hacia* 140–141) [illustration equality discourse has the undoubtable advantage of being free of ambiguity, of being directly incisive and irreversibly recuperative, of having a clear polemical reference point in discussions of precise terms such as superiority and inferiority in establishing oppositions to patriarchal definitions]. Amorós immediately recognizes that such a statement could be taken as an oversimplification, and asserts that freedom from ambiguity does not mean freedom from complexity, since "el contenido mismo de la igualdad es un cajón de sastre tan confuso como ambiguo es el de la diferencia" (142) [the very content itself of equality is a jumble that is just as confused and as ambiguous as difference]. At the end of her essay, she attempts to find a way to validate both difference and equality. Quoting Hegel as saying that the road to the spirit is a "rodeo" [roundabout], she postulates the road to women's liberation as a "rodeo de los rodeos" [roundabout of roundabouts] in which theorists will have to move beyond difference and equality to draw on both discourses as they are modified by practical experience (142). Such a route was not taken, although several Spanish feminist theorists (Justa Montero and Marina Subirats, among others) have attempted to negotiate this middle road since the mid-1990s. In the meantime, the division between equality and difference feminists deepened and grew more hostile as difference feminist theory began to be cultivated by autochthonous Spanish thinkers.

The following year (1982), Amorós continued her conciliatory approach. In "Feminismos ilustrados y feminismos helenísticos" [Illustration feminisms and Helenistic feminisms] she casts difference feminism as ambiguous and equality feminism (or *el feminismo ilustrado*) as confused ("los contenidos de tal discurso de la igualdad distan de ser cartesianamente claros y distintos" (*Hacia* 157) [the contents of such equality discourse are far from being Cartesianally clear and distinct]. However, she now assumes a somewhat more aggressive stance vis-à-vis difference feminism, which she says, perhaps in reaction to Sendón de León's attack on equality feminism, "recoge resonancias ancestrales, caras a la sensibilidad romántica como lo abismático, lo misterioso, lo incontrolable, lo insondable" (*Hacia* 148) [gathers up ancestral resonances in the face of the romantic sensibility like the abysmal, the mysterious, the uncontrollable, the unfathomable]. She also allies difference feminism with ancient philosophies such as cynicism, epicureanism, and stoicism. Even though she believes difference feminist theory falls into impasses that echo those of some ancient philosophies, she does accept difference feminists' notion of self-affirmation, which can provide the oppressed with mechanisms to combat their marginalization.

Nineteen eighty-three saw the founding of the Instituto de la Mujer by the recently elected Spanish Socialist Party—a seminal event in the development of democratic-era Spanish feminism. The express purpose of the Instituto was to promote women's equality. Equality, as defined in the Constitution, figures prominently in its mission statement: "El Instituto de la Mujer es un organismo autónomo dependiente del Ministerio de Igualdad, a través de la Secretaría General de Políticas de Igualdad"[2] [The Women's Institute is an autonomous organism under the Ministry of Equality, through the General Secretariat of Equality Politics]. The purpose of the Instituto is described as the promotion and encouragement of "las condiciones que posibiliten la igualdad social de ambos sexos y, por otro, la participación de la mujer en la vida política cultural, económica y social. Por tanto, es el organismo del Gobierno central que promueve las políticas de igualdad entre mujeres y hombres" (http://www.migualdad.es/mujer/quien/historia.htm) [the conditions that make the social equality of both sexes possible and thus the participation of women in political, economic, and social life. As such, it is an organism of the central government that promotes the politics of equality between men and women]. Its rationale specifically notes that its principles are tied to the 1978 Constitution whose promulgation "supuso el reconocimiento de la igualdad ante la ley de hombres y mujeres como uno de los principios inspiradores de nuestro ordenamiento jurídico" (http://www.migualdad.es/mujer/quien/historia.htm) [meant the recognition of equality of men and women before the law as one of the inspiring principles of our juridical order]. In a clause that appears to recognize some of difference feminists' arguments about the problems of legislation as a sole avenue to women's having a proper place in all spheres of life, the statement recognizes that equality cannot be achieved by legislative means alone: "Para que las mujeres accedan a la igualdad no bastan los cambios legislativos. Hay que remover los obstáculos para que éstas participen en la cultura, el trabajo y la vida política y social" (http://www.migualdad.es/mujer/quien/historia.htm) [For women to achieve equality legislative changes are not enough. We must remove the obstacles to allow them to participate in culture, work, and political and social life]. All the references to equality and the Instituto's presumed independence from the government (at the time dominated by the Socialist Party) did not inspire difference feminists' confidence.[3]

In 1986, Celia Amorós, repeating some of the ideas of the 1982 lecture about parallels between difference feminism (which she calls a "curiosa combinación de elementos ideológicos" ["Algunos aspectos" 53] [a strange combination of ideological elements]) and dead-end classical philosophies, names Victoria Sendón de León overtly. Taking the high road and avoiding Sendón de León's stridency, Amorós calls Sendón's book *Sobre diosas, amazonas y vestales* "vibrante" and "una reelaboración relativamente original" [a relatively original reelaboration] of difference feminism. Amorós then deconstructs Sendón's central ideas. She notes that while Sendón argues against the rational logos as a patriarchal invention, she proposes the very Cartesian "autoconciencia feminista transparente y directa que saltaría por encima de mediaciones definitorias de la propia cultura patriarcal . . . para que la mujer se autorreconociera «a partir de sí misma» en ese cuerpo marcado" ("Algunos aspectos" 53) [transparent and direct feminist self-consciousness that would skip over the defining mediations of the patriarchal culture itself . . . so that women would recognize themselves "from themselves" in this marked body].

Nineteen ninety-eight marked a turning point in the equality/difference standoff in Spanish feminist theory of the democratic era. In that year Marina Subirats published *Con diferencia* [With difference], an attempt to reconcile the two positions, and Cristina Caruncho and Purificación Mayobre edited the essay collection *Entre igualdad e a diferencia* [Between equality and difference]. The attempt to find ways around the seeming impasse was already evident in the 1994 special issue of *El Viejo Topo*. There, Justa Montero asserted that a pragmatic feminism must overcome the philosophical differences of the several Spanish feminist groups to continue to make concrete gains for women in the real world. Montero argues for a common philosophical position that blends important elements of equality and difference feminisms. Pointing out that all egalitarian suppositions implicitly or explicitly begin by recognizing difference since what is being called for is equal consideration for those who do not enjoy it, precisely because they are not identical: "hemos entendido la lucha por la igualdad de derechos, que durante estos años ha desarrollado el movimiento feminista, unida a la reafirmación de nuestra identidad como mujeres y la autonomía de las mujeres" (40) [we have understood the struggle for equality of rights, which during these years the feminist movement has developed, as united to the reaffirmation of our identity as women and the autonomy of women]. Montero rejects the idea, implied by both equality and difference feminists, that equality means assuming a traditionally masculine identity, "una falsa analogía entre igualdad e identidad" (41) [a false analogy between equality and identity].

Marina Subirats, once director of the Instituto de la Mujer, suggests eliminating genders from our thinking, and replacing all references to "hombres y mujeres" [men and women] with "«individuos» de experiencia diferenciada, y diferenciada en tanto que individuos, no en tanto que seres pertenecientes a un género" (25) ["individuals" with different experiences, and differentiated as individuals, not as beings belonging to a gender].[4] Subirats goes beyond the legal issues and arguments that normally limit equality feminist thinking and programs to include interior transformations, and unlike difference feminists, she points out the need for men as well as women to reshape their consciousnesses. She affirms that in order for every human being to achieve status as an individual, there must be absolute parity in all life's arenas, not just the public sphere. Equality feminism's focus on legal parity has a hard time reaching into the private sphere where such matters as shared domestic duties are negotiated, immune from the long arm of the law. In this area perhaps the difference feminists have an edge in their concentration on fortifying women's inner selves.

In *Democracia feminista* (2003), political theorist Alicia Miyares proposes a feminist democracy to replace the two basic democratic models—liberal democracy and social democracy—in the Western world, neither of which, she argues, allows women to achieve equality. For Miyares, feminism is political and is centered on achieving equality as she defines it. She begins her study with a discussion of the notions of liberty and equality so fundamental to the 1978 Constitution. She attempts to find means to reconcile these two heretofore irreconcilable political models, asserting that for a political feminism a defense of equality must also be the defense of liberty, and all equality is liberty while all inequality is a deficit of liberty (154). Her reconciliation, however (again echoing an unacknowledged Rousseau), tips in favor of equality over liberty: "el cambio institucional que facilita la cohesión social no depende del énfasis que pongamos en la idea de libertad, sino en la idea de igualdad. La igualdad ha de presidir todas las instancias por las que nos socializamos y si no hay igualdad la cohesion social no será posible y la libertad será cosa de muy pocos" (13) [the institutional change that facilitates social cohesion does not depend on the emphasis that we put on the idea of liberty, but rather on the idea of equality. Equality must preside over all the instances for which we are socialized, and if there is no equality, social cohesion is not possible, and liberty will belong to very few]. She further observes that in a feminist democracy, both individual liberty and profound institutional change are necessary. To achieve the liberty/equality integration, she relies on the key concept of "sexual consciousness" (conciencia de sexo), which she believes joins "tanto libertad individual como igualdad en el completo sentido distributivo y de reconocimiento" (13) [both individual liberty and equality in a complete distributive and recognition sense]. She offers "sexual consciousness" as an alternative to "gender," a concept she claims "está totalmente despoliticizado y parece referirse únicamente a cierta identidad cultural que implica la aceptación de la mal denominada «cultura femenina»" (137) [is completely depoliticized and seems to refer only to a certain cultural identity that implies the acceptance of the misnamed "feminine culture"]. Sexual consciousness, which she defines as both men and women understanding that reality cannot be determined by sexual categories, dissolves any link between liberty and stereotypical roles. Thus, equality is freed from normativity, and sex has no place in the discussion of relations between women and men, the resources for obtaining work, and the ways intimacy or religiosity are carried out (171). For Miyares, sexual consciousness politicizes discussion of the sexes with respect to equality; it is as essential to feminism as class struggle is to Marxism or individualism to liberalism.

Miyares proposes "recognition" (reconocimiento), "la capacidad para abatir las designaciones sexuales" (154) [the capacity to tear down sexual designations] as a fundamental aspect—along with liberty and equality—of sexual consciousness. Despite her attempts to incorporate the difference feminist emphasis on the interior realm into her theory, her aversion to difference feminism is nonetheless evident. In an overt jab against difference feminism, which had so triumphantly announced the end of patriarchy in 1996, she sardonically observes that the burial of an ideology does not imply the death of the hierarchical family. She believes that through the concepts of oppression and domination, sexual justice can make visible injustices that were traditionally considered part of private life and cultural values: "La justicia sexual aborda principalmente la injusticia del poder sexual y la división sexual del trabajo" (31) [Sexual justice principally addresses the injustice of sexual power and the division of sexual work]. Her study includes a thorough analysis of the negative consequences for women of both liberalism and socialism. Liberalism, based as it is on personal realization, "el pacífico goce de la independencia privada" (47) [the peaceful joy of private independence], which produces self-esteem pertaining to the realm of private life (private life understood as "las relaciones que no determinan en absoluto la organización del Estado . . . caracterizada por el lenguaje emocional . . . relaciones mediadas por los afectos y los sentimientos negativos o positivos" [61]) [the relations that certainly do not determine the organization of the State . . . characterized by emotional . . . relations mediated by affections and negative or positive sentiments]. Private life is governed by custom rather than civil law, and thus women's lives have been subject to emotional rather than civic education. Liberalism does not recognize that the private sphere has been a realm of injustice for women ("todo apunta a que la esfera privada está regida por la jerarquía y la desigualdad" [50] [all points toward the private sphere being governed by hierarchy and inequality]). Personal realization depends on the well-being of society as a whole, a fact that requires a redefinition of privacy: "La libertad, por lo tanto, ha de salir de los reductos de la privacidad y asentarse sobre la ciudadanía" (49) [Thus liberty must emerge from the realm of privacy and install itself in the citizenry].

Her solution to women's submission to the cultural normativity and inequality of private family life is to make private life public: "La base del cambio en la familia se halla en que sea tomada como esfera pública y, por lo tanto, susceptible de cualquier regulación jurídica y valorativa que la convierta en una instancia igualitaria. La base de la familia ha de ser el reconocimiento" (121) [The basis for change in the family is that it be considered as part of the public sphere and thus susceptible to any juridical and evaluative regulation that converts it into an egalitarian case. The basis of the family must be recognition]. Recalling some of Empar Pineda's arguments in 1980, in Miyares's version of political feminism, equality should change everyone's position, both men's and women's. No one particular measure can be directed only toward modifying women's attitudes; men must always be part of the equation. She argues that the aura of privacy surrounding the family and the dependence of women's subjectivity on emotional relationships leads women to put up with domestic violence. In addition she cites a passage from Milagros Rivera to demonstrate how defense of the privacy of family life can lead to what she calls "posiciones erráticas" [erratic positions]. She quotes Milagros Rivera's *Mujeres en relación* on the dignity of battered woman, "su ofrendarse, a mantener viva la memoria de la importancia del vínculo, de su amor al vínculo" (Rivera 37) [their offering themselves to maintain the memory of the importance of the tie, of their love of the tie]. In a number of Miyares's statements she is responding directly to difference feminists' positions. She also calls perverse a political theory that conceives of an unchangeable women's culture focused on love, intimacy, and caregiving that one must adapt to, noting that "segregación es un modo de adaptación" (139) [segregation is a means of adaptation].

Finally, she declares herself completely unable to understand why difference feminism cannot accept an individualism unconditioned by sex (140). Miyares's solution to all human being's situation seems just as utopian as difference feminists' notion of a separate female culture. She idealistically proposes that it is possible for a person to be simultaneously caregiving and ambitious, to raise children and be civically engaged, to combine affect with efficiency and sacrifice with authority.

The principles of sexual consciousness and recognition move Miyares toward her "third-way" feminist democracy, which, unlike either liberalism or Marxism, is inclusive. Liberalism cannot take women into account because its notion of the person is based on property-holding, and Marxism does not consider women a social class.[5] She avers that sexual consciousness derives from individualism in that sex is no longer a differentiating trait for men and women; it also derives from equality because it allows the process of recognition between individuals to take place (171). Thus sexual consciousness operates at different levels of reality, allowing for the recognition of both individuality and equality. A feminist democracy would reduce the private sphere to intimacy and beliefs; it would not allow media entertainment to use women as sexual objects or religious motivations to enter the public sphere and exacerbate conflicts between the sexes. Feminist democracy would give absolute parity to both sexes, and women would have access to the political power denied them because of their family responsibilities. In combining the opportunities for personal self-development that liberal autonomy offers via the wedding of state and civil society in social democracy: "Vincula . . . autonomía de los individuos con compromiso cívico y constata que la amplia definición de privacidad debilita el estatus de las mujeres" (189) [(It) unites individual autonomy with civic responsibility and affirms that the wide definition of privacy weakens women's status].

The Spanish feminist polemic over equality and difference is far from over. Books that address gender equality and difference continue to appear. In her *Rebeldes. Hacia la paridad* (2000) [Rebels: Toward parity], Amelia Valcárcel maintains that equality goals have not been achieved. Victoria Sendón de León's *Marcar las diferencias* (2002) [Marking the differences] continues to vigorously defend difference feminism, although she now complicates her arguments and modulates her tone with Sartrean notions of the *en soi* and the *pour soi*. Carlos Lomas's 2004 *Los chicos también lloran. Identidades masculinas, igualdad entre los sexos y coeducacion* [Boys cry too. Masculine identities, equality between the sexes and coeducation] brings a male perspective to the polemic. Also focusing on education is Ylanda Herranz Gómez's *Igualdad bajo sospecha: El poder transformador de la educación* (2006) [Equality under suspicion: The transformative power of education]. And María Elena Simón Rodríguez's *Hijas de la igualdad, herederas de injusticias* [Daughters of equality, inheritors of injustices] considers the second generation of democratic-era women who have lived under legal parity. Carlos Lomas again takes a male viewpoint in *¿El otoño del patriarcado? Luces y sombras de la igualdad entre mujeres y hombres* (2008) [The autumn of the patriarchy? Lights and shadows of equality between men and women].

Equality feminists might seem to have gained an official victory with the establishment in 2008 of the Ministerio de Igualdad, although an article in the Madrid daily *ABC* "La Comisión de Igualdad se aburre" [The Equality Commission is getting bored] reported that the congressional organ charged with overseeing equality had fewer issues on its agenda than any other commission, except housing. The official and theoretical work regarding equality begun several years before the 1978 Constitution and ratified by the document is not yet completed. It is perhaps safe to say that the debate over equality and difference will be a subject of interest to Spanish feminist theorists for some years, although the debate will doubtless take into consideration other dimensions of the subject.

Epilogue

Toward a Better World

This book must remain open-ended. New topics in Spanish feminist theory will continue to arise as the old ones play themselves out. Surely, the whole matter of immigrant women and their particular problems and viewpoints, which I have barely touched on here with references to Najar El Hachmi's journalism, will find voices that must be taken into account. Another new strand that has attracted essayists is ecofeminism. This body of theory is especially promoted in Spain by political philosopher Alicia Puleo, who was an early member of Celia Amorós's University of Madrid Seminario Permanente Feminismo e Ilustración (1987–1994) [Permanent Seminar Feminism and Illustration] continued as Proyecto de Investigación: Feminismo, Ilustración y Postmodernidad (1995–1999) [Research Project: Feminism, Illustration and Postmodernity]. Ecofeminists are concerned about both ecological and feminist matters and combine the two interests in their thinking, writing, and/or activism. These areas of interest were first brought together in 1974 by Françoise d'Eaubonne, who believed that the hierarchy of social domination over women could be compared to the exploitation of the environment. Ecofeminists argue that considering feminism and ecology together reinforces certain aspects of their concerns that otherwise remain in the shadows. For example, looking at environmental deterioration from a gendered perspective highlights the fact that women's health can be particularly compromised by the presence of estrogen-like toxins in soil and water. The hope from both the environmental and feminist sectors is that the alliance of the two will raise global consciousness of the many environmental and feminist issues remaining to be solved and that these will be addressed in ways that protect both the environment and women's rights.

As Alicia Puleo has demonstrated in her many writings on the history and theory of ecofeminism, in its some forty-year history, the concept has manifested itself in different ways in various parts of the globe, from a more mystical orientation in places such as India (Vandana Shiva is Puleo's primary example) to anarchist and socialist political affiliations (Carolyn Merchant and Mary Mellor are her representatives of politically leftist ecofeminists). Puleo has written about and critiqued these orientations since the early 1990s and has developed her own approach to ecofeminism that integrates ideas she has adopted from her association with equality or enlightenment feminists such as Celia Amorós. Puleo's latest book, *Ecofeminismo: Para otro mundo posible* (2011) [Ecofeminism: For another possible world], is her most intensive and extensive consideration of an Enlightenment (or critical) ecofeminism. It synthesizes her earlier historical-critical writings on the subject and proposes a new position that mediates between the rational and affective approaches of historical ecofeminisms.

The cornerstone of Puleo's mature concept of ecofeminism is the notion of women as individuals on a universal scale. Puleo has argued for ecofeminism's potential to overcome the divide between equality and difference feminism. She judges difference feminism to coincide with early ecofeminism's tendency to equate women with nature, thus underwriting traditional belief in ontological differences between the sexes. Ecofeminism, she proposes, has the potential to change the human paradigm and overcome the tradition of equating the generically human with the masculine. *Ecofeminismo: Para otro mundo mejor* affirms that the task of our time is to "superar la ignorancia, combatir la injusticia y cultivar la sensibilidad moral. ¿Acaso no es un buen lema ilustrado? Las luces se curan con más luces. Hoy, feminismo y ecología pueden revitalizar el impulso emancipatorio ilustrado." (*Ecofeminismo* 146) [overcome ignorance, combat injustice, and cultivate moral sensibility. Can there be a better enlightened motto? Enlightenment is cured with more Enlightenment. Today feminism and ecology can revitalize the emancipatory Illustration impulse]. Alicia Puleo's critical ecofeminism, as fully elaborated in *Ecofeminismo*, is a capacious theory that embraces a wide array of principles—reason, emotions, equality, freedom, ethics of care, politics—brought together in a dialectical relationship in which each is tempered by the others. Puleo observes that ecology and women's concerns emerged at the same historical juncture in the eighteenth century, which saw both the rise of reason and a concern for animal feelings (she gives the example of eighteenth-century women's horror at the practice of vivisection). Reason—critical reason—she posits, must always include an ethical dimension. This fundamental insight allows Puleo to accomplish the fusion of reason and affect at the heart of her mature ecofeminist position. To this end

> es necesario favorecer el desarrollo conjunto de la razón y la emoción y abandonar lo que el ecofeminismo ha llamado «lógica del dominio». Razón y emoción tienen que estar conectadas para que los humanos seamos seres equilibrados capaces de alcanzar una calidad de vida que no pase por la multiplicación *ad infinitum* de los objetos materiales, sino por la mejora de las relaciones interpersonales en la igualdad por disponer de más tiempo libre y ser capaces de usarlo de maneras no alienadas. (*Ecofeminismo* 17)

> [we must enable the joint development of reason and emotion and abandon what ecofeminism has called "the logic of domination." Reason and emotion have to be connected so that we humans can be balanced beings capable of achieving a quality of life that isn't just limited to the infinite multiplication of material objects, but that improves the equality in interpersonal relations so that there is more free time that can be used in nonalienating ways.]

Puleo's reading and research have reached beyond philosophy, feminist theory, ecological theory, and ecofeminist theory into neuroscience, whose recent finds indicate that some animals practice an ethics of care. Thus such comportment may have evolutionary value, which makes it worth universalizing as a human practice.

Puleo joins a long list of Spanish feminists, including María Martínez Sierra, Rosa Chacel, and María Zambrano, who subscribe to "la idea radical de que las mujeres somos personas" (*Ecofeminismo* 265) [the radical idea that women are persons]. In her insistence on viewing women as persons, she turns her critical reason on a number of recent social and theoretical trends that are legacies of postmodern philosophy. For example, when examined from her critical perspective, transgressive sexual acts, which now seem socially acceptable for women, only confer pseudo-liberation. Viewing such acts as liberating for women merely adopts male standards and reinforces the nature/culture divide. These observations lead Puleo into a critique of queer theory for its perpetuating constructivist notions of the subject that deny both female and homosexual identities. And she also engages with Donna Haraway's notion of the cyborg for its exclusionary notion of the Other. Puleo concludes that the poststructuralist tendency to deny "toda instancia natural es problemática para la ecología. La reducción de la realidad a construcción discursiva es falsa e incita a intensificar los procesos de colonización de la Naturaleza" (*Ecofeminismo* 252) [all natural entreaty is problematic for ecology. The reduction of reality to a discursive construction is false and incites the intensifying of the process of colonizing nature]. For Puleo, transgression is not invariably to the good, and one must distinguish between transgressions that are genuinely emancipatory and those that ignore nature and bring suffering, disease, and death.

Puleo has made a bold statement and added significantly to previous ecofeminist theories from her unique position informed by Spanish equality feminism. In moving beyond the polarizing division between equality and difference feminism that characterized Spanish feminist theory in the 1980s and 1990s, Puleo has found ways to combine equality feminism's reason and difference feminism's affect.

Notes

Introduction

1. There are, of course, other issues or concepts I could have included, such as women's writing, although it is not as salient a topic in Spanish feminist writing as it is in American and French feminist theory. As a sample of Spanish theories of women's writing, I can point to Carmen Laforet's and Carmen Martín-Gaite's ideas on the subject. Although Laforet's ideas were not written for a general public, in 1967 she wrote in a letter to Ramón Sender: "Quisiera escribir una novela (Que no es de la célebre frase en El Banquete ¿verdad? «Tenemos las mujeres del gineceo para la casa y los hijos . . .») En verdad, es el mundo que domina secretamente la vida. Secretamente. Instintivamente la mujer se adapta y organiza unas leyes inflexibles, hipócritas en muchas situaciones para un dominio terrible . . . Las pobres escritoras no hemos contado nunca la verdad, aunque queramos. La literatura la inventó el varón y seguimos empleando el mismo enfoque para las cosas. Yo quisiera intentar una tradición para dar algo de ese secreto, para que poco a poco vaya dejando de existir esa fuerza de dominio, y hombres y mujeres nos entendamos mejor, sin sometimientos, ni aparentes ni reales, de unos a otros . . . tiene que llover mucho para eso. Pero ¿verdad que está usted de acuerdo, en que lo verdaderamente femenino en la situación humana las mujeres no lo hemos dicho, y cuando lo hemos intentado ha sido con lenguaje prestado, que resultaba falso por muy sinceras que quisiéramos ser?" (*Puedo contar contigo* 97) [I would like to write a novel (but not for two years or so) about a world that is not known except from the outside because it has not found its language . . . The world of the gynaeceum. (Which is not from the famous sentence from The Banquet, right? "We have women of the gynaeceum for the home and children . . .") In reality, it is the world that secretly dominates life. Secretly. Instinctively women adapt themselves and organize some inflexible, hypocritical laws, often for a terrible domination. . . . We poor writers have never told the truth, much as we might wish to. Literature

was invented by men, and we continue to employ the same viewpoint]. In a series of lectures from the mid-1980s Carmen Martín Gaite, who had come into contact with Anglo-American feminist theory while teaching at Barnard College in 1980, gives a brilliant feminist reading of Rosalía de Castro's novel *El hombre de las botas azules* [The man in the blue boots], in which she finds that Castro inverts the typical romantic trope of the female muse and invents a male muse for a woman ("El hombre musa"). She had used the same strategy herself in her novel *El cuarto de atrás*, published in 1978. Emilie Bergmann aptly calls Martín Gaite's writings on literature "Narrative Theory in the Mother Tongue." Another example of Spanish women's theorizing about women's writing is the statement by Soledad Puértolas quoted in the text.

2. Mary Nash ("Experiencia") traces the alternate route that nineteenth-century Spanish feminism traveled, developing as it did within the Spanish Catholic tradition and within a political system that lacked a notion of universal suffrage even for men.

3. Carmen Alcalde also defines Spanish feminism as activism. Alcalde shifted her view as to whether or not there had been a "feminist movement" in Spain before the Civil War, centering her argument on the theoretical matter of whether feminism entails individual or group efforts: "Lo que pasa precisamente es que la Guerra frustró completamente al feminismo, lo cortó. Entonces vino la reacción y la mujer volvió al hogar. Quizás ahora lo ampliaría más y quizás lo trasladaría mucho más a la política, al problema del no feminismo en España. . . . Yo no sé en esos momentos qué se entiende por feminismo, porque me parece que está muy confuso todo esto. Si lo entiendes como un movimiento militante, no sé hasta qué punto lo somos. Ahora, si el feminismo se entiende simplemente a nivel individual, la realización verdadera de la mujer como ser, entonces yo creo que no se puede decir que no hubo feminismo en España. Creo que hubo feminismo. Lo que pasa es que España lleva un lastre de un siglo y más, de mucha castración y mucha reacción. Entonces no hay posibilidad de feminismo en un clima de reacciones imposibles" (Levine and Waldman 27–28) [What happened exactly is that the War completely interrupted the feminist movement; it stopped it. Then came the reaction and women returned to the home. Perhaps now it will be amplified, and perhaps it will be transferred to the political arena, because it seems to me that all of this is very confused. If you understand it as a militant movement, I don't know to what point we are. Now, if feminism is simply understood at the individual level, the true realization of the woman as a being, then I believe that we can say there was feminism in Spain. I believe there was feminism. What happened is that Spain carries the burden of more than a century of castration and reaction. Thus there is no possibility for feminism in a climate of impossible reactions].

4. Glenn also quotes Cristina Fernández Cubas as having emphatically declared "[n]inguno de nuestros libros se puede considerar feminista. . . . Y es

que literatura y feminismo no tienen nada que ver" (374) [none of our books can be considered feminist. . . . And it is that literature and feminism have nothing to do with each other].

5. Wadda Ríos-Font carefully examines Trigo's works to discover that his self-proclaimed feminist stance is not borne out by his narrative strategies.

6. Interestingly and not surprisingly, the studies of Concepción Arenal from the Franco era emphasize her Catholicism and elements in her feminist thought (women as emotional and caring) that are compatible with a conservative social agenda. Simultaneously, they deny all connections of her work to Krausism, which in the Franco era was considered liberal and subversive just as it was in the pre-Republican era of the 1860s. Jesús Tobio Fernández, for example, is pleased to note that "[s]u feminismo es decidido, pero no avanzado. Merece en todo el calificativo de «aceptable» que le aplicó el padre Alarcón" (Las ideas sociales de Concepción Arenal 110) [her feminism is firm, but not advanced. It entirely deserves the qualification of "acceptable" that Father Alarcón applied to it]. He was equally happy that she attacked with "hábil y poderosa dialéctica contra las concepciones utópicas de la sociedad, «los idilios sociales compuestos de los que no saben lo que pasa» y ataca también las ideologías subversivas del anarquismo y el comunismo y, en particular las figuras de Proudhon, a quien llama «una gran caverna con muchos errores», y Fourier" (19) [able and powerful dialectic against utopian conceptions of society, "the social idylls composed by those who do not know what is happening," and she also attacks the subversive ideologies of anarchism and communism, in particular the figures of Proudhon, whom she calls "a great cavern of many errors," and Fourier]. Tobio Frenández goes on to assert, without any proof, that "[d]el krausismo, felizmente, no se advierte en su obra vestigio de influencia alguna" (21) [happily, we cannot detect any influence at all of Krausism in her work]. Juan Antonio Cabezas in *Concepción Arenal o el sentido romántico de la justicia* places Arenal within early-nineteenth-century Spanish Romanticism, thus making her thought sound archaic, even though it was an important inspiration to the Spanish feminist movement of the 1920s and 1930s, which disappeared by 1940. However, in *Concepción Arenal en su aspecto pedagógico*, Manuel Casas Fernández does allow that "Aquella idea de Krause de constituir la Sociedad científica (Wissenschafthund) de la cual todos forman parte no es ajena al deseo de Concepción Arenal de que la ciencia se extienda a todos los hombres sin distinción de clases; porque la cultura y la educación son las dos paralelas que señalan el camino de la perfección individual y social" (57) [That idea of Krause to constitute the scientific society of which we all form a part is not far from Concepción Arenal's desire for science to extend to all people without differentiation of classes because culture and education are two parallels that point toward the road to individual and social perfection].

7. The essay was published along with others by Rafael Salillas and Sánchez Moguel in a collection titled *Doña Concepción Arenal y sus obras*.

8. "Entre los «papeles» de Azcárate aparece, entre otras, la autógrafo de doña Concepción Arenal a doña Constancia Caveda dándle el pésame por la muerte de su esposo don Anselmo Cifuentes, veradero modelo en su género; carta que con toda seguridad dio a Azcárate su cuñada doña Constancia Cifuentes, hija de don Anselmo, y que Azcárate conservó como una verdadera reliquia" (Azcárate 32) [Among Azcárate's "papers" there appears, among other things, a signed letter to Constancia Caveda expressing her condolences for the death of her husband Anselmo Cifuentes. His sister-in-law Constancia Cifuentes, Anselmo's daughter, surely gave the letter, a real model of its genre, to Azcárate, who conserved it as a true relic].

9. López Morillas particularly mentions 1857 until Sanz del Río's death in 1869 as the reigning years of his influence.

10. Lou Charnon-Deutsch points out the importance of the nineteenth century in the history of Spanish and other feminisms: "The nineteenth century is one of the favored test periods feminism uses to confront patriarchal values because the ideologies of gender are so heavily inscribed in its discourses and because as Carolyn Heilbrun argues, it is a century of such great sexual polarization (*Towards a Recognition* 54)" (*Gender and Representation* xii).

11. See Carmen Martín Gaite (*Usos amorosos de la posguerra en España*) for an account of women's lives under the dictates of Sección Femenina ideology.

12. For example, Mary Lee Bretz cogently analyzes Margarita Nelken's argument from history: "early in the text [*La condición social de la mujer en España*], the blame for the lack of women's advancement in Spain is attributed equally to the Moorish influence and a narrow-minded anti-Christian Church (13), but in a subtle textual about-face, in a later discussion, the text speaker points out that under the purported antifeminine Moorish regime, there were several famous women doctors at the University of Córdoba (44). The reader is left to surmise that the major contributor to the Spanish woman's developmental lag is the Church" (103). Michael Ugarte observes that Carmen de Burgos "takes great care to distance herself from the popular anticlerical discourse that was crucial to the understanding of the history of the Spanish left. On the contrary, in *Modern Woman*, she uses examples from the lives of Jesus, the saints, and certain teachings of theologians as allies in her arguments for the social and legal rights for women" (63).

13. Her historical approach is very similar to Simone de Beauvoir's in *The Second Sex*, which she quotes in chapters 3, 4, and 5.

14. See Shirley Mangini (129–32) for an analysis of the seeming inconsistencies and contradictions in Chacel's arguments in "Esquema de los problemas prácticos y actuales del amor," as she attempts to overcome the male-female polarity: "One of the concepts Chacel argues most insistently is found in 'Outline' is the adherence to the belief that woman's intellectual development has been

hampered by the quagmire of social institutions; nevertheless, she systematically refuses, in all her writing about women's inferior role in culture and society at large, to point the accusatory finger at the instigators and defenders of those institutions" (132). Mangini also suggests the importance of Chacel's essays as "theoretical frameworks for understanding the ambiguous, shifting realities of her fictional characters" (132).

15. Vanessa Knights and Mercedes de Grado cover some of this terrain. They summarize the history of the equality/difference debate beginning in the late Franco era up to 1996 and 2000, respectively. De Grado's essay contains a great deal of useful information, but it sides with equality feminism. The point of Knights's fine article is to demonstrate how knowledge of the equality/difference debate can shed new light on women's fiction of the democratic era; thus, half of her essay is devoted to novelists. I concentrate on feminist theory as such rather than how feminism is encoded in literary works, and I emphasize different writers and their historical and philosophical roots.

Chapter 1

1. For example, Luis de Góngora's best-known poems are titled *Las soledades* [The solitudes], and Geoffrey Ribbans has studied the melancholic tone of Antonio Machado's *Soledades* [Solitudes]. Interestingly, the female protagonist of Juan José Millás's novel *La soledad era eso* [That is what solitude was] defines solitude as follows: "Bueno, pues la soledad era esto: encontrarte de súbito en el mundo como si acabaras de llegar de otro planeta del que no sabes por qué has sido expulsada. Te han dejado traerte dos objetos (en mi caso, la butaca y el reloj) que tienes que llevar a cuestas como una maldición, hasta que encuentres un lugar en el que recompones tu vida a partir de esos objetos y de la confusa memoria del mundo del que procedes. La soledad es una amputación no visible, pero tan eficaz como si se te arrancaran la vista y el oído y así aislada de todas las sensaciones exteriores de todos los puntos de referencia, y sólo habitar y que te habita. ¿Qué había en esto de literario, qué había de divertido? ¿Por qué nos gustaba tanto?" (133–34) [OK, well solitude was this: to find yourself all of a sudden in the world as though you had just arrived from another planet from which you have inexplicably been expelled. They have allowed you to bring two objects (in my case, the easy chair and the grandfather clock), which you have to carry on your back like a curse until you find a place in which you can reconstitute your life based on these objects and the fuzzy memory of the world from which you came. Solitude is an invisible amputation, which is just as effective as if they had removed your sight and hearing, and thus isolated from all external sensations of all points of reference, and you just inhabit and

are inhabited. What was literary in that; what had amused you? Why do we like it so much?] With these words the protagonist echoes many Spanish feminists' assertions since the 1920s, especially in the last twenty years.

2. Since I am interested primarily in thought, I limit myself to theoretical or philosophical texts and must necessarily leave out the many literary works pertinent to the subject. If I were including fiction in this study, I would have to comment on Victor Català's novel *Soledad* (1905), which chronicles the life of Mila, married to Matias. The couple become caretakers of a religious hermitage in the Catalonian mountains. Matias is a lazy ne'er-do-well who takes to gambling and leaves Mila to do all the work related to the religious site. In that sense her solitude is less positive than that of the writers I describe in this chapter. However, at the end of the novel, after Mila is raped by a vicious local man with whom Matias is friendly (the rapist takes advantage of Matias's being absent because he is gambling), Mila leaves Matias to begin a new life alone, in some sense a more positive state than that in which she has lived since marrying Matias.

3. There is only one word in Spanish for the English concepts "solitude," which can have positive and negative connotations, and "loneliness," which indicates a lack of someone or something and is more negative. Thus, *soledad* in Spanish is more ambiguous and must be interpreted in each context in which it appears. Linda Chown writes of her surprise when she asked her students at a Basque university if they understood the difference between "loneliness" and "solitude" in English, and they had no idea what "loneliness" meant: "in fact, the very idea of loneliness made no sense either conceptually or emotionally" ("Solitude/Identity" 197). Toward the end of this chapter, more recent feminist writers (Rosa Montero, Carmen Alborch), perhaps influenced by English meanings and/or French existentialism, appear occasionally to adopt "loneliness" as a standard meaning for *soledad* in Spanish.

4. I am grateful to my University of Kansas colleague Janet Sharistanian for pointing me toward Stanton's speech.

5. It should be noted, however, that Emilia Pardo Bazán allied herself indirectly with Feijoo in naming the journal she founded and wrote entirely herself *Nuevo Teatro Crítico* [New critical theater], echoing the general title Feijoo gave his complete works *Teatro crítico universal* [Universal critical theater].

6. The enlightenment and Krausism have rationalism in common. As a neo-Kantian philosophy, the rational has a prominent role in Krausism; "reason is the seat of rectitude, in the dual sense of integrity and discipline" (López Morillas 38).

7. In formulating her concept of the woman, Arenal prefers the term "social" instead of "relacional," which for her has a more negative connotation than Alda Blanco gives the term. According to Blanco, "[f]eminismo relacional y feminismo individualista conviven en la Europa decimonónica y elaboran

diferentes representaciones ontológicas de la mujer" (*Textos* 453) [relational feminism and individualist feminism coexisted in nineteenth-century Europe and elaborated different ontological representations of women]. Concepción Arenal ingeniously marshals the relational (or social) dimension of women's lives in order to get them out of the house; she argues that women can do much social good by visiting the poor and engaging in other charitable activities.

    8. Concepción Arenal also read Rousseau, but I cannot find any indication as to her opinion on the social contract, although her theoretical orientation seems to agree with this philosophical concept.

    9. María Martínez Sierra likewise argues the same position in *Cartas a las mujeres de España*.

    10. As I noted in the "Introduction," one can defend literature as a source of Spanish feminist thought (especially in periods such as the Franco era when openly feminist essays were difficult to get past the censors), but here I limit myself to nonfiction.

    11. Nineteenth-century poet Carolina Coronado also approaches an aspect of female solitude or individuality—liberty—from a political viewpoint in her 1846 poem "Libertad." Women were not included in the political liberties so celebrated by men of the Romantic era: "Mas por nosotras, / las hembras, / ni lo aplaudo ni lo siento, / pues aunque leyes se muden, / para nosotras no hay fueros. / ¡Libertad! ¿qué nos importa? / ¿qué ganamos, qué tendremos?. . . . ¡Libertad! ¿de qué nos vale, / si son los tiranos nuestros / no el yugo de los monarcas, / el yugo de nuestro sexo?" (*Poesías*, 1853 edition, qtd. in Kirkpatrick 319) [But for us, / the women, / I neither applaud nor regret it, / since, although the laws are mute, / for us there are no rights. / Liberty! What do we care? / what do we gain, what will we have?].

    12. María Martínez Sierra (María de la O. Lejárraga) was married young to childhood sweetheart Gregorio Martínez Sierra. They collaborated together on theatrical projects; María wrote plays under Gregorio's name, and Gregorio produced them on stage. Gregorio left María when his lover, the stage actress Catalina Barçena, became pregnant. Even though Gregorio lived with Barçena after the birth of their daughter, he and María continued their theatrical collaborations.

    13. See Shirley Mangini (130–32) for a discussion of possible ambiguities in Chacel's argument.

    14. In using the term "man" to refer to all humanity, as was the custom in philosophical texts at the time, Chacel writes that "al decir el hombre, lo hago con sentido estrictamente humano. El problema, el *pathos* de esta lucha, lo llevan igualmente en su fondo íntimo el hombre y la mujer" (168, emphasis in original) [in saying man, I do so in the strictly human sense. The problem, the *pathos*, in this struggle essentially belongs to both men and women].

    15. One can hear echoes of Scheler's distinction between humans and animals in this statement.

16. See the correspondence between Ramón Sender and Laforet, published in *Puedo contar contigo* (edited by Israel Rolón Barada) and in letters to Roberta Johnson in Rolón Barada ("La correspondencia").

17. For example: "Yo estoy deseando quedarme sola, decir a todo el mundo que me he marchado o marcharme de verdad si fuera posible y terminar mi famoso libro" (Rolón Barada, "Letter 38" to Father Arrizabalaga, 7 February 1964); "Las vacaciones de Semana Santa fueron un paréntesis muy bueno, lleno de descanso y lujo spiritual y material también porque tenía sol, soledad en el bosque cuando quería y compañía de viejas amigas al atardecer y decidí olvidar toda preocupación de todas clases en aquellos días" ("Letter 39" to Father Arrizabalaga, 7 April 1964); "He alquilado una casita en Cercedilla para que la familia pasemos todos los domingos y vacaciones posibles en el campo y yo los días a la semana o el tiempo seguido que necesito para escribir lejos del teléfono y las complicaciones. Mi idea es estar al menos tres días a la semana allí y aprovechar esos tres días de silencio para el trabajo intensivo" [I am feeling the need to be alone, to tell everyone that I have gone away or to actually go away, so I can finish my famous book. . . . The Easter vacation was a good break, full of rest and spiritual and material luxury, because I had sun, solitude in the forest, and when I wanted it, the company of long-time women friends in the afternoon, if I decided to forget all my worries during those days. . . . I have rented a little house in Cercedilla so that the family can go there on Sundays and for vacations in the country, and I will go during the week or for a period of time when I need to write far from the telephone and complications. My idea is to be there at least three days a week and during those three days of silence to work intensively.]

18. See Arsova for a discussion of Fuertes and the theme of solitude.

19. Montserrat Roig writes that "Las «heroínas» de la Sección Femenina eran en el orden religioso, «mártires, las vírgenes y, en general, todas las santas, cuya vida fue un total renunciamiento para llegar a Cristo». En la pirámide de la santidad, del máximo valor, estaba la virginidad. Cuando era una niña, siempre me pareció más santa Lucía, sin ojos, o santa Eulalia, sin pechos, que no santa Francisca viuda. Esta última, por muy santa que fuese, no dejaba de estar «contaminada»" (66) [The "heroines" of the Sección Femenina were religious types, "martyrs, virgins, and, in general, all saints, whose lives were a total renunciation in order to reach Christ." In the pyramid of sainthood, virginity had the greatest value. When I was a girl, I always thought more highly of Saint Lucía without eyes or Saint Eulalia without breasts, than of the widow Saint Francisca. The latter, however saintly she might have been, seemed somehow "contaminated"].

20. In *Desde la ventana* Carmen Martín Gaite quotes Judith Fetterley, Sandra Gilbert and Susan Gubar, Adrienne Rich, and Elaine Showalter, and in *Solas* Carmen Alborch mentions Helen Gurley Brown, Kate Millett, E. A.

Kaplan, Susan Faludi, Toni Morrison, Gloria Steinem, Lillian B. Rubin, Naomi Wolf, Ann Kaplan, and Betty Friedan.

Chapter 2

1. There are some differences between this definition and the one that appears in the eighteenth edition of 1956 and later editions. For example, the fourth definition of 2001 is found in the second position in 1956, and the fifth in third place. The third definition does not exist in the 1956 edition. Joaquín Sánchez de Toca employs the term *personalidad* in an essay titled "El matrimonio" [Matrimony] from 1973. Although his message is not exactly feminist, it does allow for women to have a personality distinct from that of a man: "Desde el punto de vista ideal, el marido y la mujer no forman más que un mismo ser: el amor conyugal confundió su carne y su espíritu, y de las dos criaturas distintas se formó una sola persona moral que sólo tiene una misma voluntad, un mismo afecto, idénticos sentimientos, iguales deseos, las mismas penas y los mismos placeres. Pero esto no es más que un ideal irrealizable, pues de otro modo la unión conyugal no constituiría una sociedad, porque para la existencia de cualquier sociedad se necesitan varias personas, varias voluntades distintas individualidades unidas en el logro del mismo objeto; considerada la unión conyugal como antes la considerábamos, no formarían ambos cónyuges más que una misma personalidad, un mismo ser moral. Aun en el seno de la más íntima unión conyugal concebimos al marido y a la mujer como dos personalidades distintas: indisoluble aparece su unión, eterna fuerza del amor que las enlaza, sorprendente la misteriosa unidad que entre ellas reina; pero en el fondo resulta siempre distinta la individualidad de los seres. Y al mismo tiempo que la razón nos dice que son ambos cónyugues dos personalidades diversas, y nos los senseña como iguales entre sí, como complemento uno de otro, y como miembros de una sociedad, vemos por otro lado que la idea de autoridad entraña la idea de superioridad, y consiguiente aquél de los dos que tenga la autoridad, debe por lo tanto poseer también superioridad" (*La mujer en los discursos de género* 84) [From an ideal point of view, man and woman do not form more than one and the same being: conjugal love melded their flesh and spirit, and a single moral person with only one will, one affection, identical sentiments, the same desires, the same pains and the same pleasures were formed from the two different creatures. But this is only an unrealizable ideal, since if it were any other way, the conjugal union would not constitute a society, because in order for a society to exist, there must be various persons, several different individuals united in achieving the same object. As the conjugal union was formerly considered, both partners in the conjugal union would constitute only one personality, one morality. Even in the heart

of the most intimate conjugal union, we conceive of the husband and wife as two distinct personalities. Their union seems undissolvable, the love that binds them eternally, and the mysterious unity that reigns between them surprising. However, in the end their individuality is always different. At the same time that reason tells us that both married persons have different personalities, we see them as equals, as complements one of the other, and as members of a society, we also see that the idea of authority includes the idea of superiority, and thus the one that has authority should therefore also be superior].

2. Interestingly, Emilia Pardo Bazán in her summation at the end of the 1892 Congreso Pedagógico, which Arenal was unable to attend for reasons of health, pays special homage to the founding mother of Spanish feminism "El Congreso, señores, tributaría a la autora de las *Cartas a los delincuentes*, de la *Cuestión social* y del *Visitador del pobre*, el homenaje debido a la dama insigne, a quien leen, traducen y consultan los sociólogos de Alemania y de Inglaterra, y a quien corona ya, con la augusta diadema de los años, el lauro de la sabiduría y la gloria del más ejemplar empleo de las facultades afectivas e intelectivas, no de una *mujer*, sino, como ella quiere que se diga, de una *persona*" (*La mujer española*) [The Congress, gentlemen, would like to pay homage to the author of "Letters to the prisoners," "Social question," and "Visitor of the poor," an homage due a notable woman, who German and English sociologists read and who is now crowned with the august diadem of the years, the laurel wreath of wisdom and the glory of the exemplary affective and intellectual faculties, not of a *woman*, but, as she would have it, of a *person*].

3. María Zambrano's concept of the soul is feminine. See my article "El concepto de persona."

4. See Christine Arkinstall ("Writing") for more information on Rosario de Acuña's life and thought.

5. In the mother's trial for Hildegart's murder, the word *personalidad* comes up often: "Había una lucha entre la personalidad de la madre y la hija, predominando la de la madre. . . . Hildegart, que tenía personalidad suficiente para vivir emancipada de la madre, quisiera separarse de ella. . . . el deseo de Hildegart de independizarse de su madre, recobrando su pesonalidad. . . . Hildegart quería tener una personalidad propia ya que la madre absorbía la suya" (*Hildegart Rodríguez* 180, 185) [There was a battle between the mother's personality and that of the daughter in which the mother's personality dominated. . . . Hildegart, who had sufficient personality to live emancipated from her mother, wanted to separate from her. . . . Hildegart's desire to become independent of her mother, recovering her personality. . . . Hildegart wanted to have her own personality because her mother absorbed hers].

6. See my article "María Zambrano's Solitude."

7. The concept of a being or a person and his or her surroundings that María Zambrano elaborates in *Persona y democracia* combines Unamuno's intimist

approach and the more historical view of her teacher and dissertation director José Ortega y Gasset in order to arrive at a truly original notion of the human being as an individual in relation to society.

8. See Meredes Carbayo Abengózar (43–73) for a discussion of the influence of European existentialism on Martín Gaite and other writers of her generation.

9. The references that Martín Gaite makes to the public feminist demonstrations indicate that it is toward the end of the 1960s or beginning of the 1970s, the year that the author separated from her husband Rafael Sánchez Ferlosio.

Chapter 3

1. As Lidia Falcón will do in the late twentieth century, Arenal places women alongside the working class as a parallel social entity that requires attention: "La cuestión social de la mujer, si no formalmente como la del obrero, está esencialmente planteada, y que, como todas las cuestiones que se plantean en la sociedad, es preciso resolverlo" [The social question of women, if not formally like that of the worker, is essentially posed, like all questions posed in society, in order to resolve it].

2. San Martín adds that "Así, pues, tratándose de mujeres, esta información requiere más amplitud que en lo referente al trabajo de los hombres; porque hay seres más desgraciados que el obrero., la mujer y la hija de éste, y hay todavía mujeres más desamparadas que las obreras: la viuda y la huérfana de las clases medias trabajadoras" (qtd. in Nash, *Mujer* 342) [So, when it comes to women, this information requires greater scope than in the case of men's work, because there are human beings who are less fortunate than the male worker—his wife and daughter. And there are women who are more helpless than working-class women—the widow and orphan of the working middle classes].

3. The article was published in Spanish the following year in *La España Moderna* XVII (1890): 101–13; XVIII (1890): 5–15; XIX (1890): 121–31; XX (1890): 143–54.)

4. Maryellen Bieder ("Women, Literature, and Society" 39–40) points out that Pardo Bazán follows the format of the painting of national types study so common in nineteenth-century Spain, although in this essay Pardo Bazán attempts to give her analysis a scientific veneer.

5. I should note that Geraldine Scanlon believes that Pardo Bazán's position coincides with that of a bourgeois liberal: "She is aware of the class-bound character of the anti-feminist discourse which identified 'woman' with the middle-class woman but her own ideological position is that of a bourgeois liberal feminist, a remarkably radical position for late nineteenth-century Spain, which lagged far behind other European countries on this matter" ("Gender and Journalism" 231–32).

6. See my *Gender and Nation* (13–14) for a discussion of women portrayed as national stereotypes in late nineteenth- and early twentieth-century Spain.

Chapter 4

1. Martínez Veiga notes that this division into domestic and extradomestic had legal implications when in 1900 the law of accidents was promulgated. It covered all workers who worked outside the home, leaving most women uncovered by the law.

2. Lou Charnon-Deutsch covers much of the same ground on Arenal's ideas on women and work, albeit in a somewhat different manner. Charnon-Deutsch is particularly good in analyzing Arenal's use of language in her arguments.

3. Throughout his narrative on Spanish women's work in the last part of the nineteenth century, San Martín (in Mary Nash, *Mujer, familia y trabajo* 315–342) maintains a neutral tone, although his statistics on the number of hours women work and the unhealthy nature of some of the jobs they perform (for example, making artificial flowers with materials that contain arsenic) are condemnatory. The passage from Dr. F. Carreras's *A la dona gràvida* (see Nash 354–360) provides more scientific details on the health dangers of a number of jobs that women perform.

4. In *Las damas del liberalismo respetable* Mónica Burguera covers much of the same ground about women in the tobacco industry in Spain (see especially "El trabajo femenino industrial y la reforma moral de las cigarreras madrileñas" 115–47). Burguera adds some interesting statistics, such as the fact that in the early nineteenth century, there were tobacco factories in nearly all Spain's major cities—Alicante, Barcelona, Cádiz, La Coruña, Gijón, Madrid, Santander, Seville, and Valencia; thus thanks to cigar-making, women's paid work outside the home was present throughout Spain in the early 1800s. In addition she includes important material on tobacco factories' providing care and education for workers' children.

5. Already in 1910 the CNT (Confederación Nacional de Trabajo [National Confederation of Work]) issued a "Dictamen sobre el trabajo de la mujer" [Pronouncement about women's work] that "Entendiendo que para lograr su independencia la mujer necesita del trabajo y por consiguiente éste es penoso y mal retribuido. Proponemos: a) Que el salario responda a su trabajo con idéntica én la proporción al del hombre. b) Que sea deber de las entidades que integran la C.N. del T Española, se comprometan a hacer una activa campaña para asociar a las mujeres y para disminuir las horas de labor" (qtd. in Mary Nash, "Mujer, familia," 365) [Understanding that in order to achieve her independence women need to work and thus the work is difficult and poorly paid. We propose: (a) That the salary for her work be identical to that of the man. (b) That the entities that make up the Spanish CNT promise to make an active campaign to unionize women and to lower their work hours].

6. Blanco's article provides a detailed analysis of many of the literary strategies, such as the epistolary form, Martínez Sierra employed to convince her audience. Blanco also outlines the salient theoretical issues in Martínez Sierra's feminist writing, including "the theoretical possibility of wedding femininity to feminism" (89), the importance of developing consciousness (90), the place of feelings and passions (91), the necessity for "every woman's desire for solidarity" (93), "social emotions" (94), and divorce (97).

7. Geraldine Scanlon, referencing Emilia Pardo Bazán, notes the omission of Arenal's feminist work from commentaries on her at the time of her death on 4 February 1898: "Not only, she [Pardo Bazán] observes, do these lectures and the obituaries of Arenal tend to omit any mention of her views of female emancipation, hiding them as if they were a crime, but they actually portray her as devoted to the 'labores de su sexo' [housewifely duties], converting her into a type that she herself described as an erroneous ideal" ("Gender and Journalism" 232).

8. The number of women entering the Spanish workforce after 1975 was astronomical. Laura Nuño Gómez in *El mito del varón sustentador* summarizes "desde el año 1981 se ha producido una masiva incorporación de las mujeres españolas al mercado laboral. En concreto, según los datos de la EPA para el período de referencia las tasas de actividad y de ocupación femenina han experimentado un crecimiento de 22,5 y 20,8 puntos porcentuales, respectivamente. . . . la vinculación de las mujeres españolas con la actividad económica se ha ido aproximando a la pauta observada entre los varones. De forma que, si en etapas precedentes se constaba una retirada del mercado tras el matrimonio o la maternidad, esta práctica, aunque todavía presente, ha ido perdiendo vigencia a lo largo del período, siendo cada vez menos habitual" (271) [since 1981 there has been a massive entry of women into the Spanish labor market. According to data from the EPA for the period, the rates of [economic] activity and female employment have experienced a growth of 22 1/2 and 20 3/4 percent respectively. . . . the ties between Spanish women and economic activity have been approaching the rate among men. So that, if in previous periods there was a withdrawal from the market after marriage or maternity, this practice, although still present, has been losing ground throughout the period, becoming less and less the case].

9. Martínez Veiga's book contains a thorough examination of piecework that women carried out in their homes rather than in factories, and the problems of wages, sanitation, and other regulation that such work arrangements incurred.

Chapter 5

1. For later studies that rely on Durán and Gallego's chronology, see Folguera, Brooksbank Jones (*Women*), Knights, and de Grado. Brooksbank Jones's rendition is rather schematic; de Grado's is more detailed. According to

Durán and Gallego, "The two main tendencies that appeared after 1975 (double and single militancy feminism) turned out to be irreconcilable. . . . Besides the dichotomy of double and single militancy, the debate on 'equality' v. 'difference' feminism was sour and intense" (213). Both Brooksbank Jones and de Grado note that difference feminism arose in part from the disillusion Spanish feminists experienced after the first exhilaration of the democratically sanctioned feminist movement wore off, and the movement fragmented into various factions. (This statement makes it clear that Krausism's long history of providing a vocabulary for Spanish feminism has come to an end. Here "harmony" is no longer a positive, but a negative [or at least, ironic] term.)

2. Mercedes de Grado defines the schism as between "feminismo socialista y el radical" (29) [socialist and radical feminisms].

3. See Brooksbank Jones (1–6) for a summary of the origins of post–Civil War Spanish feminism in oppositional activities to the Franco regime.

4. The "absence of a strong feminist tradition" is not quite accurate, since, as Geraldine Scanlon has amply demonstrated, a major Spanish feminist movement in the 1920s had an important role in promulgating the Second Spanish Republic in 1931 and in women's receiving the vote in 1932. Underground feminist activity tied to clandestine opposition parties during the Franco era continued some feminist presence during the dictatorship.

5. Italian difference feminist Carla Lonzi's *Escupamos sobre Hegel* [Let's spit on Hegel] was available in Spanish translation (published in Buenos Aires) in 1975, and Luce Irigaray's *Speculum* was published in Spanish in Madrid in 1978.

Chapter 6

1. Rosa Chacel made a similar point in her 1931 essay "Esquema" and again in *Saturnal*.

2. This *dependencia* is recent; the Instituto began as a dependencia of the Ministerio de Asuntos Sociales and was later moved to Asuntos Sociales y Trabajo when these were consolidated in 1997; the Ministerio de Igualdad was created in 2008 http://www.migualdad.es/mujer/quien/historia.htm).

3. Even though the Institute was conceived as an autonomous agency, as Anny Brooksbank Jones notes, the Institute's "critics represented the Institute as a channel for the implementation of PSOE government policy on women and questioned its assumption that new institutional structures and priorities would win more supporters for women's causes. . . . Difference feminists have castigated institutional feminism . . . for failing to meet its commitments to women, for purporting to speak on behalf of women who do not share its priorities, and for colluding with capitalism through measures that are themselves potentially oppressive" ("Spain's Institute" 262). The Institute issued general plans in 1988

and 1993. The first, which supplements article 14 of the Constitution, states that "Socialist governments see the removal of social inequalities as a priority, and always direct an important part of their actions and policies toward securing greater equality of opportunities for women, particularly the most disadvantaged" (qtd. in Brooksbank Jones, "Spain's Institute" 263). Brooksbank Jones cites María Morón on the underlying masculine model for the Institute's policies: "The discourse of equality as it emerges from institutional policies, and the legislative changes which promote more just, nondiscriminatory laws, combine to obscure the discourse of difference. It is true that there have been changes which have contributed to gender equality, but their point of reference remains the hegemonic masculine model" (265). She adds that "Difference feminists' opposition to the Institute is grounded in the belief that existing political parties will never be able to come to terms with the legitimacy of the women's movement without a thoroughgoing and principled reformulation of their androcentric assumptions" (265). According to Brooksbank Jones, "The Institute for Women is increasingly turning its attention to the materialization of what remain, in many cases, merely formal rights. This emerges most clearly from its second Plan. This covers the period 1993–95 and its primary focus is no longer 'equality before the law' but 'genuine, real-life equality'" (Instituto de la Mujer, 1993: 33, qtd. in Brooksbank Jones, "Spain's Institute" 266). The new emphasis is on the "unequal distribution of domestic responsibilities, which is characterized as 'the principal [cause] of women's inequality'" (Brooksbank Jones, "Spain's Institute" [267]).

4. Much earlier María Martínez Sierra argued for women as human beings: "¿No soy un ser humano, mundo dentro del mundo. Compendio de humilde pero firme grandeza? . . . ¿Por qué no he de lograr, si únicamente de mí depende, esa eminencia impasionable?" (Feminismo 42) [Am I not a human being, a world within a world? Compendium of humble but firm grandeur?]. This concept is akin to the notion of "persona" that María Zambrano developed in the 1950s. (See Juan Fernando Ortega Muñoz for a discussion of Zambrano's "persona" as a philosophical category.)

5. Surprisingly, Miyares does not invoke Lidia Falcón, who has meticulously argued for women as a social class. Clearly, the amnesia on the part of later Spanish feminists regarding their forebears has become a habit, even in today's climate of accessibility.

Works Cited

Acuña, Rosario. "Discurso pronunciaado en el acto de la instalación de la logia femenina «Hijas del Progreso»." Avilés: Imprenta de E. Suárez Puerta, 1889. Print.

———. *Obras reunidas*. III. *Prosa*. Ed. José Bolado. Gijón: Instituto Asturiano de la Mujer, KRK Ediciones, 2008. Print.

Alborch, Carmen. *Solas: Gozos y sombras de una manera de vivir*. Madrid: Ediciones Temas de Hoy, 1999. Print.

Alcalde, Carmen. Interview. Levine and Waldman. 25–38.

Álvarez, Lilí. "Masculinismo y feminismo." *Antología del pensamiento feminista español*. Eds. Roberta Johnson and Maite Zubiaurre. Madrid: Cátedra, 2012. 339–42. Print.

Amar y Borbón, Josefa. *Discurso sobre la educación física y moral de las mugeres*. Madrid: Benito Cano, 1790. Print.

Amorós, Cèlia. "Algunos aspectos de la evolución ideológica del feminismo en España." *La mujer española: de la tradición a la modernidad (1960–1980)*. Eds. Concha Borreguero, Elena Catena, Consuelo de la Gándara, and María Salas. Madrid: Tecnos, 1986. 41–54. Print.

———. "Feminismo: discurso de la diferencia, discurso de la igualdad." *Hacia una crítica de la razón patriarcal*. 132–42. Print.

———. "Feminismo y perversión." *Sexo y esencia: De esencialismos encubiertos y esencialismos heredados: desde un feminismo nominalista*. Ed. Luisa Posada Kubissa. Madrid: horas y HORAS, 1998. 130–41. Print.

———. "Feminismos ilustrados y feminismos helenísticos." *Hacia una crítica de la razón patriarcal*. 143–58. Print.

———. "La política, las mujeres y lo iniciático." *El Viejo Topo* 100 (1996): 63–71. Print.

Arenal, Concepción. *La emancipación de la mujer en España*. Ed. Mauro Armiño. Madrid: Júcar, 1974. Print.

———. *La mujer del porvenir*. Madrid: Castalia, 1993. Print.

———. *La mujer de su casa. La emancipación de la mujer en España.* Ed. Mauro Armiño. Madrid: Biblioteca Júcar, 1974. 189–284. Print.

———. "El trabajo de las mujeres." *Boletín de la Institución Libre de Enseñanza* XV (1891) *La emancipación de la mujer en España.* Ed. Mauro Armiño. Madrid: Júcar, 1974. 83–95.

Arkinstall, Christine. "A Feminist Press Gains Ground in Spain, 1822–1866." Bermúdez and Johnson. 111–25. Print.

———. "Forging a Nation for the Female Sex: Equality, Natural Law, and Citizenship in Spanish Feminist Essays. 1883–1920." In Bermúdez and Johnson. 147–57. Print.

———. *Histories, Cultures, and National Identities. Women Writing Spain, 1877–1984.* Lewisburg, PA: Bucknell UP, 1984. Print.

Arsova, Jasmina. "Gloria Fuertes: Self-Portraits of a Fertile Spinster." *In Her Words: Critical Studies on Gloria Fuertes.* Ed. Margaret H. Persin. Lewisburg, PA: Bucknell UP, 2011. 52–81. Print.

Azcárate, Gumersido de. *Estudio bibliográfico documental, semblanza, epistolario.* Madrid: Tecnos, 1969. Print.

Bachelard, Gaston. *The Poetics of Space.* Tr. Maria Jolas. Boston: Beacon Press, 1964. Print.

Baroja, Pío. *El mundo es ansí.* 4th ed. Madrid: Espasa-Calpe,1966. Print.

———. *Paradox, rey.* Ed. José Antonio Pérez Bowie. 9th ed. Madrid: Espasa-Calpe, 1990.

Beauvoir, Simone de. *The Second Sex.* Tr. Constance Borde and Sheila Malavany-Chevalier. New York: Alfred A. Knopf, 2009. Print.

Bergmann, Emilie L. "Narrative Theory in the Mother Tongue: Carmen Martín Gaite's *Desde la ventana* and *El cuento de nunca acabar*." Glenn and Mazquiarán de Rodríguez. 173–97. Print.

Bermúdez, Silvia, and Roberta Johnson, eds. *A New History of Iberian Feminisms.* Toronto: U Toronto P, 2018. Print.

Bieder, Maryellen. "Carmen de Burgos: Modern Spanish Woman." Vollendorf. 241–59.

———. "Women, Literature, Society: The Essays of Emilia Pardo Bazán." Glenn and Mazquiarán de Rodríguez. 25–54.

Blanco, Alda. "A las mujeres de España: The Feminist Essays of María Martínez Sierra." Glenn and Mazquiarán de Rodríguez. 75–99.

———. "Teóricas de la conciencia feminista. Introducción." *La mujer en los discursos de género. Textos y contextos en el siglo XIX.* Barcelona: Icaria, 1998. 445–467. Print.

Bofill, Mireia. Interview. Levine and Waldman. 39–50.

Bolufer, Mónica. "Neither Male, Nor Female: Rational Equality in the Spanish Enlightenment." *Women, Gender, and Enlightenment.* Eds. Barbara Taylor and Sarah Knott. London: Palgrave, 2005. 389–409. Print.

———. "New Inflections of a Long Polemic: The Debate between the Sexes in Enlightenment Spain." Bermúdez and Johnson. 38–49. Print.
Borderías, Cristina, Cristina Carrasco, and Carmen Alemany. "Prólogo." *Mujeres, trabajos y políticas sociales: una aproximación al caso español*. Madrid: Instituto de la Mujer, 1997. Print.
Bretz, Mary Lee. "Margarita Nelken's *La condición social de la mujer en España*: Between the Pedagogic and the Performative." Glenn and Mazquiarán de Rodríguez. 100–26. Print. Brooksbank Jones, Anny. *Women in Contemporary Spain*. Manchester, UK: Manchester UP, 1997. Print.
Bundgård, Ana. *Más allá de la filosofía: Sobre el pensamiento filosófico-místico de María Zambrano*. Madrid: Trotta, 2000. Print.
Burgos, Carmen de. *La mujer moderna y sus derechos*. Valencia: Editorial Sempere, 1927. Print.
———. *El divorcio en España*. Madrid: Viuda de Rodríguez Sierra Romero, 1904. Print.
Burguera, Mónica. *Las damas del liberalismo respetable: Los imaginarios sociales del feminismo liberal en España (1834–1850)*. Madrid: Cátedra, 2012. Print.
Cabezas, Juan Antonino. *Concepción Arenal o el sentido romántico de la justicia*. Madrid: Espasa-Calpe. 1942. Print.
Campo Alange, Countess. María Lafitte. *La secreta guerra de los sexos*. Madrid: Edi 6, 1948. Print.
———. *La mujer como mito y como ser humano*. Madrid: Taurus, 1961. Print.
Campoamor, Clara. *El voto femenino y yo. Mi pecado mortal*. Madrid: horas y HORAS, 2006.
Camps, Victoria. *El siglo de las mujeres*. Madrid: Cátedra, 1998. Print.
Capel Martínez, Rosa María. "Life and Work in the Tobacco Factories: Female Industrial Workers in the Early Twentieth Century." *Constructing Spanish Womanhood: Female Identity in Modern Spain*. Eds. Victoria Lorée Enders and Pamela Beth Radcliff. Albany, NY: SUNY P, 1999. 131–50. Print.
Capmany, Maria Aurèlia. *De profesión mujer*. Barcelona: Plaza y Janés,1971. Print.
———. *El feminismo ibérico*. Barcelona: Oikas-Tau, 1970. Print.
———. "Prólogo. Un libro polémico sin polémica." Margarita Nelken. *La condición social de la mujer en España*. Madrid: CVS Ediciones, 1975. 9–25. Print.
Caruncho, Cristina, and Purificación Mayobre Rodríguez, eds. *Entre a igualdad e a diferencia*. Vigo: U of Vigo, 1998. Print.
Casas Fernández, Manuel. *Concepción Arenal en su aspecto pedagógico*. Madrid: Librería General de Victoiano Suárez, 1954. Print.
Chacel, Rosa. *Desde el amanecer*. Barcelona: Bruguera, 1981. Print.
———. "Esquema de los problemas prácticos y actuales del amor." *Revista de Occidente* 31 (1931): 141–80. Print.
———. *Saturnal*. Barcelona: Editorial Seix Barral, 1972. Print.

Charnon-Deutsch, Lou. "Concepción Arenal and the Nineteenth-Century Spanish Debates about Women's Sphere and Education." Vollendorf. 198–216. Print.

Chown, Linda E. "American Critics and Spanish Women Novelists, 1942–1980." *Signs: Journal of Women in Culture and Society* 9 (1983): 91–107. Print.

———. "Solitude/Identity: New View of American Critics and Spanish Women Novelists." *La mujer hispana en el mundo: Sus triunfos y sus retos/Hispanic Women en the World: Accomplishments and Challenges.* Ed. Jorge H. Valdivieso, L. Teresa Valdivieso, and Enrique Ruiz-Fornells. Phoenix, AZ: Editorial Orbis Press, 2000. 194–201. Print.

Cibreira, Estrella. *Palabra de mujer: Hacia la reinvindicación y actualización del discurso feminista español.* Madrid: Fundamentos, 2007. Print.

"La Comisión de Igualdad se aburre." *ABC* (Sept. 2009): 20. Print.

Davies, Catherine. "Feminist writers in Spain since 1900: From political strategy to personal inquiry." *Textual Liberation: European Feminist Writing in the Twentieth Century.* Ed. Helena Forsås Scott. London: Routledge, 1991. 192–226. Print.

de Grado, Mercedes. "Encrucijada del feminismo español: Disyuntiva entre igualdad y diferencia." *La mujer en la España actual: ¿Evolución o involución?* Barcelona: Icaria, 2004. 25–58. Print.

Diccionario de la Real Academia de la Lengua. 22nd ed. Madrid: Real Academia de la Lengua, 2001. Print.

Dorado, Pedro. *Concepcióon Arenal: estudios biográficos.* Madrid: La España Moderna, 1892. Print.

Durán, María Ángeles, ed. *Mujeres y hombres: La formación del pensamiento igualitario.* Madrid: Castalia, Instituto de la Mujer, 1993. Print.

Durán, María Ángeles, and María Teresa Gallego. "The Women's Movement in Spain and the New Spanish Democracy." *The New Women's Movement: Feminism and Political Power in Europe and the USA.* Ed. Drude Dahlerup. London: Sage, 1986. 200–16. Print.

El Hachmi, Najat. "La discriminación positiva no tiene como objetivo hacer que mujeres ineptas y mediocres ocupen puestos relevantes solo por ser mujeres." Web. http://www.elperiodico.com/es/opinion/20170225/malentendidos-sobre-el-feminismo-5858118.

Ema, Charo. Interview. Levine and Waldman. 51–66. Print.

Enders, Victoria Lorée, and Pamela Radcliff. *Constructing Spanish Womanhood. Female Identity in Modern Spain.* Albany, NY: SUNY P, 1999. Print.

Extebarria, Lucia. *La futura Eva. La letra futura.* Barcelona: Destino, 2000. Print.

Extebarria, Lucia, and Sonia Nuñez Puente. *En brazos de la mujer fetiche.* Barcelona: Destino, 2003. Print.

Fabio Fernández, Jesús. *Las ideas sociales de Concepción Arenal.* Madrid: CSIC, 1960. Print.

Falcón, Lidia. *Los derechos civiles de la mujer*. Barcelona: Ediciones Nereo, 1962. Print.

———. *Los derechos laborales de la mujer*. Barcelona: Ediciones Montecorvo, 1963. Print.

———. Interview. Levine and Waldman. 67–85. Print.

———. *Mujer y sociedad*. Barcelona: Editorial Fontanella, 1969. Print.

———. *La razón feminista: La mujer como clase social y económica. El modo de producción doméstico*. Barcelona: Fontanella,1981. Print.

Feijoo, Benito Jerónimo. *Defensa de las mugeres. Discurso XVI. Teatro crítico universal* I. Madrid: Joachin Ibarra, 1773. 325–98. Print.

Fernández Tobio, Jesús. *Las ideas sociales de Concepción Arenal*. Madrid: Estudios Histórico-Sociales, 1960. Print.

Folguera, Pilar, ed. *El feminismo en España: Dos siglos de historia*. Madrid: Fundación Pablo Iglesias, 1998. Print.

Forest, Eva. Interview. Levine and Waldman. 98–109.

Formica, Mercedes. "Simone de Beauvoir. *Le deuxième Sexe I les faits et les Mythes*." Paris, 1949. *Clavileño* No. 49, 1950. Print.

Friedan, Betty. *The Feminine Mystique*. New York: Norton, 1963. Print.

Gilbert, Sandra, and Susan Gubar. *Madwoman in the Attic. The Woman Writer and the Nineteenth-Century Literary Imagination*. New Haven: Yale UP, 1981. Print.

Gimeno de Flaquer, Concepción. "El problema feminista." *Antología del pensamiento feminista español*. Ed. Roberta Johnson and Maite Zubiaurre. Madrid: Cátedra, 2012. 105–33. Print.

Glenn, Kathleen M. "Voice, Marginality, and Seduction in the Short Fiction of Carme Riera." Glenn and Mazquiarán de Rodríguez. 374–89. Print.

Glenn, Kathleen, and Mercedes Mazquiarán de Rodríguez, eds. *Spanish Women Writers and the Essay: Gender, Politics, and the Self*. Columbia: U Missouri P, 1998. Print.

González-Allende, Iker. "*Vivir sola no es lo mismo que estar sola*: Carmen Alborch y el compromiso de la soledad." *Escritoras y compromiso. Literatura española e hispanoamericana de los siglos XX y XXI*. Eds. Ángeles Encinar and Carmen Valcárcel. Madrid: Visor, 2009. 743–756. Print.

Haidt, Rebecca. *Women, Work and Clothing in Eighteenth-Century Spain*. Oxford, UK: Voltaire Foundation, 2011. Print.

Heranz Gómez, Yolanda. *Igualdad bajo sospecha: El poder transformador de la educación*. Madrid: Narcea, 2006. Print.

Herr, Richard. *Spain*. Englewood Cliffs, NJ: Prentice Hall, 1971. Print.

Hyland, Christy Presson. *Emilia Pardo Bazán and the Sexing of the Soul* (Unpublished PhD dissertation). University of Virginia, Charlottesville. 2002. Print.

Instituto de la Mujer. Web. Accessed July 2009.

Jaffe, Catherine M. "From the Traps of Love and the Yoke of Marriage to the Ideal of Friendship: Women Writers in the Eighteenth Century." Bermúdez and Johnson. 67–76.
Johnson, Roberta. "The Concept of Gender Equality in Constitutional Spain." *Revista de Estudios Hispánicos* 44 (2010): 613–633. Print.
———. "Fashion as Feminism." *Studies in Honor of Maryellen Bieder*. Lewisburg, PA: Bucknell UP, 2019. In press.
———. "La filosofía de María Zambrano y el pensamiento feminista europeo." *Antígona* 3 (2009): 196–206. Print.
———. *Gender and Nation in the Spanish Modernist Novel*. Nashville, TN: Vanderbilt UP, 2003. Print.
———. "María Zambrano's Solitude: The Silver Age Continued." *Anales de la Literatura Española Contemporánea* 38 (2013): 149–74. Print.
Johnson, Roberta, and Maite Zubiaurre. *Antología del pensamiento feminista española 1729–2011*. Madrid: Cátedra, 2012. Print.
Kirkpatrick, Susan. *Las Románticas: Women Writers and Subjectivity in Spain 1835–1850*. Berkeley: University of California Press, 1989. Print.
Knights, Vanessa V. "Feminismo de la igualdad/Feminismo de la diferencia?: A Study and Bibliography of the Debate and Its Implications for Contemporary Spanish Women's Narrative." *Hispanic Research Journal* 2.1 (2001): 27–43. Print.
Irigaray, Luce. *This Sex Which Is Not One*. Ithaca, NY: Cornell UP, 1985 [1977]. Print.
Johnson, Roberta, and Maite Zubiaurre, eds. *Antología del pensamiento feminista español 1700–2012*. Madrid: Cátedra, 2012. Print.
Labanyi, Jo. *Gender and Modernization in the Spanish Realist Novel*. Oxford, UK: Oxford UP, 2000. Print.
Laforet, Carmen. Nada. Ed. Rosa Navarro Durán. Barcelona: Destino, 2010. Print.
———. *La correspondencia de Carmen Laforet (1939–1991): Razones de una novelista*. Edited by Israel Rolón Barada (Unpublished PhD dissertation). University of Málaga. 2008. Print.
Laforet, Carmen, and Ramón J. Sender. Puedo contar contigo: Correspondencia. Ed. Israel Rolón Barada. Barcelona: Destino, 2003. Print.
Lafuente, Isaías. *La mujer olvidada: Clara Campoamor y su lucha por el voto femenino*. Madrid: Temas de Hoy, 2006. Print.
Lamas, Elisa. Interview. Levine and Waldman. 110–21. Print.
Levine, Linda Gould, and Gloria Feiman Waldman. *Feminismo ante franquismo*. Miami, FL: Ediciones Universal, 1980. Print.
Lewis, Elizabeth Franklin. *Women Writers in the Spanish Enlightenment. The Pursuit of Happiness*. Burlington, VT: Ashgate, 2004. Print.
Lomas, Carlos. *Los chicos también lloran: Identidades masculinas, igualdad entre los sexos y coeducación*. Barcelona: Paidós, 2003. Print.

———. ¿*El otoño del patriarcado? Luces y sombras de la igualdad entre mujeres y hombres*. Barcelona: Península, 2008. Print.
López Morillas, Juan. *El krausismo español: Perfil de una aventura intelectual*. Mexico: Fondo de Cultura Económica, 1956. Print.
Louis, Anja. *Women and the Law in Carmen de Burgos, an Early Feminist*. Woodbridge, UK: Tamesis, 2005. Print.
Mangini, Shirley. "Women, Eros, and Culture: The Essays of Rosa Chacel." In Glenn and Mazquiarán de Rodríquez. 127–43.
Marañón, Gregorio. *Tres ensayos sobre la vida sexual*. Madrid: Biblioteca Nueva, 1921. Print. Martín Gaite, Carmen. *Courtship Customs in Postwar Spain*. Tr. Margaret E. W. Jones. Lewisburg, PA: Bucknell UP, 2004. Print.
———. "La chica rara." *Desde la ventana*. Madrid: Espasa-Calpe, 1987. 89–110, Print.
———. *Love Customs in Eighteenth-Century Spain*. Tr. María G. Tomsich. Berkeley: U California P, 1991. Print.
———. *Pido la palabra*. Barcelona: Anagrama, 2002. Print.
———. *Usos amorosos del dieciocho en España*. Madrid: Siglo Veintiuno, 1972. Print.
———. *Usos amorosos de la postguerra española*. Barcelona: Anagrama, 1987. Print.
Martínez Sierra, María [Gregorio]. *Cartas a las mujeres de España*. Madrid: Renacimiento, 1930. Print.
———. *Feminismos, feminidad, españolismo*. Madrid: Renacimiento, 1930. Print.
———. *Nuevas cartas a las mujeres de España*. Madrid: Renacimiento, 1930. Print.
Martínez Veiga, Ubaldo. *Mujer, trabajo y domicilio: Los orígenes de la discriminación*. Barcelona: Icaria, 1995. Print.
Mazquiarán de Rodríquez, Mercedes. "Introduction." Glenn and Mazquiarán de Rodríguez. 1–5. Print.
Mill, John Stuart. *The Subjugation of Women*. New York: Frederick A. Stokes Company, 1911. Print.
Millás, Juan José. *La soledad era eso*. Barcelona: Destino, 1990. Print.
Miyares, Alicia. *Democracia feminista*. Madrid: Cátedra, 2003. Print.
Monserdà de Maciá, Dolors. *Estudi Feminista: Orientacions pera la Dóna Catalana*. Prol. M.R.P. Miguel D'Esplugues. Barcelona: Lluis Gili, 1909. Print.
Montero, Julio, ed. *Constituciones y códigos políticos españoles, 1808–1978*. Barcelona: Ariel, 1998. Print.
Montero, Justa. "Igualdad y diferencia: Encrucijada del movimiento." *El Viejo Topo* 73 (1994): 39–44. Print.
Muraro, Luisa. *El orden simbólico de la madre*. Madrid: horas y Horas, 1994. Print.
Nash, Mary. "Experiencia y aprendizaje: la formación histórica de los feminismos en España." *Historia Social* 20 (1994): 151–72. Print.
———. *Mujer, familia y trabajo en España 1875–1936*. Barcelona: Ánthropos, 1983. Print.

Nelken, Margarita. *La condición social de la mujer en España: Su estado actual y su posible desarrollo*. Barcelona: Minerva, n.d. (c. 1919). Print.

Nieto, Laura. *Ilustración española y pensamiento inglés: Jovellanos*. Granada: U of Granada P, 2008. Print.

Nuño Gómez, Laura. *El mito del varón sustentador: Orígenes y consecuencias de la división sexual del trabajo*. Barcelona: Icaria, 2010. Print.

O'Connor, D. J. "Representations of Women Workers: Tobacco Strikers in the 1890s." *Constructing Spanish Womanhood: Female Identity in Modern Spain*. Eds. Victoria Lorée Enders and Pamela Beth Radcliff. Albany, NY: SUNY P, 1999. 151–72. Print.

Ortega Muñoz, Juan Fernando. "La persona como superación de los géneros: Un análisis sobre el pensamiento zambraniano." *Aurora* 1 (1999): 151–72. Print.

Ortega y Gasset, José. *On Love*. Cleveland: The World Publishing Co., 1967. Print.

Pardo Bazán, Emilia. "La educación del hombre y de la mujer." *La mujer española y otros escritos*. Ed. Leda Schiavo. Madrid: Ediciones Cátedra, 1999. 140–77. Print.

———. "La exposición de trabajos de mujeres." [1893]. *"La mujer Española" y otros escritos*. 163–72. Print.

———. "La mujer española." *La España Moderna* 2 (1890): 12131. Print.

———. "The Women of Spain." *The Fortnightly Review* 65 (1889): 879–904. Print.

Pérez Galdós, Benito. *El amigo manso*. Madrid: Alianza, 1972. Print.

———. *La familia de León Roch*. Madrid: La Guirnalda, 1878. Print.

Pineda, Empar. "¿El mito de la feminidad cabalga de nuevo?" *El Viejo Topo* Extra 10 (1980): 16–24. Print.

Pittaluga, Gustavo. *Grandeza y servidumbre de la mujer: la posición de la mujer en la historia*. Buenos Aires: Editorial Sudamericana, 1946. Print.

Poulain de la Barre, François. *De l'Egalité des Deux Sexes, discours phyasique et moral où l'on- voit l'importance de se défaire du prejugés*. Paris: Chez Jean du Puís, 1673. Print.

Puleo, Alicia. *Ecofeminismo. Para otro mundo posible*. Madrid: Cátedra, 2011. Print.

Radcliffe, Pamela, and Victoria Lorée Enders. *Constructing Spanish Womanhood*. Albany, NY: SUNY P, 1999. Print.

Ríos-Font, Wadda C. "'Horrenda Adoración': The 'Feminism' of Felipe Trigo." *Hispania* 76 (1993): 224–34. Print.

Rivera, María-Milagros. *El fraude de la igualdad*. Barcelona: Planeta, 1997. Print.

———. "Partir de sí." *El Viejo Topo* 73 (1994): 31–35. Print.

Rodrigo, Antonina. *María Lejárraga: Una mujer en la sombra*. Madrid: Vosa, 1994. Print.

Rodríguez, Carmen. Interview. Levine and Waldman. 135–51. Print.

Roig, Montserrat. *Tiempo de mujer*. Barcelona: Plaza & Janés, 1980. Print.

Rolón Barada, Israel. *La correspondencia de Carmen Laforet (1939–1991): Razones de una novelista* (Unpublished PhD dissertation). University of Málaga. 2008. Print.

"Rosa Montero." *La mujer feminista: Revista de Mujeres Feministas* 21 (1985): 7–10. Print.
Rosetti, Ana. Interview with the author. UCLA. January 15, 2004.
Salillas, Rafael, and Sánchez Mogul. *Doña Concepción Arenal y sus obras*. Madrid: Librería de Victoriano Suárez, 1894. Print.
Ruiz Franco, Rosario. *Eternas menores*. Madrid: Biblioteca Nueva, 2008. Print.
Sánchez Barbudo, Antonio. *Estudios sobre Galdós, Unamuno y Machado*. Madrid: Guadarrama, 1968. Print.
Sárraga, Belén de. *Conferencias sociológicas y de crítica religiosa, dadas en Santiago de Chile en enero y febrero de 1913*. Santiago de Chile: Biblioteca Nacional de Chile, 1913. Print.
Sartre, Jean Paul. *Being and Nothingness: A Phenomenological Essay on Ontology*. Tr. Hazel Barnes. New York: Washington Square Press, 1992. Print.
Scanlon, Geraldine M. *La polémica feminista en la España contemporánea (1868–1974)*. Mexico City: Siglo Veiniuno Editores, 1976. Print.
———. "Gender and Journalism: Pardo Bazán's *Nuevo Teatro Crítico*. *Culture and Gender in Nineteenth-Century Spain*." Ed. Lou Charnon-Deutsch and Jo Labanyi. Oxford, UK: Oxford UP,1995. 230–49. Print.
Schillinger, Liesl. "The Beautiful and the Damned." *New York Times Book Review*. April 16, 2006. 18. Print.
Sendón de León, Victoria. *Sobre diosas, amazonas y vestales*. Madrid: Zero, 1981. Print.
Sherno, Sylvia R. "Gloria Fuertes and the Poetics of Solitude." *Anales de la literatura española contemporánea* 12 (1987): 311–26. Print.
Simón Rodríguez, María Elena. *Hijas de la igualdad, herederas de injusticias*. Madrid: Narcea, 2008. Print.
Smith, Theresa Ann. *Emerging Female Citizen: Gender and Enlightenment Spain*. Berkeley: U California P, 2006. Print.
Stanton, Elizabeth Cady. "The Solitude of the Self." *Man Cannot Speak for Her: Key Texts of Early Feminists*. II. Ed. Karlyn Kohrs Campbell. New York: Greenwood Press, 1989. 371–84. Print.
Stanton, Elizabeth Cady, Susan B. Anthony, and Mathilde Joselyn Gage. *History of Woman Suffrage*. New York: Fowler and Wells, 1887. Print.
Stuurman, Siep. *François Poulain de la Barre and the Invention of Modern Equality*. Cambridge, MA: Harvard UP, 2004. Print.
Subirats, Marina. *Con diferencia: Las mujeres frente al reto de la autonomía*. Barcelona: Icaria, 1998. Print.
Sullivan, Constance. "Constructing Her Own Tradition: Ideological Selectivity in Josefa Amar y Borbón's Representation of Female Models." *Recovering Spain's Feminist Tradition*. Ed. Lisa Vollendorf. New York: Modern Language Association of America, 2001. 142–59. Print.
Threlfall, Monica. "The Women's Movement in Spain." *New Left Review* 151 (1985): 44–75. Print.

Tolliver, Joyce. *Cigar Smoke and Violet Water: Gendered Discourse in the Stories of Emilia Pardo Bazán*. Lewisburg, PA: Bucknell UP, 1998. Print.

Ugarte, Michael. "Carmen de Burgos ('Colombine'): Feminist *Avant la Lettre*." Glenn and Mazquiarán de Rodríguez. 55–74.

Valcárcel, Amelia. "El derecho al mal." *El Viejo Topo* Extra 10 (1980): 25–29. Print.

———. *Rebeldes. Hacia la paridad*. Barcelona: Plaza y Janés, 2000. Print.

Vollendorf, Lisa, ed. *Recovering Spain's Feminist Tradition*. New York: Modern Language Association of America, 2001. Print.

Woolf, Virginia. *A Room of One's Own*. New York: Harcourt, Brace, 1989. Print.

Zambrano, María. "A propósito de la 'Grandeza y servidumbre de la mujer.'" *La aventura de ser mujer*. 194–204. Print.

———. *La aventura de ser mujer*. Ed. Juan Fernando Ortega Muñoz. Málaga: Editorial Veramar, 2007. Print.

———. *La confesión: Género literario*. Madrid: Mondadori, 1988. Print.

———. *Confession as a Literary Genre. Two Confessions*. Tr. Noël Valis. Albany, NY: SUNY P, 2015. Print.

———. "Eloísa o la aventura de ser mujer." Zambrano, *La aventura de ser mujer*. 162–93. Print.

———. *El hombre y lo divino*. Mexico City: Fondo de Cultura Económica, 1955. Print.

———. "La metáfora del corazón." *María Zambrano en Orígenes*. Mexico City: Ediciones del Equilibrista, 1987. 1–13. Print.

———. *Persona y democracia: La historia sacrificial*. Barcelona: Anthropos, 1988. Print.

———. "Por qué se escribe." *Hacia un saber sobre el alma*. Madrid: Alianza, 1987. 31–38. Print.

Index

abortion, 17, 21
Acuña, Rosario de, 32, 64–66, 95, 140, 154–158, 218n4
  "Consecuencias," 64
Adinolfini, Giulia, 195
Alborch, Carmen, 5, 26, 51–57, 162, 214n3, 216n20
  Solas, 51–57
Alcalde, Carmen, 105, 142, 210n3
Alemany, Carmen, 118
Alicante, 220n4
Álvarez, Lilí, 5, 20, 103–104, 164, 165
  Feminismo y religion, 104
  Plenitud, 164
Amar y Borbón, Josefa de, 5, 17, 90, 91, 180
Amorós, Celia, 5, 7, 22, 149, 161 165, 170, 173–174, 175, 177, 195–198, 205
Anarchism, 11, 15, 97, 211n6
Andalusia, 106
ANME, 68
Anthony, Susan B., 154
Arenal, Concepción, 5, 13–15, 17, 23, 25, 27, 30, 32, 37, 49, 56, 60–64, 65, 66, 69, 70, 86, 92, 96–97, 108, 111, 120–124, 127, 131, 133, 137, 140, 151, 152–154, 159, 160, 184–186, 188, 190, 211n6, 212n8, 214n7, 215n8, 218n2, 219n1, 220n2, 221n7
  "La educación," 61, 186
  La mujer de su casa, 14, 28
  La mujer del porvenir, 14, 17, 28
Arkinstall, Christine, 60, 91, 180, 184, 218n4
Arrizabalaga, Bernardo de, 44, 216n17
Arsova, Jasmina, 216n18
article, 438, 17
Asturias, 119, 120
Azcárate, Gumersindo de, 14
Azorín (José Martínez Ruiz), 25

Barcelona, 220n4
Bárcena, Catalina, 215n12
Bachelard, Gaston, 170
Baroja, Pío, 10, 25
  El mundo es ansí, 10
  Paradox rey, 10
Basque Country, 89, 95, 183, 214n3
Beauvoir, Simone de, 16, 56, 81, 140, 193
  The Second Sex, 19, 212n13
Bieder, Maryellen, 10, 95, 162, 162, 189, 219n4
Bizet, Georges
  Carmen, 125

Blanco, Alda, 25, 150, 212n7, 221n6
Bofill, Mireia, 10–11, 97, 142–144
Bolufer, Mónica, 90, 102, 151, 161, 180
Borderías, Cristina, 117
Borreguerra, Concepción, 20
Bretz, Mary Lee, 9, 100, 212n12
Brooksbank Jones, Anny, 165, 221n1, 222n3
Brown, Helen Gurley, 216n20
Bundgård, Ana, 38
Burgos, Carmen de, 2, 5, 6, 7, 10, 15, 22, 23, 102–103, 108, 120, 122, 126, 132, 152, 160, 161–162, 178–179, 189, 190, 212n12
   El divorcio en España, 12, 21
   La mujer moderna y sus derechos, 12, 17, 22, 100, 126, 150
Burguera, Mónica, 220n4
Butler, Judith, 13

Cabezas, Juan Antonio, 28, 140, 211n6
Cádiz, 220n4
Campoamor, Clara, 2, 161, 178, 179, 191–193
Camps, Victoria, 147
Capdevila, Josep, 99
Capmany, María Aurèlia, 1, 90, 106, 116, 120, 136, 141, 165
   De profesión mujer, 1, 141
Carbayo Abengózar, Mercedes, 219n8
Carancho, Cristina, 198
Carrasco, Cristina, 117
Carrera, Dr. F., 220n3
Casas Fernández, Juan Manuel, 141, 211n6
Castile, 3
Castro, Ana de, 180
Castro, Rosalía de, 48, 210
Catalá, Víctor, 214n2

Catalonia, 3, 33, 89, 95, 97, 106, 107, 116, 150, 214n2
Catena, Elena, 20
Catholicism (Catholic Church), 3, 21, 40, 121, 136, 140, 151, 152, 166, 184, 186, 191, 211n6, 212n12
Caveda, Constancia, 212n8
Cavia, Mariano de, 9
Chacel, Rosa, 3, 4, 5, 6, 7, 8, 15, 32, 34–36, 37, 43, 49, 50, 53, 54, 56, 69, 70–71, 73, 105, 107, 123, 138, 164, 207, 215n13, 215n14, 222n1
   "Esquema de los problemas," 22, 26, 70, 212n14
   Saturnal, 6
Charnon-Deutsch, Lou, 212n10, 220n2
Chodorow, Nancy, 13
Chown, Linda, 25, 26, 214n3
Christianity, 66, 118, 123, 127, 186–187
Cibreira, Estrella
   Palabra de mujer, 2
Cifuentes, Anselmo, 212n8
Cifuentes, Constancia, 212n8
Cixous, Hélène, 13, 170
Conde, Carmen, 21
Confederación Nacional de Trabajo (CNT), 220n5
Constitution (1931), 179
Constitution (1978), 165–166, 199, 203
Congreso Pedagógico, 29, 32, 61, 95, 186, 218n2
Coronado, Carolina, 32, 215n11
Countess of Campo Alange. *See* María Laffitte

Dante, Elzira, 189
Davies, Catherine
   "Feminist Writers," 2, 16–17, 19

democracy, 104, 144
Descartes, René, 41, 149, 161
d'Espluges, Miquel, 64
Díaz Gutiérrez, Ana María, 145
difference, 2, 3, 6, 22–23, 37, 149–176, 213n15
divorce, 17, 99, 192
domesticity, 9, 16, 19, 23, 35, 49, 151
double militancy, 9, 10, 11, 97, 104
Durán, María Ángela, 8, 165, 181, 221n1
  Mujeres y hombres, 8

ecofeminism, 205–208
education, 2, 4, 61–62, 93–94, 98–99, 107, 124, 135, 143, 145, 151, 152, 157, 160, 184, 186, 188, 202–203
El Hachmi, Najat, 7–8, 205
Ema, Charo, 105, 113, 193
Enders, Victoria Lorée
  Constructing, 3
Enlightenment, 17, 27, 214n6
Enlightenment Feminism (Feminismo de la Igualdad), 23
equality, 2, 3, 4, 6, 16, 17, 22, 23, 31, 35, 177–204, 213n15
Etxebarria, Lucía, 5, 10, 162
existentialism, 15, 64, 72, 81, 83, 170, 214n3

Falcón, Lidia, 2, 5, 7, 9, 10, 12, 16, 17, 22, 104, 105, 107–113, 118, 219n1
  La razón feminista, 107
  Los derechos civiles, 20
  Los derechos laborales, 20, 141
  Mujer y Sociedad, 12, 17, 10, 104, 123, 141–142
  women as a social class, 11–12, 15
Faludi, Susan, 217n20

Feijoo, Benito Jerónimo, 5, 27, 90, 92, 108, 111, 118, 120, 124, 152, 159, 161, 169, 177, 180, 181–183, 185, 188, 190, 214n5
  Defensa de la mujer, 17
femininity, 9
feminism
  definition, 7
Fernández, Jesús Fabio, 141
Fernández Cubas, Cristina, 210–211n4
Fetterly, Judith, 16, 216n20
Folguera, Pilar, 5, 221n1
Formica, Mercedes, 140
Forest, Eva, 12–13, 142
Franco, Francisco, 4, 5, 6, 7, 17, 18, 21, 22, 44, 81, 82, 92, 143
  censorship, 43
  dictatorship, 26, 54, 104, 114, 122, 123, 136, 139–142, 143–144, 162, 164, 166, 167, 176, 211n6, 213n15, 222n4
Francos Rodríguez, José, 126
Freud, Sigmund, 110, 169
Friedan, Betty, 16, 17, 56, 117n20
Fuertes, Gloria, 44, 50

Gage, Elizabeth Joslyn, 154
Galicia, 3, 95, 106, 107, 119, 120
Gallego, María Teresa, 165, 221n1
Gilbert, Sandra, 16, 216n20
Gándara, Consuelo de la, 20
Gijón, 220n4
Gilligan, Carol, 13
Gimeno de Flaquer, Concepción, 140, 158–159
Giner de los Ríos, Francisco, 14, 27, 152
Glenn, Kathleen, 8, 210n4
Gómez de Avellaneda, Gertrudis, 180, 184
Gómez de Baquero, Eduardo, 8

Góngora, Luis de, 25, 213n1
González-Allende, Iker, 57
Grado, Mercedes de, 167, 213n15, 221n1, 222n2
Granada Jornadas Feministas, 166
Gubar, Susan, 16, 216n20
Gustavo, Soledad, 6

Haidt, Rebecca, 120
Hegel, Georg Wilhelm Friedrich, 196
Heidegger, Martin, 170, 174
Heilbrun, Carolyn, 212n10
Herr, Richard, 119
Herranz Gámez, Ylanda, 203
Hicky, Margarita, 180
Hyland, Christy Presson, 178

individualism, 52
Instituto de la Mujer, 196
Irigaray, Luce, 13, 16, 56, 222n5

Jaffee, Catherine, 102
Jiménez, Juan Ramón, 25
Jiménez Bermejo, María, 20
Johnson, Roberta, 216n16
Jovellanos, Gaspar Melchor de, 119, 183–184
Joyes y Blake, Inés de, 17, 178
Junta de Damas, 91
Jung, Carl, 34, 70

Kant, Emmanuel, 27, 92, 121, 149
Kaplan, Ann, 217n20
Karr de Lasarte, Carme, 127
Kent, Victoria, 18
Kirkpatrick, Susan, 32
Knights, Vanessa, 213n15, 221n1
Krausism, 13–15, 27, 66, 92, 96, 123, 131, 152, 157, 160, 189, 211n6

Labanyi, Jo, 89, 152–153
Gender and Modernism, 15

La Coruña, 220n4
Laffitte, María (Countess of Campo Alange), 5, 19, 20, 63, 81–82, 103, 162–164
La mujer como mito, 20, 103
La secreta guerra, 19, 103
Laforet, Carmen, 2, 5, 26, 32, 43, 44–47, 49, 56, 82, 86, 209
chica rara, 43
Nada, 19, 43, 44
LA MAR, 167
Lamas, Elisa, 18, 123, 142–143
Lewis, Betsy Franklin, 102, 159
liberalism, 1, 107 191, 202
Lomas, Carlos, 202, 203
Lonzi, Carla, 150, 193, 222n5
López Morillas, Juan, 14, 15, 121n9
Louis, Anja, 161, 162

Machado, Antonio, 25, 213n1
Madrid, 220n4
Malabranche, Nicolas, 181–182
Mangini, Shirley, 112n4, 115n13
Marañón, Gregorio, 35, 141, 162
marriage, 9, 45, 54, 69, 82, 86, 89, 98, 99, 101, 103, 122, 126, 127, 136, 149, 158, 182–183, 184, 192, 193, 221, 229
Martín Gaite, Carmen, 2, 5, 16, 26, 32, 33, 37, 43, 46, 47–49, 50, 54, 60, 69, 72, 80, 83–86, 209n1, 210n1, 218n8, 218n9
La búsqueda de interlocutor, 83
chica rara, 19, 43
El cuarto de atrás, 43
Desde la ventana, 85, 216n20
Love Customs, 83, 212n11
on solitude, 26
Martínez Ruiz, José. *See* Azorín
Martínez Sierra, Gregorio, 215n12
Martínez Sierra, María (Gregorio) (María de la O. Lejárraga), 5, 6, 9, 10, 31, 33–34, 43, 69–70,

97, 125, 126, 127–132, 178, 189, 207, 215n12, 221n6, 223n4
Cartas a las mujeres de España, 126, 159–161, 193
Feminismo, 17–18, 126
Nuevas cartas, 33, 67, 69, 126
and the Socialist Party, 11
Martínez Veiga, Ubaldo, 93, 118, 146, 220n1, 221n9
Marxism, 15, 97, 169, 170, 200, 202
Masonry, 64, 65, 138, 157, 180
Matute, Ana María, 26, 43
Primera memoria, 43
Mayobre, Purificación, 198
Mazquiarán de Rodríguez, Mercedes, 8
Mellor, Mary, 206
Merchant, Carolyn, 206
Millás, Juan José, 25, 213n1, 223n5
Mill, John Stuart, 13, 15, 27, 30, 33, 92, 178
Millet, Kate, 216n20
Ministerio de Igualdad, 203, 222n2
Miyares, Alicia, 5, 199–202
Moebius, Paul Julius, 162
Monserdà, de Maciá, Dolors, 64, 66, 99–100
Estudi Feminista, 64
Montero, Justa, 196
Montero, Rosa, 2, 5, 10, 26, 50
Montseny, Federica, 2, 5, 6, 9, 15, 18, 43, 97, 193
Montseny, Joan, 6
Morón, María, 223n3
Morrison, Toni, 117n20
motherhood (maternity), 3, 19, 35, 62, 63, 68–69, 127, 135, 179
Muraro, Luisa, 16, 150, 170, 175

Nash, Mary, 1, 2, 5, 22–23, 92, 150–151, 179, 210n2
Nelken, Margarita, 2, 5, 6, 7, 10, 15, 18, 43, 212n12

and the Communist Party, 11
La condición social, 12
and the Socialist Party, 11
New History of Iberian Feminism, A, 1, 180, 184
Nietzsche, Frederich, 39
Nuño Gómez, Laura, 126, 221n8
"Experiencia y aprendizaje," 1
nuns, 95, 98, 99

O'Connor, D. J., 125
Ortega Muñoz, Juan Fernando, 72, 223n4
Ortega y Gasset, José, 6, 22, 26, 34, 35, 36, 37, 38, 39, 63, 64, 164, 170, 218n7

Pardo Bazán, Emilia, 5, 6, 8, 13, 17, 23, 25, 27, 29, 30–32, 33, 37, 47, 49, 50, 54, 90, 92, 93–95, 97, 120, 124, 140, 151, 178, 186–189, 214n5, 218n2, 219n4, 219n5, 221n7
Nuevo teatro crítico, 8
"The Women of Spain," 93–95, 108
Pasionaria, La, 18
Pérez Galdós, Benito
El amigo manso, 14
La familia de León Roch, 14
Pérez Seonae, Carmen, 20
personality, 3, 6, 27, 28, 33, 59–87
definition, 59–60
phenomenology, 64
Pineda, Empar, 193–194
Pittaluga, Gustavo, 71, 72
Grandeza y servidumbre, 71
Poststructuralism (postmodernism), 16, 174
Poulain de la Barre, François, 16, 161, 179–180, 181, 190
Prat, José, 98–99
Primo de Rivera, Miguel, 10, 72

Proyecto de Investigaciones: Feminismo, Ilustración y Postmodernidad, 205
Puértolas, Soledad, 2, 8, 210
Puleo, Alicia, 5, 205–208

Quiroga, Elena, 26

Radcliff, Pamela Beth
  Constructing, 2
Republic. *See* Second Spanish Republic
Ribbans, Geoffrey, 213n1
Rich, Adrienne, 16, 216n20
Ríos Font, Wadda, 211n5
Rivera, Milagros, 5, 7, 150, 170, 172–173, 175–176, 201–202
Robinson Crusoe, 53
Rodrigo, Antonina, 178
Rodríguez, Carmen, 114, 144
Rodríguez, Hildegart, 5, 6, 68–69, 70, 80, 82, 161, 218n5
Rodríguez Campomanes, Pedro, 118–119
Rodríguez Carballeira, Aurora, 68, 218n5
Roig, Montserrat, 2, 5, 10, 26, 37, 49–50, 216n19
Rolón-Barada, Israel, 44–46, 216n16
Rossetti, Ana, 54–55
Rousseau, Jean Jacques, 30, 39, 40, 41, 54, 56–57, 149, 199
Rubin, Lilian B., 217n20

Sábato, Ernesto, 49
Saint Augustine, 39, 40, 41, 182
Saint Eulalia, 216n19
Saint Francisca, 216n19
Saint Lucía, 216n19
Saint Teresa, 47, 54
Salas, María, 20
Salas, Pura, 20

Salillas, Rafael, 211n7
Salmerón, Nicolás, 14
Sánchez-Barbudo, Antonio, 72–73
Sánchez de Toca, Joaquín, 217n1
Sánchez Ferlosio, Rafael, 219n9
Sánchez Moguel, Eduardo, 211n7
San Martín, Alejandro, 92, 119n2, 220n3
Santander, 220n4
Sanz del Río, Julián, 14, 15
Sanz de Soto, Emilio, 46, 82
Sárraga, Belén de, 66–68
Sartre, Jean Paul, 72, 74, 75, 76, 77, 79, 81, 170
  bad faith, 74
  Being and Nothingness, 40, 75, 76
Scanlon, Geraldine, 130, 219n5, 221n7, 222n4
  La polémica feminsta, 4, 5, 8
Scheler, Max, 15, 35, 40, 71, 123, 164, 170, 215n15
Schelling, Friedeich Wilhelm Joseph, 27
Sección Femenina de Falange, 16, 19, 20, 43
Second Spanish Republic, 3, 4, 6, 17, 18, 43, 56, 104, 179
Seminario de Estudios Sociológicos sobre la Mujer (SESM), 20, 164
Seminario Permanente Feminismo e Ilusttación, 205
Sender, Ramón, 209, 216n16
Sendón de León, Victoria, 5, 89, 113–114, 150, 154, 167–172, 197–198, 202
Seville, 220n4
Sharistanian, Janet, 214n4
Sherno, Sylvia, 44
Shiva, Vandana, 206
Showalter, Elaine, 216n20
Simmel, Georg, 22, 35, 71, 105, 138
Simón Rodríguez, María Elena, 203

Smith, Teresa Anne, 91, 183
social class, 3, 4, 6, 9, 10–11, 13, 19, 31, 89–115, 117, 170
socialism, 15, 97, 169, 172, 200
Sociedades Económicas Amigos del País, 183
solitude, 3, 6, 25–57, 59, 69, 85
Spanish Civil War, 4, 5, 6, 19, 26, 43, 56, 72, 97, 104, 109, 139, 210
Stanton, Elizabeth Cady, 27, 32–33, 46, 53, 154, 178, 189
Steinem, Gloria, 117n20
Subirats, Marina, 5, 196, 198–199
suffrage, 2, 4, 23, 191
Sullivan, Constance, 91
Stuurman, Siep, 179

Threlfall, Mónica, 166
Tobio Fernández, Jesús, 211n6
Tolliver, Joyce, 5
Trigo, Felipe, 10, 211n5
Tusquets, Esther, 2

Ugarte, Michael, 212n12
Unamuno, Miguel de, 25, 72–73, 81, 86, 218n7
  La tía Tula, 55

Valcárcel, Amelia, 149, 155, 194–195, 202
Valencia, 220n4

Vollendorf, Lisa
  Recovering, 3

Weininger, Otto, 162
Wolf, Naomi, 217n20
Woolf, Virginia, 27, 38, 43, 49, 56
work, 3, 4, 6, 19, 20, 21, 47, 64, 102, 108, 109, 111, 113, 114–115, 117–147
  tobacco factory, 125–126, 136, 139, 220n4

Zambrano, María, 2, 3, 4, 5, 6, 7, 8, 15, 26, 32, 36–43, 46, 49, 60–62, 64, 66, 68, 69, 71–80, 81, 83, 86, 107, 109, 123, 138, 150, 156, 164, 169–170, 175, 207, 218n3, 218n6
  La confesión, 37, 39
  "Eloísa," 37, 81, 174
  hombre y lo divino, El, 37, 41–42, 72
  Horizonte del liberalism, 75
  "La metáfora del corazón," 41
  "La soledad enamorada," 39
  La tumba de Antígona, 79
  Persona y democracia, 6, 37, 71, 75, 77–79, 83, 218n7
  "Por qué escribimos," 37
  "Respuesta," 37, 71
Zubiaurre, Maite
  Antología, 3

www.ingramcontent.com/pod-product-compliance
Ingram Content Group UK Ltd.
Pitfield, Milton Keynes, MK11 3LW, UK
UKHW041940140426
5217IPUK00014B/576